THE
BOOK OF
ISAIAS

...

Isaias plays guitar in his room. *(Photo by Karen Pulfer Focht/The Commercial Appeal)*

THE
BOOK OF
ISAIAS

...

A Child of

Hispanic Immigrants

Seeks His Own America

...

DANIEL CONNOLLY

ST. MARTIN'S PRESS

NEW YORK

www.stmartins.com

Designed by Kathryn Parise

LIBRARY OF CONGRESS CATALOGING-IN-PUBLICATION DATA

Names: Connolly, Daniel, author.
Title: The book of Isaias : a child of Hispanic immigrants seeks his own
   America / Daniel Connolly.
Description: New York, NY : St. Martin's Press, 2016.
Identifiers: LCCN 2016018423| ISBN 9781250083067 (hardback) |
   ISBN 9781250083074 (e-book)
Subjects: LCSH: Ramos, Isaias. | Mexican American students—Biography. |
   Children of immigrants—United States—Biography. | Minority college
   students—United States—Biography. | Talented students—United
   States—Biography. | Memphis (Tenn.)—Biography. | BISAC: BIOGRAPHY &
   AUTOBIOGRAPHY / Personal Memoirs. | SOCIAL SCIENCE / Emigration &
   Immigration.
Classification: LCC E184.M5 C658 2016 | DDC 305.235/1092 [B]—dc23
LC record available at https://lccn.loc.gov/2016018423

First Edition: October 2016

10 9 8 7 6 5 4 3 2 1

For my mother, Candida Connolly (1941–2002),
who told me, "You're a hard worker!"
Thank you for believing in me.

CONTENTS

...

PROLOGUE   Gold in a Green Town   1

ONE   Chaos and Hope   31

TWO   Outclassed   56

THREE   Rain   73

FOUR   A Deck of Cards   94

FIVE   Horse to Water   104

SIX   Motivation   134

SEVEN   Intervention   158

EIGHT   Bianca the Guide   176

Contents

NINE A Funeral in Mexico 188

TEN Victory 206

ELEVEN A Locked Door 213

TWELVE Dustin's Destiny 222

EPILOGUE 234

Acknowledgments 241

Notes 245

THE
BOOK OF
ISAIAS

...

PROLOGUE

...

Gold in a Green Town

IF YOU FLY OVER MEMPHIS in an airplane in the springtime and look out the window, you will see a lush carpet of green trees extending to the horizon, with a few tall buildings sticking through. Entire neighborhoods disappear under the forest canopy. And if you land and take a taxi to one suburban neighborhood in the eastern part of the city, you will notice its distinctive features: small, square brick homes under the oak trees, gray satellite dishes bringing in Spanish-language channels, gang graffiti spray-painted on the wooden fences. And soon you will spot a building that you might have missed from the air: Kingsbury High School, a two-story brick structure with decorative white columns at its porch-like entrance.

It was in this school one spring afternoon that a teenaged boy raised his hand in an English class to ask a question. "Have you thought about being a teacher, Isaias?" the boy asked. He used the English pronunciation, "Eye-ZAY-us."

"I did," Isaias said, standing at the front of the classroom. "I didn't like it."

The boy continued. "Don't he sound like a teacher?" he asked his classmates. "I learned so much from him, fool."

Isaias laughed. "Thanks a lot."

The question might have sounded like a taunt, but it wasn't. At Kingsbury, many kids admired Isaias and treated him like a leader. Isaias was 18, relatively short in stature, with glasses and dark brown hair that tended to puff up on its own. He had just delivered a talk to his classmates as part of his senior project, standing behind a podium in his school uniform of khaki pants and white shirt and occasionally pointing out images projected on a screen. He spoke English with the slightest trace of a foreign accent, and he bounced from topic to topic: religious freedom, the Libyan dictator Moammar Gadhafi, energy conservation, a defense of abortion rights and stem cell research. He said that during the financial crisis, every conservative in the world had wanted to save failing banks, but he praised Iceland's government for taking a different approach. "In Iceland, not only did they not bail out the banks, the bankers—but they actually sent them to prison for using people's money like that."

Tying it all together was Isaias' call for political liberalism. He defined liberalism as critical thinking rather than blindly following tradition. "That could take us so much farther, to make us progress so much more as a world," he said. "Not as a country, not as individuals, but as a world, united against human suffering, against human injustice."

Perhaps if Isaias had made this presentation in college, a professor would have raised questions—was it really true, for instance, that *every* conservative supported bailing out the banks? And did liberals *really* possess the solution to all the world's problems? Yet it was impossible to miss his love of learning and his excitement at engaging with ideas.

Every Kingsbury student had to complete a capstone project and class presentation to graduate, and some of Isaias' fellow students had simply copied material off the Internet and read it out loud in class without absorbing its meaning. But Isaias had clearly thought through his presentation, and as he spoke, he made confident gestures with his large brown hands.

Almost all the students at Kingsbury came from poverty. Some came from worse situations, and their senior projects reflected it. One girl focused on the experience of being raped by her father. Another girl spoke about abusive relationships and told classmates she'd been in one a couple of years earlier. One boy's project focused on drug smuggling, a business he said he'd nearly joined.

For Kingsbury teachers, bright students like Isaias were a happy contrast to the school's sad stories. Isaias ranked sixth in his class and had scored a 29 on the ACT, better than 93 percent of kids in the United States. For fun, he'd taken up the viola and helped build a soccer-playing robot. He'd gone on local TV as captain of the trivia team. Adults invested their hopes in Isaias—perhaps too many hopes.

Now a girl asked him, "Have you ever thought about going for, like, government or something like that? Like a politician?"

"I thought about it as well," Isaias said. "But I didn't like it either."

Someone muttered "construction worker." The guidance counselors had wanted Isaias to apply to Harvard, yet he'd talked about joining his family's house-painting and remodeling business instead. His parents were unauthorized immigrants from Mexico and were thinking about returning to that country, leaving Isaias and his big brother, Dennis, in charge of their little brother, Dustin, still a young boy. The brothers considered Memphis home and had no plans to accompany their mother and father when they went back. If their parents went back to Mexico, the law might prevent them from returning to Memphis for years, possibly forever, and the family members might have to endure a long separation.

As Isaias saw it, college would complicate both the painting business and his duty to help raise his little brother. Perhaps more importantly, he questioned the school's go-to-college gospel, just as he had pushed against the culture of this strongly Christian city and his parents' Catholic beliefs by identifying as an atheist. He knew he wouldn't live forever, and he was saddened by the thought of spending four years of his life on college, something that he saw as ultimately a waste of time.

Or so he said. The teacher who had coached Isaias in quiz bowl wondered if this exceptional student simply believed college was out of reach. His parents had brought him to the United States from Mexico at the age of eight, and they'd crossed the border illegally, a fact that greatly complicated his search for financial aid. While some kids in this situation fought to find a way to get to college, Isaias dismissed the idea.

"It's not that I'm undocumented," he said once. "It's not that I feel *less*. If anything, I think it's the other way, maybe because I feel *above* college, or like if I went to college I'd be too confined and my mind would be too diminished, too driven in one certain path. And that's not the path I want to go on."

But Isaias had a habit of changing his mind. Perhaps he'd take the college path after all. Now, in his final year of high school, Isaias was forced to make choices that could affect his life for decades and influence the lives of his potential children and grandchildren. Dozens of his fellow seniors at Kingsbury would make similar decisions that year. So would countless legions of students like them across the country. And so will millions upon millions more in the years to come.

In that final year, Isaias would sometimes leave school without permission and eat lunch at Taco Bell. He would fall in love with one of the smartest girls in the school and caress her face with the back of his hand. He would exclaim, "I love Shakespeare so much!" and mean it. He would play the keyboard in smoky bars with a punk rock band called Los Psychosis. He would sing along to songs by his favorite artist, Björk, and her old band, the Sugarcubes. He would make a teacher cry in disappointment. He would inspire an intervention to change the course of his life, as family and friends would do for an alcoholic.

His parents worked long hours. When it came to big decisions on school and the future, they let Isaias find his own way. They didn't speak English and didn't understand the college application process. "No, we really have no idea," his father said in Spanish one day in the family's sunny kitchen. "The little that we know is that it's possible to find scholarships. If he wants to go, I told him, you must find them yourself." Isaias' father had gone only through the sixth grade, his mother through the ninth.

The people closest to Isaias often didn't know what he was thinking. Like many teenagers, he'd push back when his mother asked about his plans for life after high school.

Would Isaias make it to college? Would his family split apart? That last year of high school was a crucial time. But Isaias rarely seemed to worry about the decisions before him.

"I'm not sure at all," Isaias had said early in the year. "I kind of like it that way. Because when you're sure of everything, there's no room for surprises. That's no fun."

. . .

If you had visited the same Memphis high school some years earlier—1989, for instance—you likely would have seen no students of Mexican origin. An official report for that year placed Kingsbury students into just two groups: black and white.

But starting in the 1990s, thousands of immigrants began arriving in Memphis, many coming directly from Mexico. They made up part of a national immigration wave that was unprecedented in size. "Looking back over the entire span of U.S. history, no country has ever seen as many of its people immigrate to this country as Mexico has in the past four decades," demographers for the Pew Hispanic Center wrote in a 2012 report.[1]

The demographers later compared this modern immigration to the two previous largest waves. In the 1840–1889 wave, the leading country was Germany, which sent 4.3 million people. Ireland sent 3.2 million. In the 1890–1919 wave, the leading country was Italy, which sent 3.8 million.

Some 250,000 of the Germans who arrived in the nineteenth century were Jewish, and over 2.5 million more Jews would arrive between 1881 and 1924, mostly from Russia and eastern Europe.[2]

Modern immigration from Mexico has dwarfed all of these previous waves in raw numbers. Between 1965 and 2015, Mexicans arriving in the United States numbered 16.3 million, eclipsing each of the previously mentioned migrations by more than a factor of three, although of course today's immigrants arrive in a country with a much bigger total population. Mexican immigration and large numbers of arrivals from countries like China and India pushed the proportion of foreign-born people in America to 14 percent by 2015, nearly as high as the record 15 percent from the early 1900s.[3]

Modern migration from Mexico touched almost every part of the nation, and it was followed by births. In 2007 alone, so many Hispanic* children were born in the Memphis area that they could have filled more than three elementary schools.[4] By October of Isaias' senior year, Hispanic students made up 37 percent of the student population at Kingsbury High: 422 kids in all.

National statistics were even more dramatic. By 2010, the proportion of Hispanics among America's youth had grown to almost one in four. And demographers had pointed out a related number: if you looked at American kids of all ethnicities, not just Hispanics, the proportion with at least one immigrant parent also stood at nearly one in four.[5]

All of this would have been hard for me to imagine as a non-Hispanic white child growing up in Memphis in the 1980s. My introduction to Hispanic culture came when I was a teenager and Mexican immigrants began moving into my family's neighborhood, called Fox Meadows, or more broadly, Hickory Hill. Many immigrants attended the Catholic Church of the Resurrection, the same church my family went to. The changes in my neighborhood prompted me to learn Spanish in my college years. During my work as a news reporter in Alabama, Arkansas and Memphis in the early 2000s, I returned over and over to immigration stories. Maybe I loved these stories because I had a sense of what it was like to live in a place but think of somewhere else as home. My parents had come south from New York when my father got a job teaching German at what was then Mem-

---

* A quick word on terminology: the word "Hispanic" refers to any person who identifies with a Spanish-speaking culture, regardless of race, skin color, citizenship, nationality, or whether the person actually speaks Spanish. In Memphis, most Hispanics are Mexican immigrants or children of Mexican immigrants. Many other people might identify as Hispanic: a young man from Peru who just arrived in Alabama; an Afro-Caribbean woman from the Dominican Republic who's lived 30 years in New York; a U.S. citizen child growing up in an old Mexican-American family in Texas where everyone only speaks English. And when I refer to "children of immigrants," I mean children born in the United States as well as those like Isaias who were brought here when they were small.

phis State University, and even though I was born in Memphis, I grew up seeing the place much as my parents did, as outsiders.

In my early years of covering immigration, I almost always spoke with adults. One conversation in November 2010 would change that. I went to lunch with Mauricio Calvo, whom I'd met years earlier at the Catholic church in my old neighborhood. He'd moved from Mexico City to go to college in Memphis, and after he graduated, he ended up staying. We became friends, and in 2008 he became the director of the city's biggest Hispanic social services organization, Latino Memphis.

At the lunch, Mauricio said he worried about immigrants' children. Adults worked long hours away from kids, domestic violence broke homes, parents were separating, many mothers were raising sons and daughters on their own, and in some cases children were abused. Workers in medicine, social services and mental health weren't trained to deal with first-generation immigrants. Now children of immigrants were getting older and often dropping out of school. *"¿Qué nos espera?"* Mauricio asked—what awaits us?

Nationwide, others were raising similar concerns. Historically, few Hispanics had gone far in school, which held back their social and economic progress. Only 14 percent of adult Hispanics had a college degree in 2012, compared to 19 percent of African-Americans, 33 percent of whites and 51 percent of Asians.[6] Though people in power frequently talked about immigration, they were usually talking about adults. But the demographic changes raised another question: Would the huge new generation of immigrants' children do better than their parents?

Given the sheer number of children of immigrants in America, you might imagine governments and social organizations were devoting plenty of resources to supporting them. Not so. On a trip to Washington, D.C., in 2012, I visited the offices of some of the leading organizations that focused on Hispanic education. The White House Initiative on Educational Excellence for Hispanics had an impressive name, but just three employees. Another leading group, *Excelencia* in Education, had a staff of six.

The tiny staffs of these organizations drove home the point that in the eyes of the broader society, the education of immigrants' children just wasn't that important. Except that it *is* important. Higher levels of education generally lead to higher wages, more tax income, more demand for goods and services and more money to fund Medicare and Social Security. These young people will not just work. They will fight America's wars, play its sports, fill its churches, elect its leaders, sing its songs. And they will raise the next generation of children.

Failure can echo for decades, but so can success. I can point to a case from my own family: my mother's father. I knew him as a short-statured, very quiet man with blue eyes and white hair. He was a child of Italian immigrants and the first in his family to go to college, and through a series of high-paying engineering jobs, he accumulated wealth. My grandfather died when I was a teenager, and when my mother and grandmother passed away years later, I inherited part of his earnings. The money would help cover my expenses during the early stages of writing this book.

My grandfather's life is an example of how higher education can vault children of immigrants into the American mainstream and influence the generations that follow, a fact that's worth remembering as our nation seeks to absorb the great wave of Mexican immigration.

One factor complicates the process of helping immigrants' children: the ongoing fight over illegal immigration, a fight in which some people have argued that these parents and kids don't belong in America at all. In Memphis and across the country, Mexican immigration differed from previous waves not just in size, but in immigration status—in 2012, the Pew researchers said that more than half of Mexican immigrants had "unauthorized" immigration status, which most often meant they'd overstayed visas or entered the country illegally.[7] Away from the border, the government rarely enforced immigration law, and these newcomers lived in a legal gray zone, neither fully accepted nor fully rejected.

Isaias and some of his peers at Kingsbury High had illegal immigration status. But theirs wasn't the only story at Kingsbury, of course. Some Hispanic students at Kingsbury were born in the United States, which automatically made them U.S. citizens under the Fourteenth Amendment of the nation's Constitution. Indeed, most Hispanic kids across the country enjoyed citizenship.

Regardless of citizenship or ethnicity, many Kingsbury students did poorly. The overall graduation rate for the 2011–2012 school year was only 61 percent. Many adults at the school were fighting to improve the bad outcomes. It was a struggle that had relevance for the rest of the country, and I wanted to watch it happen. I asked Kingsbury principal Carlos Fuller for permission to report within the school for a year, and he said yes. Mr. Fuller hoped to highlight the troubling stories of good students with immigration problems, and because he supported the project, the school system agreed. I took a leave of absence from my newspaper job and reported full-time within Kingsbury High, observing classrooms, faculty meetings, the principal's office and the guidance office.

I kept up with students outside of school, too, visiting them and their parents at home and following kids on field trips, to soccer games and on college tours. After my time inside Kingsbury ended in 2013, I kept talking with some of the students and adults for more than two years. I stayed in especially frequent contact with Isaias.*

Children of immigrants will form part of our society for decades. Their numbers are too big to ignore, and they hold great potential that our society should help develop. America is beginning to look more like Kingsbury High. Isaias isn't a prophet, but he's named after one, and his story can show us the future.

• • •

When I first met Isaias' parents in 2012, his father, Mario Ramos, was 51, with a soft voice, bright eyes and a large stomach. His wife, Cristina Vargas, was nearly a decade younger, pretty, with flecks of white paint in her hair from work. Mario liked to make jokes about her. A novelty license plate hung on the decorative wrought-iron front door of their house: "Never

---

* This is a work of nonfiction. I have used people's real names, and at the rare times that wasn't possible, I have simply left names out rather than inventing pseudonyms.

mind the dog—beware of my wife!" It had originally said "ex-wife," but the "ex" had been painted over.

Jokes aside, they clearly loved one another. They had been married for 22 years. "Most people ask us, 'And you haven't killed each other?'" Mario said. Cristina said, "It strengthens you a lot. That's the way I see it."

We spoke at a table in their kitchen, and Mario and Cristina sometimes sat so close to one another that their elbows touched. Early in their relationship, Mario had followed Cristina everywhere. "We got married and my father told me, 'Enough, leave her alone! Separate! Because if she goes to grind some dough, you go. If she goes to cook food, you go. If she goes to the bathroom, you go!'"

On painting jobs, they acted like work colleagues, and sometimes they spoke harshly with each other, jokingly, Cristina said. She might tell him, *"¡Agárrale, pendejo!"* Grab that thing, you dumbass! Away from work, they sometimes fooled around like children. Their sons heard them laughing behind their bedroom door. What are you doing? they'd ask. The answer: we're playing!

The chain of events that brought the family to Memphis had begun a decade earlier in a village nestled amid a landscape of rolling green hills, rough footpaths, grazing sheep and agaves, which look like giant aloe vera plants.

The cluster of buildings in central Mexico's Hidalgo state is called Santa Maria Asunción. A tall tree looms over the town square, an Asian variety called *alcanfor,* or camphor. The tree can produce medicine. But the people of the town sometimes put it to a different use. Over a period of many years, residents occasionally dragged people accused of theft, rape or other crimes to the tree. Sometimes the crowd beat the troublemaker or they'd toss a rope over a branch and hoist him into the air by the wrists, where he would hang with arms wrenched painfully behind him, screaming. Such vigilante actions happened as recently as 2013, when police officers were accused of trying to extort money from the owners of one of the many tiny factories in the village that produced clothing for open-air markets across Mexico. A crowd hauled the officers to the tree, and a local news photographer took pictures of the frightened figures with bowed heads. Before the punishment could start, other policemen saved them.[8]

The punishment tree and the bell tower of a white adobe church stand a few feet away from an elementary school where one-story classroom buildings open out into a central courtyard with trees. As a child, Isaias sometimes hid among the small trees during recess with his best friend, Ponchito. Sometimes when the other kids went back to class, they sneaked away to play with marbles, tops or yo-yos. They'd play together outside school, too, each shadowing an older brother. The four boys caught frogs, floated paper boats down a creek and built dirt racetracks for their toy cars. Their mothers joked to one another, "Either you have to come live in my house, or I'll go live in yours, because we can't separate the children."[9]

Inside their cinder block house with its corrugated metal roof and a big satellite dish, Isaias' mother, Cristina, joined other women pushing cloth through whirring sewing machines, and little Isaias amused himself nearby, listening to a radio play Mexican and American songs.[10] Isaias' parents owned this in-home shop and lived with their children in the other rooms. When Dennis and Isaias were both very young, Dennis couldn't pronounce his little brother's name, and called him Chaias. The name stuck, and at home the family members called Isaias "Chay." They pronounced it "chai," like Indian tea.

The family had drinkable water and a television. Mario had a guitar, too, and played it, until baby Dennis broke it, ending his dad's musical career. Despite all they had, Mario wanted the family to progress economically. "Mexico gave us enough to live," he said years later. "But you can only live up to a certain level. You can't go beyond it." The house that they were living in had belonged to Mario's parents, and Mario and Cristina wanted their own. Buying or building a house would cost serious money—money Mario could earn outside Mexico.

In 1998, Mario crossed the border illegally into the United States by himself. He worked hard jobs, tending fruit trees and laboring in an icy cold lumber mill near Gettysburg, Pennsylvania, picking blueberries near

Atlantic City, New Jersey, and finally on construction jobs in Fort Myers, Florida.

Dennis remembered his father's phone calls from those distant places, and his absence. On the last day of fifth grade, the kids were told to bring their fathers for a ceremonial sanding and painting of the desks. Dennis had to go by himself, and it hurt.

Mario's mother died while he was away. Cristina cared for the two children on her own, living like a single mother. She said she wouldn't wish the separation on anyone. Mario said the lonely years in America were a terrible time. After about three and a half years, he finally returned to Cristina and his children in 2002. "When we got back together, I told her, never again will we separate. No matter what."

At first, Mario didn't want to go back to the United States. But the basic economics of their situation hadn't changed. Cristina wanted funds to re-model their house. Mario would say later that he wanted a better educa-tion for the two boys. The year after Mario returned, he and Cristina made plans. They would go together to America, spend three years there, earn money and come back. They didn't realize Cristina was pregnant.

One day at recess when Isaias was eight, he told his friend Ponchito that he was going to America with his family, walking through the desert. At first, Ponchito didn't believe it. Then Isaias said it again, more seriously, and with more detail: his mother, father and 12-year-old brother would travel light and carry water.[11]

Mario and Cristina knew a woman who had recently emigrated to the United States: Paulina Badillo Garcia. She had sewed men's button-down shirts in the Ramos family shop until the work slowed down. Mario and Cristina had lost contact with her, but Mario went to Paulina's parents in town, got her number and called her. He said he wanted to go to the United States but didn't know where exactly. Paulina said they were welcome to stay with her, in the city of Memphis.

The boys packed their toys into a storeroom: bicycles, a toy truck, a top, a dinosaur. They wouldn't be gone for long, and they planned to open the storeroom and play with the toys when they came back. A human smuggler who lived nearby agreed to take the family's sewing machines as payment for the crossing.

Mario and Cristina each prepared a backpack with a few items for survival: water, Gatorade and the sweets known as *alegrías*, clusters of small seeds stuck together with honey or sugar. The family members brought no clothes other than what they wore because in the desert, every ounce counted.[12]

Shortly before they left, a woman they had met through the sewing business asked them to come to her house in Mexico City. She knew they were leaving and gave them blessed items to protect them on their journey, including a small wooden plaque that showed an image of Christ with the words *"Jesús, yo confío en Ti."* Jesus, I trust in you. Cristina put the image in her backpack.

Isaias remembered walking in darkness, seeing strange shapes in the nighttime landscape of the desert: walls, castles, and at one point a racetrack with a Formula One car. He got closer, and the racetrack became a cactus and a little ditch. He had imagined it. Dennis would remember more: a stop at a border town to buy supplies, walking at night with a group of migrants, resting under trees in the early morning, the sand beneath him still warm, getting up to walk in the sun, fleeing at the sound of a helicopter, the group running low on water, then stumbling upon a cache of water jugs someone had left in the desert. Spending a night in an abandoned, half-burned house, crawling through a tunnel to get from one side of a highway to another, the sand cold this time. Then huddling on the floor of a pickup truck with a crush of other migrants on top of him, learning that the truck was stolen, seeing that the driver turned the ignition not with a key but with a big knife.

Cristina remembered that the border itself was marked by a fence so low she could practically step over it. Mario said that on both sides of the border, the desert landscape looked exactly the same.

It was March 2003, and the temperature in Arizona was moderate, with highs in the 70s.[13] As the temperature began to rise later in the year, migrants died in the heat. That year alone, about 200 corpses were found in southern Arizona. A reporter for the *Tucson Citizen* newspaper told the story of one man named Alfredo who searched for the body of his brother Rafa.[14] Surviving migrants had told Alfredo where to look, and after days of seeking, he found a skeleton that wore the same brown pants his brother had worn when he left home. Upon seeing the skeleton, Alfredo vomited and began to weep.

The Ramos family arrived at a hotel in Phoenix and rode eastward in a van. The vents in the van blew hot air, which impressed Dennis because in Mexico, he'd grown used to vehicles whose heating systems didn't work. The van slid off the road in snow near Denver. A tow truck pulled it out, and they stopped for a day to wait for the snow to melt.[15] Dennis and Isaias played in the first snow they had ever seen.

The van that carried the Ramos family rolled east on Interstate 40 across the country. As they left the flatlands of Arkansas at night, Dennis saw a big bridge lit with electric bulbs and beyond it, the skyscrapers of a modern metropolis. To Dennis, Memphis seemed like the mother of all cities.

. . .

The van that carried the Ramos family across the Mississippi River represented a tiny drop in a great wave. The Ramos family joined an estimated 570,000 Mexicans who arrived in the United States in 2003—an astounding number, but far fewer than the 770,000 who had arrived in 2000, the peak year.

Economic factors pushed Mexicans north. Mexico's peso crisis of 1994–1995 had increased the price of imported goods and led to a recession and unemployment. The wage difference between the United States and Mexico rose dramatically. In 2004, I traveled to Acambay, Mexico, with photographer Jacquelyn Martin, who snapped a picture of a man climbing high into a tree to chop down dead branches, his only support a rickety ladder of boards nailed to the trunk.[16] "It's good work," he told her. "I make ten pesos an hour." That was about 87 U.S. cents. In Mexico, he was risking a deadly fall to earn the equivalent of roughly $7 for a full day's work. In just one hour of work in America, he could easily earn the same amount or more.

Mario would later say that he and Cristina hadn't fully known the long-term consequences of an illegal crossing. "When you're in Mexico, you don't know anything about this country," he said. "So you don't know that crossing illegally can cause you problems. You don't know this. You just know that everyone's going—or anyone who wants to go does it and comes back, and nothing happens."

That statement might strike some people as strange. How could he possibly think that breaking immigration law was no big thing? Laws are laws—right?

Two facts to point out: First, Mario had lived most of his life in Mexico, where corruption was common, the justice system barely functioned, and laws often meant little. Second, the U.S. government often didn't take its own immigration law very seriously. Not only did the government rarely enforce immigration law in the interior of the country; for decades, border enforcement had been light, too, so much so that it had really been no big deal for men to enter the United States illegally, work for a while, return to Mexico, then do it again. By 2003, border enforcement had already been increasing for years, and crossing was becoming much harder—that's why smugglers had shifted from traditional urban crossing points like El Paso and were now taking people through a remote Arizona desert, and why men were beginning to bring their families. Crossing back and forth to visit loved ones was now too difficult.[17]

Mario said in hindsight that it would have been better to go to the consulate and get a visa. But if Mario and Cristina had tried to get a visa to enter the United States legally, they almost certainly would have failed.

They had no family connections in the United States, which shut off a major route to legal immigration. Some visas were available in agriculture and other seasonal work, but they lasted only a few months. Mario and Cristina could have tried to get an employment visa. But there were only 10,000 such visas available each year to unskilled laborers worldwide, said Greg Siskind, a Memphis attorney and expert on immigration law.

And only 7 percent of those employment visas could go to Mexicans, which meant that the number available could be as low as 700. The Ramos family would also have to find a U.S. employer to sponsor them through the application process. That would cost the employer thousands of dollars and take roughly eight years. As late as 2015, the country was still operating under immigration quota numbers that had been set 25 years earlier. Efforts to change the system had failed in Congress.

Paulina, the woman who had worked in the Ramos family sewing shop, was waiting for them on the night of their arrival in Memphis in 2003. Mario gave the driver Paulina's address, not far from Kingsbury High School. It was late at night, and the driver couldn't find the address, so they stopped at a gas station and telephoned Paulina, who came to meet them.

Including bus rides in Mexico and waiting for transportation, the Ramos family had been under way for about 20 days. Paulina would remember how exhausted they were. She brought them home. A total of six people were already crowded into her small two-bedroom house. They included two of Paulina's brothers, a sister, a cousin, and Paulina's infant daughter. The Ramos family took up residence in the living room, the boys on a couch, Mario and Cristina sleeping on the floor.

Mario and Cristina had bet everything on America, and by extension, on Memphis. They'd left friends and family and their home culture and language. They had crossed a desert with two young boys. Not everyone would run such risks, but from an early age, both husband and wife had shown an unusual independence and willingness to take chances.

Mario was lucky to be alive at all, since most of his brothers and sisters had died young. I wouldn't understand how this happened until one day in Mario's home village I spoke with one of his cousins, Margarita Tellez Vargas, whom Mario respectfully called Señora Mago. She was 68, with gray hair and a brown, lined face, a clear voice and a keen memory. In the back room of her family's paper products store, she told me the sad story of Mario's mother, Carmen Tellez.

Mario's mother made a living selling vegetables and she spoke both Spanish and Nahuatl, the language of the Aztecs, a language Mario would never learn. Mario's mother had many children, but they kept dying. They were born *"al valor mexicano,"* or with Mexican courage, meaning without a doctor's care, Señora Mago said. Many were stillborn. Those who survived the birth died later of something as simple as a fever. The older ones, like Bonfilio, who died about the age of nine, and Margarita, who died around the age of four, were remembered in nine days of prayer. Señora Mago went to their wakes.

So many died that Señora Mago lost track. "I think it was 16 children ... Of course we cried. We felt the loss of these little ones." Carmen Tellez's husband Juan Vargas blamed her for the deaths and sometimes slapped her—Señora Mago said she saw the violence herself.

Then Juan Vargas died, and Mario's mother married Eduardo Ramos, who had children from a previous marriage. Eduardo was a better husband who didn't hurt his wife. More children were born, but Mario was the only one who survived. Señora Mago described the difference: another woman, Mario's godmother, helped care for him and took him to the doctor.[18]

The story of the deaths reflected Mexico's lagging development in health, education and infrastructure. Electricity didn't come to the village until Mario was seven or eight years old. He remembered going to a neighbor's house to watch part of the 1968 Olympics in Mexico City on TV, then the moon landing in 1969.

Mario said his mother's vegetable and fruit sales brought in enough money for the family to survive. They always had food, shoes and clothing, but few opportunities. When Mario finished sixth grade, he wanted to continue studying, but the closest middle school was in a nearby big town, Tulancingo, and his family couldn't afford to send him. So his formal education ended.

His parents kept him busy with chores. He'd walk far into the forest to find firewood, cut it and haul it back. He recalled conversations he'd have afterward.

"Are you tired, my son?"

"Yes, I'm tired."

"Good, as a way to take a rest, grab two buckets and go fetch some water. Then feed the donkeys, the pigs and the chickens."

Mario said his mother had a generous spirit and opened their home to other kids who needed a place to stay. But she also had an explosive temper and would smack him if he did something wrong. Otherwise, he got along well with his parents. Yet he chafed under the orders and heavy work. He felt used. "When you're a child, you want to play. You don't want to do work. So it was very hard for me as a child.

"I decided to escape."

One incident played a role—he was in the forest cutting wood when he badly sliced the back of his left thumb with a machete. He would carry the scar the rest of his life. He rode a donkey back home, holding up his bleeding thumb. His mother wasn't sympathetic. She said he'd cut himself on purpose to avoid work. That hurt him a lot, and he left.

Twelve-year-old Mario gathered some pesos he'd saved, folded a few pieces of clothing into a bundle and bought a bus ride to Mexico City. People in Santa Maria Asunción had many ties to the giant city just a few hours' drive down the road. Men would sometimes part from their families for a time and work there, much as international migrants would travel to the United States in the decades that followed.

When Mario arrived in the capital, he slept in the bus terminal. The people on the cleaning crew approached him. "What are you doing here, son?" He wanted to stay in the bus terminal indefinitely, but the cleaning staff said he couldn't, and eventually the adults tracked down one of Mario's half brothers, his father's son from a previous relationship. The half brother took Mario in and brought him to work in a shop where he learned to paint cars. He worked there for about two years.

But Mario didn't like to take orders and rebelled against the half brother, too. He found another job, this time making cabinets.

Mario came back to Santa Maria Asunción to visit and, seeing that his parents were now all alone, decided at age 20 to live with them and keep them company. He started a tire shop, then later helped his mother sell vegetables. Years later, he went to a party to celebrate Three Kings' Day and spoke with a girl he'd already seen in the small sewing shop run by one of his friends. She was Cristina, his future wife, and she was only 16.

Cristina had left home early, too. She had grown up as one of ten children in a little hamlet on a hillside above Santa Maria Asunción. Her mother was sickly and spent a lot of time in bed, and her father was often away in Mexico City working construction.

Cristina's brother Alberto told me that all ten children slept on the floor with their parents as well as grandparents or aunts or uncles who might happen to be visiting: "We only slept a little bit. The next day we'd get up early and work!" They kept sheep, horses, donkeys, hogs, goats and chickens. They had to walk long distances to wash clothes and fetch drinking water. Cars were a rare sight, and when they appeared, everyone feared the drivers had come to kidnap children.

Unlike Mario, Cristina experienced extreme poverty in childhood, including going hungry at times. She began looking for a way out.

When Cristina finished elementary school at around age 11, she moved to the big town, Tulancingo, to study at a *secundaria*, or middle school. She stayed with a female doctor who had taken care of her mother. Cristina did domestic work in exchange for a place to stay: washing dishes, sweeping, cleaning up the garden and helping out in the clinic. She was a little girl working long hours, and the doctor didn't pay her. Cristina now describes the arrangement as exploitation. She later went to work for a family that gave her room, board, and some cash. Cristina's move to the big town paid off—she managed to finish the ninth grade. Among her nine siblings, only Alberto had done the same. At 15, Cristina wanted to move to Mexico City and keep studying, but her mother felt afraid and said no. So Cristina came back to the village, learned to sew, and that's how she landed in the little clothing factory where Mario first saw her. Roughly a year after they started talking at the party, they married. She was 18, he was 27.

And now, all these years later, they were sleeping on a floor in Memphis, Tennessee.

. . .

Soon after the Ramos family left Santa Maria Asunción in 2003, Ponchito and his older brother bombarded their mother with the same question. "When are they coming back? When are they coming back?" Almost every day, Cristina called Ponchito's mother. One time Cristina almost cried: she had trouble adjusting to new foods, the boys stayed inside instead of wandering outdoors, and she washed clothes by machine rather than in the creek. The changes in daily life overwhelmed her. "I can't stand it," Ponchito's mother recalled Cristina saying. But as the family gained a shaky foothold in America, the distance asserted itself and the phone calls tapered off.

In 2003, the Mexican-born population in the United States reached 10.7 million, the highest in recorded history at that point, and it continued to grow for years thereafter, peaking at 12.6 million in 2007.[19] After the 2007–2008 financial crisis, the Mexican-born population declined as fewer immigrants arrived and some went home. Most lived in the United States illegally.[20]

Eight-year-old Isaias had expected America to be a magical place, like the one he had seen on the British TV show *Bernard's Watch*. The houses and neighborhoods in the show looked well maintained and uniform, and the boy named Bernard used a special timepiece that could freeze time itself. Memphis wasn't like that. It was more like Mexico. Kind of like real life.

Dennis, Isaias and their mother Cristina on a cold day at Shelby Farms Park in Memphis, Tennessee, around 2004. *(Photograph courtesy of the Ramos family)*

Dennis and Isaias had been brought to the country illegally, but they could still go to school. The 1982 Supreme Court ruling *Plyler v. Doe* had mandated that governments provide unauthorized immigrant students with a basic education—in practice, that meant through twelfth grade. The ruling struck down a 1975 Texas law that blocked Mexican children from going to school if they couldn't prove legal status.

Justice William J. Brennan, Jr., wrote the court's majority opinion, saying that there was no rational or legal basis for the Texas law, which placed a "lifetime hardship" on children who couldn't control their own immigration status or their parents' conduct.

Isaias' parents put him in the local elementary school right away, during the middle of the academic year, and he had to repeat third grade. He quickly began to learn English. A few grades ahead of him, so did Dennis.

Paulina had fond memories of the Ramos family's early days in Memphis, how everyone in the crowded house gathered each night to eat dinner together. After a month of sleeping in Paulina's living room, the Ramos family began renting one bedroom in a house nearby. Later in 2003, Cristina gave birth at a Memphis charity hospital to a boy. They named him Dustin.

In the earliest days in Memphis, Mario went to seek jobs as a day laborer on a rough street nearby, Jackson Avenue. Cristina went to work, too, washing dishes in a Mexican restaurant, then going out to rake leaves in nearby yards. When Cristina was working, other women in the neighborhood took care of Dustin. Later, Dustin stayed at a church day care. The older brothers watched him, too.

One day the Ramos family went shopping at Walmart. Little Isaias walked up to a white American woman and asked if she'd take their picture. Of course she would. She accepted the disposable camera, and Isaias' family lined up between racks of clothes, arranging themselves around a fully loaded grocery cart with a big tub of ice cream. The stranger raised the camera. Isaias looked straight ahead, his expression neutral, hands behind his back. His mother leaned on a three-wheeled stroller with the infant Dustin, the American boy with a single American name. Mario had

(Photograph courtesy of the Ramos family)

given the older brothers double names, one Mexican, one American: Dennis' other name was Adolfo, Isaias' other name was Kenneth.

The shutter clicked.

The stranger gave back the camera. The family wanted to send the picture to the people they left behind in Mexico, to show *we're together and we're all right*. The picture of the healthy family with the full grocery cart didn't tell the whole story—they were still poor, wearing clothes from a dollar store. Both parents were busy, and they never got around to sending the photo.

When Mario began working with another man named Manuel painting houses, Cristina said she wanted to join them. Mario didn't like the idea at first. Dustin was a baby, and he thought she should stay home with him. And he didn't want his wife to enter construction, a man's world full of foul language and crude comments. But Cristina kept asking, and Mario relented. Soon, both Mario and Cristina were working with Manuel, who taught them basic painting techniques.

Through the work with Manuel, Mario and Cristina met a young woman who needed a house painted. They saw the job as their chance to start working independently, which could mean more money and could protect them from being ripped off by bad bosses. The construction business in Memphis attracted some questionable people. Once, Mario earned $200 on a job, and the boss didn't pay. Some contractors took payments from clients, didn't finish the work, then disappeared.

Most top-level general contractors were American-born, but many immigrants occupied the subcontracting levels just below them. Lawbreaking was rampant. I spent time on a construction site with a homebuilding subcontractor from Mexico who openly acknowledged that he hired unauthorized immigrants and didn't pay overtime or workers' compensation insurance. Such practices allowed him to lower his prices and helped him win contracts.

He and others could break rules because the government rarely enforced immigration law, unions lacked clout, big contractors shielded themselves from subcontractors' actions, and local and state inspectors had limited resources and authority.[21]

Mario and Cristina didn't speak English, so when they met the young woman at the house she wanted painted, they brought Dennis along to interpret. It worked. The woman was so satisfied with the painting job that she referred them to other clients, who in turn referred them to others. For this crucial first client and those that followed, Mario also used a cell phone with an unusual feature: a built-in voice recorder. When clients called, Mario would offer a memorized response. "I'm driving now. Give me your phone number and your name, and I'll call you back." He'd turn on the voice recorder and use his limited English to prompt the client to repeat the address and other details several times. Then at home, he'd play the recording for his sons to translate.

Mario and Cristina gained a reputation for quality work, and when people began asking them to expand the scope of their duties—by installing a fan, for instance—they said yes. At first, Mario and Cristina didn't know how to do these things. But they knew that every piece of hardware or paint came with instructions that were often printed in Spanish, and they could decipher some written English, too. They read the instructions, did the jobs, and their skills grew. They didn't just paint, they laid down floors, repaired cabinets, did carpentry or virtually anything else the client needed.

Mario and Cristina thought it was best to paint a client's house with as much care as they spent on their own. "You do it for the love of what you're doing," Cristina said.

They kept moving to better housing: a two-bedroom apartment, then a rental house where they lived for several years. By 2011, they'd earned enough money to buy a foreclosed house near Kingsbury High School for a bargain price: $20,500. They had held on to the image of Jesus that Cristina had carried across the desert in her backpack, displaying it in the places they had lived in Memphis, and now they hung it in the kitchen of their new home.

. . .

They were building a long-term home in Memphis, a city full of both problems and potential. The city's modern history dated to 1819, when developers carved up newly purchased Indian land on high bluffs along the Mississippi River.[22]

For decades, Memphis relied on the cotton trade and the large population of African-Americans who worked the nearby fields, first as slaves, then as oppressed laborers. Through the years, many Memphis whites worried about a black uprising, said local historian G. Wayne Dowdy. They had "this deep-seated fear that if you let them up, they're not going to be satisfied with being equal to you," he said. "They're going to want to take over."

Fear of a black uprising contributed to the city's deadly violence of 1866. A large group of African-American soldiers had just been discharged from the Union army and were drinking heavily when a brawl escalated into a gunfight with white police officers. That night, a large group of whites began burning buildings and killing every black person they saw. As Dowdy put it, it wasn't a riot, it was a massacre. Over three days of bloodshed, two whites and 46 African-Americans died, and five black women were raped. Even in 1942, during the Second World War, the Memphis mayor had to publicly deny rumors of a brewing black revolt.

The fear of black people had a curious consequence, Dowdy said. Most of the original white settlers of Memphis were English and Scotch-Irish, but since they viewed the world through the prism of black and white, they generally accepted any foreigners not of African origin as "white." That included the Irish, Italians, and German Jews. In the nineteenth century, white schools also accepted children of Chinese descent.

Memphis had experience with Mexican immigration, too, though it was temporary. In the late 1940s, thousands of Mexican workers known as "braceros" toiled in the fields around Memphis under federal contracts, and Mexico's government opened a consulate in Memphis to serve them. The braceros program ended in the 1960s. "There is very little work here for a Mexican consul nowadays," the last consul told a local newspaper in 1971, not long before the office closed.

In the late 1960s, the city saw tentative progress in race relations. For instance, in 1967, three African-Americans were elected to the City Council, the first time since the 1880s they had been represented there. But in 1968, civil rights leader Martin Luther King, Jr., came to Memphis to support a sanitation workers' strike, and an assassin shot and killed him. The killing would harden racial resentments for decades. The decline of downtown Memphis accelerated as whites moved farther and farther from the core city.

The 1990 Census found that for the first time in Memphis history, the majority of the population was black. In 1991, city schools superintendent Willie Herenton gave up his post to run for mayor and won by only 142 votes, becoming the city's first elected black executive.

Mayor Herenton would gain white support and win election four more times. But scandals and his sometimes abrasive personality hurt his popularity. Critics called him racially divisive. In 2009, he unexpectedly announced his retirement in the middle of his fifth term.

At the end of the mayor's almost 18-year tenure, the city still struggled with low education levels, a high crime rate, racial conflict, and poverty that was among the worst in the nation. Some in Memphis seemed to have internalized an inferiority complex, the sense that their city would always lag behind the region and the world.

Life in Memphis wasn't all bad, of course. The mayor could point to successes including a revived downtown and a new NBA team, the Grizzlies. The city also boasted a musical heritage based on the blues and Elvis Presley, and its visual arts scene grew in strength as old storefronts on South Main and Broad Avenue were transformed into galleries. The city full of trees was becoming more international, more diverse, and more interesting: whether you were into judo, salsa dancing, Vietnamese Buddhism, Japanese animation or African-American Gospel music, you could find a community of like-minded people. Despite the area's long-standing racial problems, interracial dating and marriages were relatively common. Plus, housing was cheap. I paid $530 per month for an apartment near Overton Park, the Memphis equivalent of New York's Central Park, and for more than nine years, my landlord never raised the rent.

The low rent reflected a sad fact: many people with money moved to outlying suburbs. Between 2000 and 2010, the city saw its population decline to 647,000, a drop of about half a percentage point, even though the government had annexed new territory.

In that decade, the city's black majority grew slightly, the white minority shrank—and the Hispanic population soared. The 1990 Census had recorded just 7,000 Hispanics in the county that included Memphis, less than one percent of the population. By 2000, shortly before the Ramos family arrived, the county's Hispanic population had grown to 23,000, or 3 percent. Most were immigrants from Mexico, with smaller numbers from countries like El Salvador and Venezuela. Many worked in warehouses or in construction.

By 2010, the Hispanic population had more than doubled again, to 52,000, or 6 percent of the county population. Many of them lived within the core city, and by Isaias' senior year, Hispanics made up nearly 10 percent of students in the urban Memphis City Schools system: more than 10,000 Hispanic kids.

Beginning early in the immigration wave, Catholic churches and evangelical congregations began offering services in Spanish. Spanish-speaking businesses sprang up quickly to meet immigrants' needs: newspapers and radio stations, restaurants and grocery stores, lawyers, mechanics, medical clinics, nightclubs, hairstylists and wedding photographers.

Hispanics moved primarily into two Memphis neighborhoods: the suburb where my family lived, Hickory Hill, and the neighborhood around Kingsbury High. People called this neighborhood by different names: Highland Heights, Nutbush, Graham Heights, the National Cemetery area, and sometimes simply Kingsbury.

As Memphis struggled with its old problems of racial tension, poverty and crime, the city's leadership remained split between blacks and whites. Many immigrants came to the country illegally, which meant they couldn't vote, and no one of Hispanic descent was elected to office. At City Council meetings there were no Hispanics on the dais, rarely any in the audience, and the politicians seldom talked about immigrants except to make general statements of support. The population of tens of thousands of people was largely ignored.

Being ignored had a benefit: though some people in Memphis made anti-immigrant remarks, no one organized a serious anti-immigrant movement. By contrast, not far away in majority white Nashville, the state legislature passed a series of mostly symbolic measures against illegal immigration, and a conservative group campaigned unsuccessfully to limit most local government communications to English.

Being ignored also had a downside. Memphis immigrants complained that when it came to commitment of government money and resources, they were skipped. For instance, in 2007 the city office dedicated to helping immigrants had just two employees, and neither spoke Spanish.[23]

. . .

Isaias and Dennis started working with their parents when they were teen-agers, and Mario and Cristina relied on them as interpreters, too, because their own skills in English remained limited. The parents could say hello, exchange a few words with clients about a job, read a little bit. But they couldn't conduct a real conversation in English. Learning a language as an adult was hard, especially for those who had little formal education. It re-quired many hours of study, time that many immigrants simply didn't have.

Mario and Cristina would get home in the evening after a long day at work, prepare something to eat, check on the children and then go to sleep before getting up and doing it all again. The boys would ask their parents why they didn't learn English, and Mario would say: "How about you go to work, and I'll go to school for six years? And I'll learn English." Churches offered some English-as-a-second-language programs that met the needs of working immigrants, but they varied widely in quality. In Memphis and around the nation, many newcomers stayed within the Spanish-speaking universe, and when they ventured outside it, they often did so with the help of their children.

Dennis played an increasingly important role in the family business. At 22, he looked and sounded like an older, larger version of Isaias: the same glasses, the same very slightly accented English, the same love of music, the same curiosity about the world. He hadn't made it to college, but it was easy to imagine him there.

One time he and Isaias started talking about the situation in Gaza while they took down a gutter on a house they were preparing to paint.

"The problem is that they're already moving troops to the edge. It's escalating," Dennis said.

"Wow! It's war," said Isaias. He asked if the U.S. government had said anything. Dennis said, "No. They condemned the Palestinians, but—" Isaias interrupted with a sarcastic "Ooh."

"They don't talk about Israel," said Dennis. He wielded a whining elec-tric drill to unscrew the gutter. The brothers switched to quick bursts of Spanish as they eased the metal to the ground.

Dennis had hoped to become an engineer in the army after graduating from Kingsbury in 2009, but his immigration status stopped him. He applied to state colleges, but he would have had to pay expensive out-of-state tuition. His parents told him they'd be willing to help pay for college. He said later that he just couldn't do that to them. As he saw it, it was their money. They had lives of their own and things they wanted to do.

As Isaias drew closer to high school graduation, Dennis doubted his brother's chances of getting to college. "I don't want to tell this to Isaias, but I just don't see many opportunities out there," Dennis said at one point. "I really hope he gets one and I think he's talking to people that may be able to help him. But I saw it. And there's just no way. No one helps you."

In 2010, Dennis traveled to New Mexico because it was one of the only states where he could get a driver's license without a Social Security number. He ended up staying with a group of young men for several weeks and became close friends with one of them, who taught him about atheism. "He looked at me in the eyes one day and told me, 'You're going to die and that will be okay. I will die. So instead of praying for a better life in the afterworld, which we're not even sure exists, let's just make the best out of our lives that we know exist now.'"

Dennis began watching online videos featuring atheists. Many of the atheists were political liberals, and Dennis began to identify with liberal politics, too. And he came across a website that sold car magnets that parodied the Christian symbol of the fish by adding legs to it and writing the word "Darwin" inside. Dennis ordered one of the Darwin fish and put it on his truck. "That represents me and what I believe," Dennis said. "And I believe in science. And my fish wasn't created. My fish evolved." Dennis came home from New Mexico and told Isaias about atheism. Isaias said he was immediately receptive to the idea because prayer had always struck him as silly. "And right there it just seemed like, duh, I've been thinking this my whole life," Isaias said.

I asked Mario and Cristina much later about their sons' atheism. They said they accepted it.

"They're free," Mario said. "They can make their own decisions." Mario and Cristina had helped lead a Christian group in Mexico. They still considered themselves religious, but now they only went to nearby St. Michael's Catholic Church once or twice a year. When Dennis had a tire blow out on his truck while he was driving, Mario made him go with him to the church to give thanks that he hadn't died: "This is my belief and I want you to go with me." Dennis didn't want to, but he eventually relented and went with his father. He said he didn't feel anything at church but was glad the tire blowout hadn't hurt him or anyone else.

Cristina said she sometimes threw holy water at the boys when they made her mad. Or she'd say, *"Cruz, cruz-que se vaya Isaías y que venga Jesús."* Cross, cross—go away Isaias and come here, Jesus.[24] Generally, though, the parents maintained a warm relationship with their children. They didn't believe atheists were bad people. Cristina thought her sons' views might change as they got older and life became harder.

Isaias' parents recognized the potential in their middle son. "I see in him a hidden artist," his father said. "You just have to find him. I don't know. He has something. He's special." Much later, they told the story of how Isaias was born—how Cristina's labor pains began at home and she went with her husband to the nearest clinic, walking because they had no money and no other transportation. They arrived to find the clinic empty. The bishop had come to town, and the clinic staff had gone to the celebration. Mario left Cristina waiting there and raced to the nearby church, where he found the nurse and the doctor and hurried with them back to his wife. The doctor was still putting on gloves when the child emerged and fell into his father's hands.

"He caught me by surprise," Cristina said. "He caught us all by surprise." Cristina believed that from that moment of birth, Isaias was destined for something unusual.

Chapter One

. . .

CHAOS AND HOPE

Summer 2012:
About nine months before graduation

Isaias spent the summer before his senior year working with Dennis and his parents on painting jobs, and in one house in Germantown, a well-to-do suburb, he used his cell phone to take a picture of himself in a mirror, then posted it on Facebook—his glasses off, a serious expression, his head haloed by light streaming from a window behind him, his shirt paint-spattered. After school started, he continued to do painting jobs on the weekends.

One day early in the school year, Isaias hurried to the vocational center near Kingsbury High to speak with Corey A. Davis, an instructor. Isaias sometimes ran from place to place, and he arrived sweating and tired, as if he'd just completed a race, Mr. Davis recalled. Isaias told him that he needed permission to sign up for the audio recording class. No problem—Mr. Davis agreed.

The class was optional, and Isaias wanted it badly. He'd sit behind an actual mixing board with knobs and sliders, learning to create songs and sound effects. He'd listen to NPR for ideas on how to edit radio stories. Every day, he would walk from the main high school building to the vocational center, and he'd stay there for about three hours, working contentedly.

But for many other Kingsbury students, the start of the school year would bring not contentment, but long hours of sitting in a gymnasium with nothing to do.

• • •

August 6, 2012, the first day of Isaias' final year of high school, dawned with a clear blue sky. The electronic sign in front of Zion Temple Church of God in Christ sent drivers a message of hope in golden scrolling letters:

GOD BLESS OUR TEACHERS

GOD HELP OUR PARENTS

A mile or so away at Kingsbury High, blue police lights flashed and an officer blocked traffic to protect students as they walked from the residential neighborhood of brick homes, crossed North Graham Street and made their way onto the school grounds. A crowd of kids milled around outside, dressed in white uniform shirts. Girls squealed as they recognized friends. "You're so gorgeous! You're so gorgeous!" "Maria!" A father pulled a red pickup truck to a stop, accordion-heavy *norteña* music playing, and a child got out. A few feet away, in front of the school, Principal Carlos Fuller, a bald, strongly built man with coffee-colored skin, shouted at a student and gestured with a small two-way radio that let out bursts of static. He greeted a boy in a wheelchair. "You have a good summer?" he asked. "Yeaaah!" the boy replied with a big smile. Mr. Fuller sent one kid straight to the office for a violation of school uniform rules. He slapped hands with other boys. "Looking good, baby, looking good."

Mr. Fuller walked into the school, passed a JROTC instructor running the metal detector check, strode into the front office and stepped to a microphone. His voice crackled over loudspeakers throughout the building.

"¡*Bienvenidos escolares y campeones!* Welcome, scholars and champions! What's up? This is going to be a great, great year!"

Mr. Fuller spoke only a little Spanish, but he made an effort, especially on the announcements. Several teachers spoke the language fluently. On this first day, Mr. Fuller talked about class schedules. "Some of your schedules may have holes. Some of you guys may not have schedules at all. Teachers, please look for your temporary schedules."

He finished with a flourish: "That being said, at the school of scholars and champions, where every day it is the sole mission of every adult in this building that at a minimum, 90 percent of our children will be proficient on all of our assessments. At a minimum, 60 percent of our children will be advanced. All of our children strive to make 30s on the ACTs. *¡Que tenga un buen, buen día!* This is going to be a great, great day, a great week, a great month, a great year! Thank you."

On nearly every other day that followed, Mr. Fuller attacked the morning announcements with similar enthusiasm. In a nod to the small number

Mr. Fuller admonishes a student early in the school year. (*Photo by Karen Pulfer Focht/The Commercial Appeal*)

of students from the Middle East, he'd often start with the Arabic phrase *"sabahu alkhayr,"* or good morning. He would clasp and unclasp his hands, opening and closing his eyes. Sometimes he'd abbreviate the last part about test scores and say, "Where every day is 90-60-30!" He'd offer life lessons: "Please surround yourselves with positive people! Every decision you make will have a positive or negative consequence. Whether it is positive or negative depends on you." He'd occasionally mix in ACT vocabulary words like "zephyr" and "yen." Even when he was having a bad day, he tried to bring excitement and energy.

Mr. Fuller made his morning announcements shortly after 7:30 a.m., but school wasn't close to really starting. The messy process of registration continued, and guidance counselors were still scrambling to put together class schedules.

Students killed time in homerooms throughout the building as a multiethnic line of parents and teens formed in the front office and stretched into the hall. A white man consulted a cell phone, a little Hispanic girl in pink with a pacifier played inside the office, an Asian father accompanied a teenaged son, and a black teenaged boy waited with his mother and two little boys. Following the announcement, dozens of other students and their families filled out registration forms in the school library, though registration had officially taken place the previous week.

Nearly two hours passed before an assistant principal made an announcement: students who had registered but did not have a schedule should receive a temporary schedule. "All other students that are not registered need to report to the gym." In the gym, students without schedules would wait in limbo. No one could say for how long.

Dozens of students walked into the hallways, past the rows of lockers and under the colorful flags of the world. Metal doors clanked open as students left the main building and walked into the midmorning heat and the buzzing drone of cicadas. They made their way to the gym, where a similar buzz sounded from one of the old lamps overhead.

Only a handful of students came in at first. Then four more girls arrived. Then more. A boy said, "I'm so glad we got here before everybody else did." The trickle became a torrent. The kids climbed up the metal steps and took seats on the maroon bleachers. By the end of the day, I counted 175 students in the gym. The good news was that they had come to school at all. Students routinely skipped school at Kingsbury, particularly on the days that everyone agreed were pointless. Given the severity of this year's scheduling problems, there were many pointless days to come.

In the school gym that first week, the kids whiled away the hours talking, sleeping, eating, lounging and playing with cell phones. One Filipino boy simply sat and stared into the distance, day after day. On Wednesday morning, the third day of school, a river of teenagers in white uniform shirts flowed back to the gym. Only one door was open, and a crowd quickly formed at the narrow entrance like water behind a dam. A tall, muscular young white teacher named Lucas Isley directed the students to points on the bleachers. "If we have a homeroom, down there. No homeroom, no schedule, right here."

This gym adjoined a smaller exercise space that Kingsbury Middle School used. On the other side of a partial barrier, younger kids killed time in a different way: walking in slow circles.

One of the 200 or so students sitting in the high school gym that day was Franklin Paz Arita, a lanky 16-year-old with large brown eyes, curly hair, an open face and a frequent smile. He was born in Honduras and smuggled into the United States as a child. His mother had endured an abusive relationship in California with a man who once threatened to kill her with a sledgehammer. Franklin said years later that he remembered the details vividly: how the man had raised up the weapon and said he'd smash her with it. Franklin was so young that he hid behind his mother, who was holding his baby sister. "My older brother basically had to talk him out of it," Franklin recalled. Meanwhile, an older sister slipped away and called the police. "And since he was drunk, a few moments later he passed out," Franklin said. "And by the time he was up again, the cops were already there."

When Franklin's mother left this man, she and her children moved from place to place before settling in Memphis. Now she cleaned houses and was raising Franklin and his two younger siblings on her own.

Two things motivated Franklin: his faith in God and his love for his mother. He liked math and science and wanted to become a detective or forensic investigator. He played soccer and tried to make money by selling sets of kitchen knives door to door. In the gym, though, he was bored and hot and wasting time.

On the first day of school, Franklin had arrived carrying a green notebook. By Wednesday, he had taken exactly half a page of notes, from when he'd sat in on an English class. He felt cheated—he'd been assigned classes that he had already taken or that he didn't need even though he'd signed up for classes before leaving school in the spring. Though hundreds of students sat in the gym, Franklin knew that many other Kingsbury students had class schedules and were already learning. It wasn't fair.

One of the teachers watching the gym, Mr. Isley, was a 26-year-old from Michigan who had gone through training with Memphis Teaching Fellows, a program for new educators. He had read a book called *Teach Like a Champion*, which told him that a teacher who found efficient ways to handle classroom chores like passing out papers could save 30 seconds per class period. At six periods a day, that added up to three minutes. Over the course of a school year, nine hours. At 1:00 p.m. on Wednesday, he calculated that the kids had sat there for between 18 and 20 hours. He didn't like it.

When the end-of-day announcements finally came on Friday afternoon, I counted 227 kids still in the gym—roughly a fifth of Kingsbury's student body. Their chatter drowned out the afternoon announcements and dismissal. Franklin left, eating a bag of crispy snack fries and planning to set up knife sales demonstrations. He carried the same green notebook as on Monday. In five days of school, he had still taken only the half page of notes. Three percent of the 180-day school year had passed. He'd start school next week.

The number of students in the gym gradually dropped until August 17, the tenth day of the school year, when Mr. Fuller walked into the guidance office and announced, "That's the last of the group! Gym is clear!"

Several factors contributed to the scheduling chaos, including students coming to school days late. But one of the primary issues was a computer problem.

Guidance counselors Tamara Bradshaw and Brooke Loeffler said many of the students who showed up at Kingsbury that August had mistakenly been assigned to another school, Douglass High. The computer records system would not allow the same student to enroll in two different schools. Until staffers at Douglass High formally dropped those students from their school's roster, the computer system wouldn't allow Kingsbury guidance counselors to build a schedule for them. During those first few weeks, schools called one another or faxed back and forth lists of students to drop.[1]

The problems that school year went far beyond Kingsbury. On September 11, dozens of students demonstrated outside another Memphis City School, Carver High, to draw attention to cuts to band and choir programs, lack of air conditioning in sweltering classrooms, and scheduling problems. Seventeen-year-old protest leader Romero Malone told the local newspaper that the chaos affected almost all the students in the school. "Ninth graders had nothing on their schedule but lunch," he said. "It lasted two to three weeks. They made the students go to a classroom where they were watched over while administrators tried to do schedules."[2]

Similar problems had cropped up elsewhere, notably in Los Angeles, where thousands of students throughout the city's public system had to deal with incomplete or inaccurate schedules in 2014, the *Los Angeles Times* reported. At that city's Jefferson High School, scheduling problems got so bad that a judge ordered education officials to fix them immediately.[3]

When I spoke with Mr. Fuller a full month after the start of the school year, he described the technical problems and also said he wasn't happy with how the guidance staff had handled scheduling. (My sense was that the guidance staff wasn't happy with how Mr. Fuller had handled it either.) Either way, he acknowledged it was a mess. "It was a headache. We're still in the process of cleaning up some schedules, which we have to do every year anyway, but we have to do it so much later because we didn't take care of it on the front end."

Registration the following year, August 2013, was far smoother, and Mr. Fuller offered an explanation: the district had expanded the length of time that the guidance counselors worked from 10 months to 11 months, which allowed them to come into school earlier and start working on the schedules.

The problems at the start of Isaias' senior year clearly hurt the students' morale and motivation. I talked with two boys who'd sat in the gym for days. They were mumbly and sullen, and I couldn't blame them. What was their impression of Kingsbury? "That this school *boring*," one boy said.

Seventeen-year-old Faith Nycole Nostrud went weeks without a real schedule, and her dad said she compounded her problems by not going to school. "If I'm going to be at school, I want to do something," she said. "It frustrates me to come to class and then just sit there the whole hour. It's like, 'Well, I could be doing this at home.'" In October, she transferred to Gateway, a private Christian school that served as a backup for many kids in the neighborhood.

English teacher Philip Tuminaro had once spent the first days of the school year trying to teach. But an ever-changing roster of students made it clear that he had to keep re-teaching the same material. So now he spent the first chaotic days of each school year reviewing material that all the students would need: preparation for the ACT test. He recognized a vicious cycle: teachers didn't teach, so students didn't come. Given the circumstances, he wouldn't come either, and he didn't know whom to blame.

Setting aside the question of blame for a moment, the organizational problems in places like Memphis and Los Angeles reflected a broader social inequality. In the 1990s, I went to the city's best public high school, White Station, and I got my schedule on the first day and went to class immediately. If I had endured weeks of chaos at the start of each year, my parents would have sent me elsewhere. Most adults with educational savvy, money and options would do the same. But many Kingsbury parents didn't have these things. Most didn't complain or pull their kids out of school.

. . .

Isaias escaped the worst of the scheduling chaos, although for some reason he spent a few weeks in precalculus, a class he didn't need. The previous year, as an eleventh grader, Isaias had taken the school's highest math course, Advanced Placement Calculus AB. He had also taken a college-level finite mathematics class and made a B. In precalculus, the teacher let him study for his other classes. Sometimes he coached other students like an assistant teacher.

Isaias eventually got his schedule changed to drop precalculus and take piano, where he practiced in a room full of expensive-looking computer screens and keyboards. That was one of the contrasts of Kingsbury—despite its high poverty rate and organizational problems, many of the classrooms were equipped with new technology, like SMART Board interactive screens.

At lunchtime on the first day of school, the students had streamed out of the main building, into the sweltering heat, up some steps and into the air-conditioned cool of the cafeteria, a space that smelled of nachos.

"I'm so proud of you! Here! Monday!" said Margot Aleman, smiling as she greeted a student just inside the cafeteria door. Margot worked for an outside evangelical Christian organization called Streets Ministries. She came to Kingsbury as a volunteer and was a constant presence in the school. She was in her thirties and often wore multicolored blouses. She continued her greetings. "Welcome to high school, baby! We're proud of you." A tall, muscular white football player with blue eyes and a big smile limped in on crutches. "Cody! Again, sweetie?" Margot said.[4]

Now the kids surged up the stairs about five or six abreast. Some Hispanic boys wore rosaries over their white uniform shirts. One wore a necklace with an image of the Virgin Mary in what looked like a tiny frame.

Some of the kids made good money working in construction. Margot pointed out a Hispanic boy at one of the round cafeteria tables who was holding hands with a younger white girl. "Him being here the first day of school, it's a lot. He made $600, $700 a week," Margot said. Another student she knew worked a night shift from 10:00 p.m. to 5:00 a.m. "At least he came to school. That's a good thing." She pointed out a bubbly ninth grader. "I got to take care of her 'cause she's cute. Guys are going to be all over her."

The kids ate in shifts, and the second group arrived shortly before noon. Again, Margot stood in the doorway, hugging students and keeping up her greetings, switching between Spanish and English. "My baby, Tri!" "How are you, Mr. Freshman?" "You are not going to skip."

As the students settled down to eat, Margot and I left the cafeteria. We walked the short distance to North Graham Street, turned to the right and continued past Kingsbury Middle School, past a church, and arrived at the Streets Ministries community center.

In 1993, *The New York Times* profiled the founder of Streets Ministries, a 35-year-old blond, bearded white man named Ken Bennett who drove an old Ford van to the city's worst housing projects and worked to bring tutoring, mentoring and love to poor kids, almost all of them black. He had married a teacher, fathered a baby daughter, and had already recruited a network of volunteer tutors.

"My faith calls me to do this, not in a romantic or martyrdom way," he said at the time. "We have two cars and a house. We don't go without. We are about spreading the Gospel of Jesus Christ, but we're not conditional." Kids could take the Gospel or leave it, he said. "We'll continue to track with them."[5] In the nearly 20 years since then, Streets had grown dramatically and now ran two multimillion-dollar community centers, one in downtown Memphis and a new one near Kingsbury High that opened in 2011. The building was equipped with spacious basketball courts, classrooms, a computer lab, an activity space for special programs and a room for nonviolent video games. Now Margot found an empty room and unpacked a toasted sandwich of tuna mixed with corn kernels—not a traditional meal, just how she liked her tuna.

She said Streets focused on the "Three E's": to engage in relationships with kids and faculty, to educate and to evangelize. But she said she rarely talked about God outside of specific events at the community center unless the students asked. "I'm not gonna pull out the Bible and start preaching to the kids," she said. "I'll lose them. But I will share my love and the reason why I'm still alive, because of God. Basically all of us do." Unlike most staffers at Streets, she did not have a bachelor's degree. "And I'm not very bright, but I can help them."

On the surface, Margot seemed all sunshine, love and cheer. But growing up in the town of Weslaco in South Texas near the Mexican border, she had lived through dark events. She said that at six, a relative raped her. At 12, someone else sexually abused her. At 13, she met her biological father for the first time. He told her three things: One, no one knows you exist. Two, your mother and I did not plan you. Three, your mother was my mistress. Margot developed suicidal thoughts as a teenager and became a "cutter," a person who inflicts wounds on herself.

When she was 17, a pastor molested her. She became a youth minister in her early twenties but around age 28 she became addicted to pills, became suicidal again and started having panic attacks. Then one day, she surrendered everything to God—again.

Margot sometimes shared her story with kids. Often they told her they had been abused, too, and sometimes they'd tell her other secrets: about a pregnancy scare, an alcoholic mother, or a dead mother and a vanished father.

She came to Memphis when the Streets founder asked a local pastor and Spanish-language radio personality named Gregorio Diaz to help him locate a Hispanic person with legal documents and experience working with youth. Mr. Diaz recommended Margot, who had also worked in Christian radio. Now she worked 50 to 60 hours per week. "We don't care. This is not work for us," she said. "This is playground. I mean, seriously: Who gets paid to take a kid out to a movie?"

She would turn 38 in a few days and said she'd found peace without a nice car, a big house, a husband, or children of her own. "I love teens. They're drama, they're crazy and they're knuckleheads, but they're great. I love them. They're my babies."

Though Margot worked for an outside agency, she played a role much like that of a guidance counselor. Kingsbury students also had counseling help from Patricia Henderson, who worked for TRIO, a federally backed program designed to help low-income students get to college. Later in the school year, the social services agency Latino Memphis used funds from the Lumina Foundation to launch a mentoring program at Kingsbury called Abriendo Puertas, or Opening Doors.

The outside staffers supplemented the four overworked guidance counselors on the school's payroll. The staff counselors not only assisted students with college applications, but administered standardized tests, set course schedules, and even sold prom tickets. Counselor Brooke Loeffler acknowledged that she didn't have enough time for the relationship building that makes a difference in kids' lives, and she regretted it. "We're doing clerical work and administrative work," she had said early in the school year. "We don't have time to sit down and have personal conversations."

Many other schools in America had fewer counselors than Kingsbury because when school systems cut budgets, guidance counselors were vulnerable. In California, the state's largest school systems lost hundreds of counselors to layoffs and attrition after the 2007–2008 financial crisis, making their ranks so thin that "most students will be hard pressed to get the personal attention they need, whether for academic or mental health reasons," the California organization EdSource wrote in 2013.[6]

In the years that followed, some California districts began to hire counselors again, a good thing, because low numbers of counselors likely meant some students wouldn't go to college. Researchers with the College Board concluded that adding an additional guidance counselor to a school staff—boosting the number from one to two, for instance—resulted in a 10 percent increase in the number of students enrolling in four-year schools.[7]

Some might worry that an evangelical Christian organization had involved itself so deeply in a secular, government-funded school. But that was like complaining that Catholic Relief Services or the Muslim Red Crescent had delivered food to survivors of an earthquake. Kids at Kingsbury needed adult guidance.

...

Another adult who interacted frequently with Kingsbury students was Eduardo Saggiante, the school's full-time Spanish interpreter, a 38-year-old former professional soccer player from Mexico with a gentle demeanor and a tired face. In the early days of school, he was busy.

Each line of the school registration forms gave instructions in both English and Spanish, but the papers intimidated one Mexican mother. She handed Eduardo the pen. *You do it.* He asked for her name, address, and countless other details and filled out her paperwork line by line. She'd only made it as far as the fourth grade.

On the second day of school, he helped orient a 15-year-old girl recently arrived from Cuba. *"Ese va a ser tu homeroom,"* he told her. This will be your homeroom. *"El locker es esto."* This is a locker. He tapped one. *Clang clang.* He'd repeat this process for days after the school year started, as students still drifted in.

Sometimes, before making a difficult call to a parent, he'd pause in the teacher's lounge to psych himself up for the moment. His wife said he took his job too personally. He couldn't help it. He'd studied economics in Mexico, not counseling. He didn't know how to deal with gangs. Yet here he had to do that and much more. He helped rescue a boy from a father who beat him. He spied on the houses that harbored kids who'd sneaked away from school to party. When girls disappeared, he'd play the role of detective, talking with the police and scouring Facebook pages. Often the girls had run off with boyfriends. One time he told a mother that no, it's not okay for a 15-year-old girl to go live with a 20-year-old man. About six girls would go missing that year. He lost count. They all turned up eventually.

· · ·

During the chaotic first days of the academic year, the administrators had a hard time keeping track of who was in the school. By October, the guidance office could confirm the stats: 422 Hispanic students made up 37 percent of the total school population of 1,143. African or African-American students made up 43 percent of the total. Whites made up 15 percent, Asians 3 percent and a small number of others were classified as American Indian or their race wasn't listed.

In the course of the year, I'd meet children of immigrants not just from Mexico, but from far-flung places including Cambodia, Iraqi Kurdistan and Ivory Coast. Many teachers also came from other states or from abroad. Tomfei Teuo-Teuo came from Togo in west Africa, taught French and also spoke fluent German. Math teacher Mamadou Diong came from Mauritania in northwest Africa; each side of his face was marked with a roughly tear-shaped scar, not far from the eye. Such decorative scarring was a custom in his part of the world.

On the sixth day of the school year, students still came to the guidance office to change schedules. Some hung around because their classes hadn't started and they had nothing better to do. Jose Perez flipped through a military recruiting magazine and pointed out a picture of a Hispanic warrior to another student. Later, Tommy Nguyen asked Jose what branch of the military interested him most. Jose's answer was certain. "I'm going to do Marines."

Of the four branches of the U.S. military, the Marines were smallest and enjoyed a reputation for elite toughness. Jose longed to become one of them.

Jose served as the highest-ranking student leader in Junior Reserve Officers Training Corps, or JROTC. His formal title was Battalion Commander—and at Kingsbury, that meant something. Far more than in most schools, the JROTC cadets in their crisp olive-green dress uniforms defined the culture of Kingsbury. For years, the school had steered almost all freshmen into the JROTC program in what Mr. Fuller described as an effort to encourage leadership skills and discipline. They did military-style exercises like shooting air rifles, and adult instructors also taught other subjects including U.S. government and personal finance. Students who showed potential could earn ranks and lead other students in activities such as precision marching and drills.[8]

The military and the school system each paid half of the adult instruc-

tors' salaries. At the start of Isaias' junior year in the fall of 2011, school
system budget cuts reduced the number of Kingsbury JROTC instructors
from four to two, and the number of students enrolled dropped from
around 400 to around 160. Still, the JROTC program remained visible at
most school assemblies and special events as students in uniform carried
out flag ceremonies. The program had a roughly even split between boys
and girls. When Congressman Steve Cohen visited Kingsbury later in the
year, a tall JROTC student named Dante Bonilla escorted him through
the school. And retired army master sergeant Ricky Williams cut an im-
posing figure as he stood at the school door in the morning and ordered
students to tuck their shirts in.

Sergeant Williams said he wanted to motivate young people to lead
productive lives after high school, and that recruiting them for military
careers wasn't the point of JROTC. Still, military recruitment and JROTC

Franklin Paz Arita (left) and Jose Perez (right). The student in the center is Astawusegne
Desalegne, better known as Ismail. *(Photo by Karen Pulfer Focht/The Commercial Appeal)*

often went hand in hand. In his junior year, Jose Perez contacted a Marine recruiter who came to the high school and talked with him.

Jose had been born in Mexico and brought to the country illegally as an infant. At the end of the conversation, Jose told the Marine that he didn't have a Social Security number, but he was working on it. The Marine said he couldn't help Jose until he took care of that.

Now Jose simply *had* to get the document.

That morning, counselor Tamara Bradshaw grew tired of Jose hanging around the guidance office. "Jose, go to class."

"We're in class?" Jose asked.

"We're in homeroom," Tommy Nguyen interjected.

"Homeroom's a class," the counselor said.

It was 9:21 a.m. School had been in session for nearly two hours, and little had happened.

The guidance counselors had asked Mariana Hernandez and Adam Truong to put course-change forms in alphabetical order. Now these reliable seniors had finished the task and sat at a table in the guidance office waiting for something else to do.

"What if we're in here 'til lunch?" Adam asked. More time passed. Mariana said, "We should see if they need anything." So she and the others started walking around the school, asking adults if they needed help.

Mariana was a slender, pretty girl who wore stylish dark-rimmed glasses and ranked among the top ten students in the senior class. She was born in Mexico; her parents brought her to the United States when she was five, and then her immigration visa expired.

She had once thought that being Hispanic and undocumented would bring bad consequences. Now, she had only a couple of Hispanic friends. Most of her friends were Asian, like her boyfriend Adam and their friend Tommy, both of whom came from Vietnamese families.

She spent a lot of time with Adam, who swam and lifted weights and liked to listen to country music and rap, especially older artists like Tupac Shakur. Mariana's parents liked Adam, and he often visited their house.

Adam Truong and Mariana Hernandez. *(Photo by Karen Pulfer Focht/The Commercial Appeal)*

Later in the year, Mariana worked in a school computer lab to fill out an application for a community college. In the box for ethnicity she marked "Hispanic." Like the U.S. Census, this form considered Hispanic ethnicity separately from race, and the computer screen wouldn't let her continue unless she also marked one of the race categories—African-American, white, et cetera. She didn't know what to do.

Beside her, Adam said, "Put Asian." So she did.

Some Mexican immigrant parents largely let their children handle school and college decisions on their own. By contrast, Mariana's parents paid close attention to her schoolwork and pushed her hard.

"You know how they make the stereotyped comments about the Asian parents being the most demanding?" she told me in June before the school year started. "Well, if my parents had to fall under some category, that would be them."

Her father had finished twelfth grade in Mexico with a technical diploma, her mother the ninth grade. They had met in Guadalajara, one of

Mexico's largest cities, and were now in their forties. Her parents both worked for a company that ran a chain of franchise restaurants, her father in the in-house construction department, her mother in one of the restaurants. Like Isaias' parents, they didn't speak much English, and I spoke with them in Spanish. "I tell Mariana that I can't give her an inheritance," said her mother, Adriana Armas. "But studying will give her what an inheritance would." She didn't want to see Mariana killing herself at work like her parents did.

Adam sometimes felt afraid of Mariana's father, Ricardo Hernandez, who was bald and often wore a severe expression. Yet his true nature was gentle, and he fully supported his daughter's education. "It would really make me sad if she can't go to the university," he said. He believed that a university degree would always help a person find a job. True, you heard stories of people who had graduated from college and worked as cashiers, he said, but even if people weren't using their educations at the moment, they could figure out a way to do so.

Mariana had scored a 19 on the ACT test, decent for Kingsbury but below the national average of 21, and her parents were upset. "They just said it was disappointing," she said. "I shouldn't be everybody else. I have to be above standards." (She eventually pulled up her score to 21.)

She signed up for all the available enrichment activities, including a Streets Ministries summer program that prepared students for college. Participants read books like *The Hunger Games, Lord of the Flies* and the Book of Romans from the Bible.[9] They studied for the ACT on the campus of the University of Memphis. In the last week of the summer institute, Mariana spent several days at the University of Alabama at Birmingham and stayed overnight in a dorm.

She signed up for hard courses like AP Chemistry, where she'd prepare for a difficult national exam. Teacher Jihad Haidar gave the students extremely tough questions, and she doubted herself. "I guess we all know we're not gonna pass this AP exam!" she said in class one day later in August. She said she found her family's expectations overwhelming.

"Because what if one day I decide to be stupid and reckless like any other teenager and I screw it up? The way that my family members view me is no longer the way that they thought I was. So everything changes completely."

And she worried about her immigration status. What if she finished high school, graduated from college and then went out into the job market and couldn't find work because she didn't have a Social Security number?

People like her who had been brought into the country illegally or on visas that expired often had no hope of ever gaining legal status. They lived for years in a legal gray zone.

Adults without papers lived the same way. Isaias' father Mario told the story of the time he was driving with Cristina and they saw a police checkpoint. They couldn't turn around. This was it. Immigration enforcement. Mario turned to Cristina and said, "I'll see you back in Mexico."

They had thought about the possibility of deportation. Since they spent so much time painting houses together, they imagined the agents might grab both of them at once, and their children might be left behind at school. At one point, they made an emergency plan with Paulina and other friends: in case of deportation, the boys would stay with the friends, who would arrange to send the children back to Mexico.

Now Mario and Cristina pulled up to the officers. It was only a seatbelt check. Someone handed them a brochure and sent them on their way.

It turned out that the government generally wasn't trying to catch people like Mario and Cristina. Large businesses with powerful friends didn't want agents to arrest and deport their workers. In 1998, the Immigration and Naturalization Service (INS) launched Operation Southern Denial, raiding Georgia fields where owners used large numbers of unauthorized immigrant workers from Mexico to grow and harvest sweet Vidalia onions. The raids made workers flee, and the onion growers complained loudly to members of Congress that their multimillion-dollar crop would rot. The feds agreed to stop the raids and give the growers temporary amnesty until the harvest came in. INS official Bart Szafnicki helped broker the deal. "I've been in this 22 years and I have never done anything like this," he told *The Chicago Tribune*. "It is absolutely unprecedented and it is very unlikely to ever happen again."[10]

But it did happen again. In 1998 and 1999, the INS launched Operation Vanguard, an effort to reduce widespread hiring of unauthorized immigrants in the meatpacking industry in Nebraska and other Midwestern states. Instead of conducting raids, the government subpoenaed the Social Security numbers and other identification that workers had presented when they applied for the slaughterhouse jobs. In theory, the law banned employers from knowingly hiring unauthorized immigrants. But the immigrants often gave them fake documents, and an employer had no obligation to investigate carefully. In Operation Vanguard, officials told workers with suspicious paperwork to come to interviews and explain themselves. Thousands quit rather than face the agents.

Again, leaders of a powerful industry complained about the enforcement. Again, lawmakers took their side. Again, the government suspended the program.[11]

Even before Operation Vanguard had run its course, the INS had decided to deemphasize worksite enforcement. A March 1999 memo made deportations of *criminal* immigrants the top interior enforcement priority. Worksite enforcement became the lowest of five priorities. "In a booming economy running short of labor, hundreds of thousands of illegal immigrants are increasingly tolerated in the nation's workplaces," *The New York Times* reported in 2000.[12] The newspaper described stepped-up border enforcement and prosecutions of companies that smuggled in unauthorized immigrants or blatantly recruited them. "But once inside the country, illegal immigrants are now largely left alone. Even when these people are discovered, arrests for the purpose of deportation are much less frequent." Such arrests had already dropped from 22,000 two years earlier to 8,600.

For people like Mario and Cristina, the chance of being pulled off a job site and deported would soon drop to almost nothing.

In a 12-month period around the time the Ramos family arrived, immigration officials arrested only 845 people on worksites nationwide. The federal government brought only a tiny number of "notices of intent to fine" against businesses for immigration violations: three, to be precise, in all of the United States.[13]

Across the country, local police generally couldn't enforce immigration law. After the September 11, 2001, terrorist attacks, the INS was broken up into different agencies. The new federal agency in charge of catching unauthorized immigrants was called Immigration and Customs Enforcement, or ICE.

In much of the United States, ICE had little manpower. When I was working in Arkansas in 2006, an ICE staffer named Rod Reyes told me the agency had about 16 agents in the entire state, fewer than the 21 sworn police officers on the streets in the small town of Hope. And ICE didn't just handle immigration enforcement, it also pursued crimes such as terrorism and child pornography. Handling the deportation of a single unauthorized immigrant could take hours of an agent's time, said Mr. Reyes, who was the resident agent in charge for ICE in Fort Smith, Arkansas. "People think that we can just pick them up and turn around and put them in a bus and ask them to leave," he said. "And it doesn't happen that way."[14]

Princeton sociologist Douglas Massey argued that many modern immigration problems could be traced to a 1986 law called the Immigration Reform and Control Act (IRCA), which, he said, had disrupted a smooth-functioning system in which Mexican men crossed the border illegally, worked, and went home. The law sought to curb future illegal immigration by expanding the Border Patrol and punishing employers who hired unauthorized immigrants. At the same time, it offered amnesty to large numbers of people who had entered illegally or overstayed visas.

Massey and his colleagues wrote that the law's combination of amnesty plus new restrictions reflected the two competing interests in the nation's immigration policy: businesses that wanted immigrant labor versus a public fearful of immigration and politicians who sought to win votes by exploiting that fear.

The problems with IRCA quickly became apparent. The 1986 law led to a black market for fake documents like the ones the immigrants were showing to get jobs at the Midwestern meatpacking plants targeted by Operation Vanguard. The 1986 law meant more risk and more paperwork for companies, and employers often responded by paying lower wages as a sort of compensation for their trouble. Some also sought to avoid the risk of sanctions by hiring through subcontractors who would take the blame if the government caught unauthorized workers on a job site. Soon, anyone who wanted a job in agriculture or construction might have to take a low-wage position or go through a subcontractor. That hurt everyone in the industry: all immigrants, regardless of legal status, and citizens, too, Massey wrote. And tighter border enforcement encouraged Mexican migrants to settle permanently in the United States. Demand for the labor of Mexican migrants continued. "If there is one constant in U.S. border policy, it is hypocrisy," he wrote. "Throughout the twentieth century the United States has arranged to import Mexican workers while pretending not to do so."[15]

People like legal scholar Eric Posner spoke of the "illegal immigration system"—an informal set of rules that allowed people like the Ramos family to live and work in America, but with limited rights.[16]

An old debate raged: Were immigrants doing jobs that Americans didn't want? Or were they doing jobs Americans wouldn't do *at that wage and under those working conditions*? My best guess is that both assertions are true to some degree, though I'll leave it for others to debate. I'm more certain of this: at its heart, the illegal immigration system exploits its workers and aims to give them as little as possible.

Justice Brennan's opinion in the 1982 school case *Plyler v. Doe* had shown a sophisticated understanding of how the desire for low-cost labor drove the system: "Sheer incapability or lax enforcement of the laws barring entry into this country, coupled with the failure to establish an effective bar to the employment of undocumented aliens, has resulted in the creation of a substantial 'shadow population' of illegal migrants—numbering in the millions—within our borders. This situation raises the specter of a permanent caste of undocumented resident aliens, encouraged by some to remain here as a source of cheap labor, but nevertheless denied the benefits that our society makes available to citizens and lawful residents."

Decades later, the specter of a permanent caste of people with limited rights was closer to becoming a reality.

Immigration enforcement statistics spiked occasionally, but in general, the government had made a quiet deal with people like the Ramos family: Do your work, avoid trouble, and you can stay. Just don't ask for too much—certainly not a trip home, or citizenship, or the right to vote. If your kids don't have papers—as Dennis and Isaias didn't—they can go to school through grade 12.

What would happen to them after that? And what would happen to children born in America, like Dustin? The leaders in the federal government didn't think that far ahead. The feds left it up to states, local governments, and school boards in much of the country to figure out how to educate a huge wave of children of immigrants. Doris Meissner, head of the former Immigration and Naturalization Service in the Bill Clinton administration, told me in 2012 that she couldn't recall any discussion among federal officials of what would happen to immigrants' children.

Young people with unauthorized immigration status, like Mariana and Isaias, were becoming an especially high-profile group. Efforts to pass a bill to regularize their status, called the Dream Act, had failed in Congress. Some young protesters called themselves Dreamers and publicly pressured the president to do more to help them. Among them were Memphis residents Patricio Gonzalez and Jose Salazar who, along with others in 2012, re-created the civil rights era march of James Meredith from Memphis to Jackson, Mississippi.

Just a few days after I spoke with Mariana in June 2012, President Obama made an announcement. His administration would grant limited immigration relief to young people without the approval of Congress. Those who met certain criteria would receive a two-year renewable work permit.

"Now let's be clear: this is not an amnesty," the president said at the time. "This is not a path to citizenship. It is not a permanent fix."

Obama's administration called the program Deferred Action for Childhood Arrivals. It was the biggest immigration legalization program since the 1980s.

Mariana, Isaias and many other Kingsbury students applied quickly. So did Dennis. The process required them to gather a wide range of records from the school system and other agencies. The families of Mariana and Isaias were among many that hired attorneys to help. Dennis and Isaias each paid a lawyer $1,000 to complete their applications, plus a fee of $465 each to the government. That fall, they traveled to the local immigration office, where they were fingerprinted and photographed. Then they waited.

. . .

On that slow day early in the school year, an administrator finally found a job for Mariana, Adam and Tommy. He brought them into the library and showed them how to cut out and laminate the numbers for the "Fight Free" board. The board posted a public count of how long each of the grade levels had gone without brawling. If the sophomores racked up enough "fight free" days, for instance, they'd win an award—maybe pizza or ice cream, or a chance to come to school out of uniform.

The three students busily went to work, cutting out numbers that ranged from zero to more than 50. Fistfights—most of them minor—broke out frequently enough among both girls and boys that the fight-free streaks that year wouldn't last very long.

Mariana often helped out adults, as she was doing now, but she could show a rebellious streak, too. For a while, she assisted Mr. Fuller with the morning announcements in the front office, reading some items over the loudspeakers in both English and Spanish before the principal started his energetic "Good morning, scholars and champions!" ritual.

One morning later in the year, Mariana came to the front office to do the announcements. She was eating an apple, and with the microphone off, the principal told her not to—he'd later say the food attracted vermin. But Mariana argued with him. "Go down to the discipline office," Mr. Fuller said. Mariana moved toward the door. On the way, in front of the principal, she took one more defiant bite.

For Mr. Fuller, this was unacceptable. "She's in the front office doing what's like a leadership role, and then gonna tell me, 'What's wrong with eating an apple in the building?'" Mr. Fuller said later. "So I had to remind her also, 'Baby, you're still a child in here, sweetie."

Why didn't she stop? "Because I was going to tell him that I needed it," Mariana said. "My blood sugar was low. I'm not going to pass out in the main office and cause more dilemma."

She ended up with an "overnight suspension," a punishment that was largely a formality. Her parents weren't upset. But Mariana wasn't eager to come back and help Mr. Fuller again. "I hold a lot of grudges," she said. And for the rest of that year, she would rarely do the announcements.

Now, though, Mariana and the others worked away. Tommy sat on the floor with a paper cutter and chopped up sheets of numbers, producing multicolored ribbons of scrap. "What if we go straight to sixth period?" Adam asked. "That would be cool."

Mariana fed the chopped-out numbers one at a time into the laminating machine, which smelled like glue. "You know, I think if we ever had our own company it wouldn't be that bad," Mariana said. "I think we could run a school, at least have it all organized."

. . .

On the second day of the academic year, guidance counselors told Isaias to start an application to a local college, Christian Brothers University, and he obeyed. But he had mixed feelings about college. "It's really interesting. But when I think a little deeper about it I think—what is it, why? Why? Why should I go to college? Why? I mean everybody tells you to get a good job, right? But I think about a good job doing what? A college degree gives you the ability, but not the actual job. And I guess from my mindset I just don't see college as being that important." He weighed becoming a civil engineer against other ideas: traveling the world as a singer-songwriter or working with his parents.

He said he'd go if he got a scholarship. "But if not, I'm not going to hassle too much, I'm not going to worry about it." Later that month, Isaias' father told me his son had changed his mind. He was trying to go to college.

Chapter Two

...

OUTCLASSED

September 2012:
Eight months before graduation

THE PLAN FOR THE STUDENT council election was simple: videotape the students' campaign speeches in advance, then play them over the old TV monitors in the classrooms. But in some classrooms, the images played with no sound. In other rooms, they didn't play at all. So Mr. Fuller ordered all the students to watch the recorded speeches on a single big screen. That meant moving more than 1,000 teenagers to the auditorium, in groups of 30 or so at a time, and everyone knew it would eat up much of the morning. "Shoot me now," chemistry teacher Jihad Haidar muttered. As the kids trickled into the auditorium, student Tri Nguyen began fiddling with a VCR and a sound mixing board. "I'm not sure where this goes," he said, holding a wire with red, white and yellow plugs. As he worked, bursts of static sounded over the speakers.

Mr. Fuller explained his reasoning to a few kids in the front rows. "The easiest thing to do is let this go, but I wanted to make sure I do right by the children," he told them. The young candidates for student council had done everything adults had asked: practiced their speeches, posted campaign signs. The least he could do was let their classmates hear what they had to say.

English teacher Jacklyn Martin saw the lengthy election process as a complete waste of time, and she knew she'd have to throw out her plans for the morning. When she'd gone to school, she'd received a higher quality of education than this. Isaias came in carrying a book he'd been reading called *Naked Economics* and took a spot in the rows of wooden folding chairs. Isaias said he saw the chaos as a sign that someone at the top was irresponsible. "Things like this happen. Very unorganized. It's always done a lot on the spot." He was used to it by now. "I don't mind anymore. It being my senior year, I don't know what it is, I just don't care much.... I don't care that the online classes still haven't gotten going. I don't care. I don't care that we're wasting a whole day here. It's like 'All right.' Plus what are you going to do, right?"

The whole process took more than three hours.

. . .

Kingsbury sometimes felt like a little world unto itself, and the most influential person within that world was Carlos Fuller.

Mr. Fuller grew up in Greensboro, North Carolina, the oldest of four brothers. His parents and his three brothers graduated from North Carolina A&T State University, a historically black college. His mother was an administrative assistant at the college, and his father worked in community relations for a county school system.

Mr. Fuller's parents emphasized education, but early in life, he didn't stay on the path they wanted. "Let's just say that I kind of drifted in and out during my college years," he said. "Trying to find my way in some cases. In some cases, hanging with the wrong people."

He described how he'd stayed in a small room in a rough neighborhood in Durham, North Carolina. "One night I just looked up at the ceiling like 'Man, it got to be a better way than this. Has to be a better way.'"

He said he found a part-time job, went back to school and registered, but still kept the same type of questionable friends. "And then my girlfriend at the time got pregnant." He was about 26, but he said he was roughly as responsible at the time as the average 18-year-old. The birth of his daughter made him take life more seriously, and though his relationship with the girl's mother didn't last, he said he continued to support the child financially. He later married another woman and had three more children.

Mr. Fuller eventually graduated from North Carolina Central University in Durham and moved with a fraternity brother to Memphis, where he started a career in education, first as a classroom teacher. He went through leadership training and served as an assistant principal and briefly as a principal of an alternative school for troubled students before taking the leadership of Kingsbury in 2008. He was a father of four and turned 50 during Isaias' senior year.

And that year, Mr. Fuller said his job was at risk. He told me much later that if the students failed to meet certain standards, he could lose his job. "Once you're a 'striving school' and you agree to come into the striving school, you sign a contract that if you don't get the scores, you can be released," he said.[1] And Mr. Fuller said one of the most important standards for keeping his job was the graduation rate. That year's benchmark was to raise the rate from 61 percent the previous year to 67 percent.

Graduating from Kingsbury was relatively easy. If students didn't do work, they got many chances to make it up. Some twelfth graders showed serious weaknesses in basic skills like reading and writing. Naturally, some teachers and counselors said the school system graduated students who were so unprepared they shouldn't have passed—and that the pressure to raise the graduation rate played a role.

"I think like most people in any other business, educators have a certain value of self-preservation," Mr. Fuller said. "And sometimes you have to do what you have to do.... I'm not telling you not to fail kids. But I am saying 'work with them.'" Mr. Fuller's view: try every intervention imaginable before giving the student a failing grade.

Mr. Fuller told me his secretary said he had attention deficit disorder. "That's what I say sometimes when I get distracted," he said once. "But I have not legally been diagnosed." Sometimes he made snap decisions that dismayed teachers.

Teachers were judged by student performance, too, and if they had less time to prepare their students, it could hurt everyone. History teacher Ron Barsotti frequently criticized Mr. Fuller's leadership and saw the wasted time at the student council election as one more count against him.

Yet Mr. Fuller often showed a fatherly interest in the students that went far beyond his job description. He routinely referred to them as "my children," and he wasn't kidding—he often worked 12-hour days and showed up at athletic and academic events on weekends.

Many months later, Mr. Barsotti, the history teacher who had criticized Mr. Fuller, told me he'd changed his mind about him and said that he'd helped the school. "He's been really good to me, and I almost feel guilty being so critical of him."

. . .

One person who knew that not every school was like Kingsbury High was 17-year-old senior Estevon Odria. Estevon had only attended Kingsbury since tenth grade, when his grandparents moved into the neighborhood to cut housing costs. "I used to go to a more organized, better-in-nearly-all-aspects public school in the suburbs of Memphis, Tennessee, until my sophomore year," Estevon wrote in an early draft of a college application essay.

At Kingsbury, Estevon said he saw that many students skipped class and seemed apathetic. He wrote in his essay that he refused to behave the same way. "I work my hardest to seize every nanosecond of my existence."

Another experience shaped Estevon's mindset: in the summer before his senior year, his grandfather drove him to the Memphis airport, where he got on a plane and flew to New England to spend five weeks at Phillips Exeter Academy, one of the nation's most prestigious boarding schools.

Kingsbury guidance counselor Tamara Bradshaw had made it happen. She had grown up in Memphis, landed at Phillips Exeter herself, and recommended that Estevon join Memphis PREP, an organization that matched local high school students with summer programs at elite colleges and boarding schools. Estevon later called the Phillips Exeter program "the most significant, life-changing experience of my life." Abraham

Lincoln sent his oldest son to Phillips Exeter. Other famous alumni included Mark Zuckerberg, the billionaire founder of Facebook.

At Phillips Exeter, Estevon went on cross-country runs four times a week with speedy students from Hong Kong. Like many of the kids from Memphis, he'd never learned to swim. Now he finally did, and he went to the beach. He explored the streets of Boston. He wrote in an essay that he considered mathematics and science "the light rays that pierce the very depths of my soul," and he took courses in calculus, astrophysics and electronics.

Normally, tuition for this summer school cost more than $7,000, but because of the Memphis program, Estevon didn't have to pay anything.

"And I realized, like, my place in the world," Estevon said later. "Like, there are these other kids who are so much more advantaged." They'd gone to boarding school not just for a few weeks, but all the time, a privilege that at Phillips Exeter cost $45,000 per year before financial aid.

Estevon's peers came from different cultures, ethnicities and religions, but as he wrote in an essay, one thing united them: the will to better themselves. "I will never forget the tears fighting to run down my face when a close friend from Beijing signed my soccer ball on the last day with the words, 'I hope you enjoyed your summer, and I know that you will make all of your dreams come…'"

And then Estevon was on a plane back to Memphis, and back to Kingsbury High, where hundreds of kids sat in the gym for days, doing nothing. He wished he were somewhere else.

What he wanted was to get out of the neighborhood—not just to go to a state university in Tennessee, but to a really good school, far away, maybe Georgia Tech in Atlanta, where a younger sister lived with her father's family, or one of those shining, hard-to-reach schools in the Northeast. He'd seen the kids at Phillips Exeter, he knew where he stood, and he realized he would have to fight harder.

He was quiet, with a dark mustache, a long nose, long eyelashes, and sometimes a sleepy expression and a shy smile. He didn't socialize much. When he talked to people, he sometimes looked away. He liked to crack

unusual jokes, and through
the course of the year, his
English teacher, Jinger Griner, kept a running list of
Estevon-isms: "Are you being cereal?" "You're my white
Mama." "My toilet paper was
moving last night." "I wish I
had gotten hit by a taco."
"I'm tired of your sass, Ms.
Griner."

Estevon Odria. *(Photo by Karen Pulfer Focht/The Commercial Appeal)*

He ranked as one of the
top five students in Kingsbury's senior class. He had
already scored a 29 on the
ACT and had loaded his
schedule for the final year with hard courses, including Advanced Placement Chemistry.

Estevon was born in Miami, which made him a U.S. citizen. It did not
guarantee an easy life. Estevon's mother, Nadine, was a U.S. citizen from
a Mexican-American family, and she had given birth to him when she was
only 16. Estevon's father, Alfred Odria, was also a teenager born in the
United States, with a mother from Cuba and a father from Peru.

Nadine married Alfred Odria. Then they broke up, and Alfred ended
up with the baby. Nadine would later say she was tricked into giving up
Estevon. By this point, Nadine's parents had moved from Miami to Memphis. The young father asked Nadine's parents for help, and they agreed
to let him take the baby to Memphis and live with them.

Estevon's father, Alfred, started working as a security guard and at one
point took classes at the University of Memphis. Then in 2000, he went
home to Florida to visit relatives. He died on Christmas Eve; he was 23.

Estevon's grandfather said Alfred's heart had given out suddenly. He
said he believed Alfred had consumed alcohol at a party and that it reacted

badly with medication he was taking. So at five years old, Estevon was left without a father. He was raised primarily by his grandparents. After Estevon's birth, Nadine went on to have three more children with three different men. She lived with her youngest child, leaving the other two to be raised by their fathers' families.

Nadine's behavior frustrated Estevon. "I really don't feel like she's my mom sometimes. Because she still acts like she's 17 years old, calling me for money, when she knows I'm trying to go to college, actually trying to do something with my life and trying to like graduate high school, which is something she never did. Like sometimes I just—I just really can't—I don't understand her." His anger was palpable.

Months later, I spoke with Estevon's mother at a restaurant. Nadine was 34, with red tint in her dark hair and an ankh tattoo on her right wrist and a rose tattoo on the left.

She said she'd fought often with her parents growing up, particularly her stepfather—Estevon's grandfather. "I left the house when I was 15 because I didn't like the way I was being raised," she said, speaking English with a slight Southern accent. "I'll just leave it at that. So that's why I married [Estevon's] dad and got emancipated and had a child, because I didn't want to be home anymore."

She had lived in Miami, Las Vegas, California, and Memphis, where at one point she got involved with an abusive man who threatened to burn down her parents' house. She left that relationship, as she had left others. "I don't put up with a lot." She had dropped out of high school, but she later earned a GED and now was taking community college classes and working in information technology for UPS.

Though Estevon's grandparents raised him, Nadine still played a role in his life. She remembered him asking her to buy him a Nintendo game system for Christmas. When she gave it to him, he took it apart to see how it worked.

"He's really smart, he has a deeper understanding," Nadine said. "He's cynical. He's got an odd sense of humor. He might be a kind of hurt, angry child too, at the same time."

She acknowledged that yes, she'd asked Estevon to lend her money. "At one time I did," she said. "Like, my lights were getting cut off or something. It was important."

Nadine said she'd sometimes thought of herself as a bad parent. In the end, though, she said Estevon benefited from living with his grandparents. "He kind of grew up better. He probably was provided for better than I could have provided for him."

Estevon lived with his grandparents in a modest white house that stood within easy walking distance of the school. Estevon's grandfather, Francisco Gonzalez, was 51, with a salt-and-pepper beard. He was born in Guadalajara, Mexico, and brought to this country at age three—illegally, he said, but it was easier to obtain papers back then, and his status was legalized when he was a teenager. His wife, Victoria, was 54 and was born in the United States near Los Angeles, where she met her husband. She had a lung condition, and an oxygen tube in her nose helped her breathe.

Estevon's grandfather had served in the army and the National Guard as an engineer surveyor and worked for many years with a company that sent him to Miami to open a warehouse, then sent him to Memphis. It was the eventual loss of the job with that company that prompted the move to the Kingsbury neighborhood. Mr. Gonzalez had considered several neighborhoods but settled on Kingsbury in part because it would give Estevon a chance to learn more about his Hispanic heritage.

Unlike many Hispanic kids at Kingsbury High, Estevon spoke English at home. He had been exposed to Spanish early in life but couldn't really speak the language until he studied it as a teenager and learned it well enough to take a part-time job as a bilingual phone operator for Pizza Hut. He used his earnings to buy ACT prep books and to pay for private cello lessons.

"We're both proud of him and where he's at right now," Estevon's grandfather said. And they wanted him to keep going. According to Mr. Gonzalez, his younger daughter—Nadine's sister—had gone to a state college and dropped out, leaving her father still paying off debt. That meant Estevon's grandparents couldn't help pay for his college education. Estevon's grandmother had completed the twelfth grade, and his grandfather had gone to junior college and hadn't finished. If Estevon could earn a bachelor's degree, he would have gone further than anyone else in his immediate family.

Estevon's story and the hard relationship with his mother reflected the difficulties of teen parenthood. In a typical year at Kingsbury High, between 25 and 40 girls gave birth during the school year or already had a child, according to Tamara Bradshaw, the guidance counselor who worked with young mothers.

Intercom announcements would bring the girls together for support group meetings: "Teen moms, at this time please report to the parent resource center. Teen moms." One day in September, six girls gathered around the table with adult counselors and volunteers for a session organized by a Christian organization called Young Life.

The counselors served pizza and did their best to keep the mood cheerful. But the girls still radiated loneliness. When one young mother talked about sharing a bed with her child, a girl named Lorena Gomez said she could relate. "I know. Last night I was thinking I need somebody to hug, so I got Bella out of the crib."

Lorena smiled often and had dyed her dark hair red. She was 16 years old, an eleventh grader with academic ambition who was trying to graduate a year early. She said the best part about being a mother was having someone to care about. "And having someone who you know is going to love you forever now."

The worst part? The unrelenting stress of meeting a child's needs while trying to study, of staying up until 3:00 a.m., then getting up a few hours later to take a test.

As I spoke with Lorena in the living room of her house one day that fall, she looked weary, with dark circles under her eyes. Little Bella ran around the coffee table in blue overalls, her shoes clomping, and then she spilled a bottle of strawberry drink all over the table and floor. Lorena gasped, then started to clean up the mess.

A moment later, Bella threw herself down and began to wail. *"Fea,"* Lorena said. The word means "ugly."

"It's fit after fit after fit," Lorena said. "And it's kind of annoying. And I guess all of that builds up anger. And I'm trying to not build anger toward her, because then I don't want her to be raised like I was raised." Lorena's own mother, Erika Gomez, was only 14 when she gave birth to Lorena. Now Erika was a grandmother at 32, and she often fought with Lorena. It got so bad that Lorena moved to Dallas for a while to stay with her dad, but she had trouble enrolling in school and came back. Lorena had a difficult relationship with the baby's father, too.

Maybe the life of Estevon's mother, Nadine, had once been as hard as Lorena's. Maybe that explained why Nadine would let her own parents raise Estevon and why, for so many years, her relationship with him was so strained.

Estevon saw the failure all around him. But he felt he wasn't alone in his quest to succeed. His dead father had left nothing else in the world but his son, and Estevon believed that even now, his father wanted him to go to college and make something of himself.

"He does not want me to give up, and I understand that," Estevon said in his grandparents' kitchen. "He's not here but I feel him. Like his spirit, his soul."

Throughout my talk with Nadine in the restaurant, her tone of voice remained level, even as she described leaving Estevon behind or how the ex-boyfriend had threatened to burn down the house. Estevon certainly felt emotions, but sometimes showed little expression, and his mother seemed to act the same way.

I asked Nadine what made Estevon so driven.

"I'm that way," Nadine said. And much as her son would do, she looked away from me, through the glass of the restaurant window and toward the parking lot.

. . .

The first few weeks of the school year passed in disorder, but finally, the class-change buzzers began to sound at normal times. School clubs started meeting, including the Knowledge Bowl team, and at one practice they played along to a video of a *Jeopardy* episode. On a Saturday in mid-September, six weeks into the school year, Isaias and the other team members went to a trivia competition at St. George's Independent School, a local institution far different from their own.

At Kingsbury, the first thing that greeted visitors at the front door was a walk-through metal detector. At St. George's, the front door led to a luxurious space something like a living room, with bookshelves and a giant slab of petrified wood that served as a coffee table. A chandelier of antlers hung from the ceiling, giving it the look of an old hunting lodge. Knowledge Bowl coach Jacklyn Martin had heard that a staffer had apologized for not turning on the gas fireplace. If Kingsbury hosted a tournament and wanted to treat visitors to a roaring fire, they'd have to play a video.

That day the Kingsbury trivia team lost its first three games. They had three more chances, but it was looking increasingly unlikely that they would make it out of the six preliminary rounds and play for the championship on the big stage. Teams got ten points for buzzing in and answering a toss-up question correctly. They then got an exclusive shot at a bonus question worth 20 points. In other words, the rules favored a team that could correctly answer more than one question in a row, something Kingsbury was having trouble doing. In the common room just beyond the hunting lodge, Mr. Fuller started strategizing with the team. Geography and social studies seemed to be sticking points. Maybe the school could start a geography class and put Knowledge Bowl kids in it. He offered some encouragement. "You guys did well though, man. I loved it! I loved it!"

They fell silent.

A screen flashed the pairings for round four. Kingsbury would face a team from Memphis University School, the city's elite private boys' institution. The kids made their way down the hall and walked into a math classroom where chairs were arranged for two opposing teams with four players each. Kingsbury had brought five players this day, so one always sat out. As the top player and captain, Isaias always stayed in and played the biggest role in the games. Mr. Fuller settled in to watch and marveled at the school's wall-to-wall carpeting.

Then the opponents walked in: two Asian boys and two white boys, freshmen, the weakest of several teams that Memphis University School brought to the tournament. They looked as though they'd barely entered puberty. Now, maybe, Kingsbury could pick up a win. Early in the game, one of the freshmen answered a question correctly and moved to the bonus. "The topic is religious edicts. In 1521, the Edict of Worms declared what German religious reformer to be an outlaw and banned the reading and possession of his writings?"

MUS conferred and missed.

"Kingsbury?" the moderator asked.

"Martin Luther?" Isaias said, his voice rising in uncertainty.

"That's correct." Surprised laughter rippled from the Kingsbury team. They seemed to expect to lose. For question six, the moderator read some lyrics and asked the students to identify the song.

Breanna Thomas buzzed in for Kingsbury. "Jambalaya?" "Jambalaya is correct!" Surprised laughter again.

The moderator read question 11. "In 2012, the U.S. Senate narrowly rejected a Republican-sponsored measure that would have bypassed the Obama administration's objections to the construction of what pipeline from Canada to..." Isaias buzzed in before she finished. "The Keystone pipeline."

"That's correct."

But by the time the moderator read question 17, the momentum had shifted. "After Thomas Jefferson was authorized to organize the Corps of Engineers, it was stationed at what New York facility to establish an American military academy?" MUS got the answer: West Point. The Kingsbury students were fading in the late stages of the game, just as they had earlier that day. Watching from the back, Mr. Fuller made a quiet sound of frustration. Within minutes, it was all over. Kingsbury's best students fell to the ninth graders, 140 to 70.

The next game, against Ridgeway High, was even worse. At one point an expression of disgust crossed Isaias' face, and he sat back with his hand on his head. The team members walked to yet another game. "Can I sit out the next one?" Isaias asked Ms. Martin.

"Why?"

"I just want to."

Ms. Martin believed the results reflected a stark difference in social class. Kingsbury was facing teams of kids from schools that set higher standards, with parents who worked as lawyers or professors and took them to the symphony or on nice vacations. And in many cases, the other students had more experience playing Knowledge Bowl. Mr. Fuller had only tapped Isaias and several other kids the previous year. If you looked at it that way, with all the obstacles the Kingsbury students faced, they did well. She knew they could improve. But she felt proud of them.

Kingsbury hadn't always been a disadvantaged school. It opened its doors in 1950 to serve a new working-class suburb. Back then, every student, teacher and administrator at Kingsbury was white.

School segregation had been enshrined in the Tennessee constitution for decades. The first class of Kingsbury twelfth graders graduated in 1959, and the yearbook showed no African-Americans other than custodians and cafeteria workers. The number of black faces increased sharply in the 1960 yearbook—not because the school had integrated, but because the students had put on a minstrel show, a crude imitation of the people then known as Negroes. According to the yearbook, the show was "a howling success."

In 1954, the Supreme Court ruling *Brown v. Board of Education* had struck down segregation, but in Memphis, neighborhood segregation kept schools separate. The NAACP filed a lawsuit in 1960 to force the Memphis City Schools to finally desegregate. By the early 1970s, the NAACP was winning the court fight, and the school system would soon start transferring kids from school to school to achieve racial balance. They would do it with buses.[2]

A mostly white organization called Citizens Against Busing rallied op-

position to the plan and organized theatrical protests and stunts, most
famously staging the public burial of an empty bus in a giant trench.

In April 1972, Citizens Against Busing urged students to stay home for
two days. Kingsbury High, one of the premier all-white schools in the
system, recorded the highest total number of absences. Including junior
high students, 2,205 kids stayed home on the second day, 84 percent of the
student body.

But the protests and lawsuits couldn't stop busing. An early round of
busing started in January 1973, and a few months later a federal judge
issued a desegregation plan he called "Plan Z," thus designated because
he hoped it would mark the end of years of bickering over the subject. A
newspaper ran two pages of small type breaking down the school-to-
school transfers. The entry for Kingsbury High was succinct: "Swaps
with Douglass; Sends 200 whites, receives 350 blacks. Projected enrollment; 355 black, 857 white."

It didn't happen like that. Instead, many white students left.

In 1970, the school system enrolled more than 71,000 white students,
48 percent of the total. By the fall of 1973, the number had dropped to
39,000, or 32 percent. At Kingsbury High, the proportion of white students
dropped from 100 percent in the early 1970s to 48 percent by the 1981–
1982 school year. In the following years, the school's white population
dropped further as whites left not just the school, but the neighborhood.
Not all the white flight out of public schools in the years after desegregation
was due to racism. Regardless of their views on race, families recognized
that the Memphis City Schools often failed to offer a good education.

In a strange way, the all-white school enabled the creation of the multicultural one that Isaias attended. If whites had not left, property values
would not have dropped, and far fewer immigrants could have afforded
homes in the area. By the time Isaias entered his senior year, handwritten
signs hung on telephone poles near the high school: *"Casas baratas"*—cheap
houses. That said, significant numbers of whites stayed in the Kingsbury neighborhood, and white youths still accounted for 15 percent of

Kingsbury High's student population during Isaias' senior year, one of the highest proportions in an overwhelmingly African-American school system. Isaias' Knowledge Bowl teammate and close friend, Daniel Nix, was white. So was a boy named Cash Price and another teammate on the Knowledge Bowl team, Skylar Sutton.

Across the country, public schools were becoming increasingly minority, and increasingly poor. In Isaias' senior year, the proportion of low-income students in American public schools reached 51 percent, marking the first time in at least 50 years that poor kids made up the majority. Public school poverty was particularly bad in Southern states. In Tennessee, 58 percent of public school students were poor. In Mississippi, 71 percent.[3]

The increasing poverty wasn't due primarily to flight to private schools, said Steve Suitts, a researcher with the Southern Education Foundation. He said that since the 1980s, the proportion of kids in private schools had remained relatively steady. Instead, Suitts pointed to other factors: national anti-poverty programs such as Aid to Families with Dependent Children were declining, and wages were stagnating. Both factors often meant that families had less money. Low-income groups had more children than higher-income groups. Internal migration increased the concentration of poverty in certain areas, and international migration played a role, too, since immigrants tended to be poorer than the native born.

Knowledge Bowl coach and English teacher Jacklyn Martin said that students sometimes assumed that her white skin and teacher's credential meant that she'd never struggled. They didn't know that although she had been born into a wealthy family, she and her mother had plunged into poverty when her parents divorced. In eighth grade, she found herself in a program for at-risk youth, and adults told her not to get pregnant. To her, it seemed that society created two tracks: a track for people expected to make something of themselves and a track for poor people to whom society sent the message "Try not to be a loser." And she saw in Isaias a smart, weird, quirky student who, like her, had landed on the second track.

They'd talked about the line Kermit the Frog sang about being different: "It's not easy being green."

"Stay green," Ms. Martin would tell Isaias.

She was in her late 20s and in her short teaching career, she'd never encountered another student so brilliant. She cared about him, too. When he won an award in her English class the year before, she offered to get him any prize he wanted. He asked for Altoid mints, the ones that come in a blue box. She had to go to three stores to find them.

Isaias became her personal symbol. "At one point I had to ask myself if I was a phony in the classroom. Here I was telling these students 'Hard work pays off!' and 'If you learn how to write this essay and you learn these skills, then you're going to have a good career and you're going to be okay, and you're gonna be able to go to college.'"

Eventually, you had to question if that was true, especially with the uncertainty around Isaias' immigration status. "Seriously, the idea of him not going to college made me not want to teach. I can't keep selling this dream to them if it's not real."

In the private school's hallway between rounds at the trivia competition, Ms. Martin convinced Isaias to keep playing. Minutes later he and his teammates faced off against suburban public Collierville High School in a biology lab. The players took seats on metal lab stools.

"The translation of the capital city of what South American nation literally means, 'The Peace?'"

Isaias buzzed in. "Bolivia."

"Bolivia is correct. Bonus round, square root." Isaias groaned.

"What is x if the square root of $2x + 15 = 5$?"

Isaias paused. "Um, 5." Correct.

Kingsbury was scoring, but not enough. "Bonus Kingsbury. Last lines. This is the last line of what Hemingway novel? 'The old man was dreaming about the lions.'"

A conference, then Isaias said, *"The Old Man and the Sea."*

"Old Man and the Sea is correct."

Both teams missed the twentieth and final question. Lab stools scraped as the students stood up. Kingsbury had lost for the sixth time in a row.

Ms. Martin tried to cheer them up. "You answered so many questions correctly." As the group moved down the hall, she told them that not so long ago, Kingsbury's Knowledge Bowl team had routinely gotten scores of zero.

The students seemed ready to think about something else. Daniel Nix announced, "I'm looking at the bear" and walked off toward a big stuffed beast mounted on all fours in a glass case. The other kids followed. Later, Ms. Martin took them to lunch at a Chinese buffet near the high school, and when they finished their meals, a waitress brought the group a plate of fortune cookies. Skylar Sutton read aloud from the white strip of paper. "You will enjoy doing something different this coming weekend." Daniel's said the same thing. They continued around the table, and Isaias read his: "You will make many changes before settling satisfactorily."

"I don't know about that," Isaias said. "I used to think these things were very accurate."

Chapter Three

...

RAIN

Late September through October 2012:
Seven months before graduation

THE BUS PULLED TO A STOP outside the college fair site at a trade show hall. Counselor Patricia Henderson rose and stood in the bus aisle, faced the students and urged them to make good use of the opportunity.

"You only have a certain amount of time," she said, projecting her voice to the back of the bus.

"How much?" student Tommy Nguyen asked.

It would turn out to be not much time at all. First, organizers led the Kingsbury students into a big auditorium with students from other schools, where they heard speakers tell them why college mattered.

Paul Fisk, a man in greenish-gray combat fatigues, took a turn. "There's a hundred vendors out there. More. How many people are serious about being here today?" Hands went up. Mr. Fisk dismissed them. "Y'all are all lying because I bet most of you are here for the free pens and goodies on the tables, aren't you?" The students laughed. "Go out there and take it serious," he said. Then he painted a bleak picture of what would happen if they didn't. "Most of you will not go to college. Most of you will serve burgers. A lot of you will be poor. How many of you want to be poor?"

Then the Kingsbury students split into groups and went into small rooms elsewhere in the building. In one room, they did a listening exercise that involved recounting the details of a story about a robbery. In another room, students heard a lecture on personal finance and watched a video on credit card debt. It featured a sexy female devil who hissed, "Charge it! Charge it!" It was unclear what any of this had to do with finding a college, but it took a long time.

Finally, the Kingsbury students were released into a cavernous space divided by blue and white fabric panels. Hundreds of chattering voices echoed loudly. Rows of recruiters stood behind tables, representing colleges, the military, and local employers. Throngs of students from throughout the school system clogged the aisles and made it hard to move.

Isaias separated from the other Kingsbury students and walked through the aisles by himself—no plan, just looking for something to catch his eye.

He found it: a booth for a student-run radio station. Isaias was spending three hours a day in a sound recording class at the vocational center near the high school. He loved the work mixing music and radio plays. Now Isaias leaned across the table to talk with an African-American man with graying hair. This man told him the school system operated its own FM radio station and that students could get training. "Through Memphis City Schools, it's free!" the man said. "Really?" Isaias asked. Bad news: it was a three-year program and Isaias couldn't do it because he was already a senior. Isaias seemed disappointed. But the radio man kept going.

"What are you thinking about doing next year?"

"Maybe college. Maybe work for a year and then college."

Just then, a loudspeaker announcement broke through the echoing shouts. "Kingsbury students move to the holding area." The students had just begun to explore the colleges, but they were already running out of time. Maybe the St. George's parents would take their children for a leisurely stroll among the aisles in the evening session of the college fair, but most Kingsbury parents wouldn't. For Kingsbury students, this was the only shot.

Isaias quickly mentioned his interest in audio recording. The man recommended audio recording programs at the University of Memphis and Middle Tennessee State University and urged Isaias to apply for scholarships. He offered his business card and Isaias took it.

Excited, Isaias walked away toward the bus. The brief conversation with the radio man had planted a seed. Of course Isaias knew about the University of Memphis campus just a few miles from his house. But until that day, he had never heard of Middle Tennessee State. For the next few months, he would focus his energy on getting there.

• • •

Attendance dropped off at Kingsbury on rainy days since most students walked to school and some had to travel a long way. But Isaias had an unusual privilege, a silver two-door Mazda coupe of his own, and tonight he was driving some friends to Kingsbury's homecoming football game. Suddenly, blue lights flashed behind him. The speed limit on the road had changed, and he'd missed it.

This could be a real problem.

Memphis had a weak public transportation system. In general, anyone who wanted a normal life had to own a car. Immigrants could buy cars without a license and even register the vehicles with the county government. But like immigrants across the United States, the Memphis newcomers wanted driver's licenses: the documents made countless other transactions easier and greatly reduced the risk of arrest in a traffic stop.

Each state in the country set its own license requirements. Tennessee had experimented with issuing licenses and more limited "driving certificates" to immigrants who lacked Social Security numbers, but after people came from other states to get them, Tennessee scrapped the programs.[1] Now Isaias' immigration problems meant he couldn't get a Tennessee license. Like many others in the Kingsbury neighborhood, he drove without a license, and without insurance.

Isaias said he sometimes enjoyed the risk of driving without a license. "I'm living on the edge!" he told Patricia Henderson once. Tonight, though, he might get arrested. And though he and Dennis had applied for Deferred Action for Childhood Arrivals, the president's new legalization program, they hadn't yet been accepted.

Relief. The officer drove away unexpectedly, perhaps to take another call. Isaias continued to the bright lights of Fairgrounds Stadium, a little field dwarfed by the Liberty Bowl Memorial Stadium a short distance away, empty tonight and looming like a warship illuminated in electric blue. The Kingsbury football players were a diverse bunch: among them Jose Garcia, the beefy kid nicknamed "Big Sexy"; Aro Nebk, the Sudanese teen who also played soccer; and Cody Sherman, the white boy with the big smile. They'd struggled all season. Going into this early October game, Kingsbury's record stood at one win, six defeats.

Kingsbury's marching band fired brassy musical volleys across the field at the band from Booker T. Washington High, another inner-city school. A boy from a Vietnamese family—Tri Nguyen, whose name was pronounced "tree win"—pounded a set of five small white drums. Mohammad Toutio, who was born in Lebanon, banged a big bass drum.

A small, delicate girl played the flute. Black bangs reached almost all the way down to her large brown eyes. She was Magaly Cruz, quiet and easy to overlook, but arguably the smartest girl in the school, an eleventh grader who would stand at the board in Advanced Placement Chemistry and work out a complex problem in front of everyone. Something had happened between Isaias and Magaly the previous year, a hint of romance that fizzled. Now they moved in the same circles and played on the same Knowledge Bowl team but kept a certain distance. They hadn't talked about it.

As the band played, Isaias and his friends took a spot in the stands. The game had already begun, and for a change, Kingsbury was winning. A cool, crisp wind picked up, and a banner at the top of the bleachers began to snap. The public address system came to life. "Attention. The game has been called." The wind began blowing trash around the field. The crowd headed down the bleachers.

And then the stadium lights went out and the rain poured down. What had seemed like an inconvenience now felt like an emergency. Jose Perez, the JROTC leader, screamed to other cadets to stay together. Tri sped to the exit and left behind his portable five-drum set. Isaias picked it up and held it over his head. He left the stadium and walked into the parking lot, where music rang from a bus in the distance: the band from the other school, still playing. Mohammad walked with Isaias, occasionally banging his big bass drum. THUMP! THUMP!

The driving rain flattened Isaias' puffy hair and spattered the lenses of his glasses. He made his way to the back of one of the yellow Kingsbury school buses that had brought students to the game and scrambled to put the bulky band instruments on board, his brown jacket offering some protection. Magaly appeared behind the bus. "This is the best homecoming ever! We won it!" She had a point: the score was 7–6 when the game was called.

The rain slowed down. Soon Mr. Fuller accounted for all the Kingsbury students, and the buses rolled out of the parking lot. The teams restarted the game days later, and Kingsbury won 38–6. The homecoming ceremonies that had been planned for halftime took place during a pep rally in Kingsbury's gym. Mr. Fuller put a crown on the head of that year's homecoming queen, Clarissa Mireles, and Mohammad, Magaly, Tri and the rest of the band rocked the gym with blaring brass and rolling drums. When the audience filed out, the band kept playing all the way to the practice room, where Mohammad jumped up and down banging his drum.

But before any of this happened, while the rain was still falling, Isaias had given his brown jacket to Magaly.

. . .

A few days later, Kingsbury took a busload of students to a local private institution, Rhodes College, as part of a series of college visits. "I feel like I'm in the scene of Harry Potter," said senior Phalander Peoples, admiring the Gothic-style buildings. The campus impressed Isaias, too. "It doesn't feel like you're in Memphis."

Isaias stuck with Magaly. They ignored the tour guide and examined the environment like children brought to the beach for the first time, picking up every seashell and piece of driftwood.

They stopped to speak with a young man with glasses who was studying sheet music. They examined a sundial. Outside the library door, Magaly pulled the handle of the book drop, swinging it open with a dull metallic clang. She tapped a tile on the floor and said, "It's hollow."

The students ate lunch in the cafeteria after the tour and were supposed to meet back at the bus at 1:00 p.m. But Isaias and Magaly were gone. Counselor Brooke Loeffler climbed onto the bus. "Okay," she told the students. "Who has a cell phone number for Magaly or Isaias?"

A few minutes later, the two of them emerged from the cluster of Gothic buildings, making their way down the green, leafy boulevard toward the bus. "We went to the library," Isaias said. Ms. Loeffler told them they couldn't do that. What if something had happened? She didn't like to see honors students wandering off. It would set a precedent for the adults to set stricter rules on college visits. And how ironic that Isaias had asked why Kingsbury couldn't be more free and open.

On the bus ride back to Kingsbury, Phalander took a window seat and Isaias sat beside him on the aisle, with Magaly on the bench behind him. She was reading *Thinking, Fast and Slow*, a book on decision making. Isaias turned toward her and she held it out in the aisle so they could read it together.

Magaly loved libraries. So when she visited Rhodes, her rapid walk-through of the library with the tour group wasn't enough. "I was like itching to see what was really in there." She and Isaias went back and explored the place on their own. They were about to leave when they found a thick book on 1920s movies and lost track of time.

Magaly's mother, Consuelo Padilla, was 44, with graying hair and twinkling eyes, and she laughed often. One day that fall I met her and Magaly at La Michoacana, a Mexican ice cream shop on Summer Avenue near Kingsbury. The shop offered unusual flavors like tequila and corn. On this day I had *piñón*—pine nut—served heaped above the rim of a

white Styrofoam cup. Magaly ate pistachio and her mother had strawberry.

Magaly's mother came from a town called Teocuitatlán in the state of
Jalisco and grew up in a family of nine children living in a little house with
just one bedroom, a small kitchen and a living room. A local school offered
a basic education, but anyone who wanted more had to go to the city. The
family lacked money, so Consuelo left school after sixth grade. In 1990, she
moved to Los Angeles, where she worked for several years taking care of
children, then as a seamstress. In Los Angeles, she gave birth to Magaly.
Magaly's father never played a role in his daughter's life, and Consuelo
said they hadn't heard from him in a long time. She turned to Magaly. "How
old are you, daughter?" she asked in Spanish. "I think it's been something
like 17 years."

Now Magaly and her mother formed a tight little family of their own.
Years earlier, a friend had brought them to Memphis, where Magaly's
mother cleaned houses.

How did Magaly get so interested in reading? "Maybe it came from her
father because it doesn't come from us," her mother said. She and Magaly
laughed, and Magaly said in Spanish, "I'm the odd one of the family." But
her mother encouraged Magaly's will to learn and wanted her to seize the
opportunities this country offered. During tough times in Los Angeles a
few years before, many people she knew had talked about going home to
Mexico. Consuelo decided not to—not for her own sake, but for Magaly's.

Unlike many other Kingsbury students, Magaly didn't work outside of
school. She'd spent the summer doing academic enrichment, including
band, an engineering program for girls and a course to prepare her for
advanced placement work in the next school year.

Magaly sometimes wrote letters to an imaginary friend, the main
character in a novel called *Interrupted: Life beyond Words* by Rachel Coker.
She wanted to become a veterinary pathologist, someone who studies
animal diseases. She liked pygmy goats. She became a vegetarian.

Magaly held many things close, and only much later did she share defin-
ing facts of her young life: how her shyness sometimes felt overwhelming, as

Isaias lets Magaly wear his jacket during a break at a Knowledge Bowl competition, with teammates Daniel Nix and Adam Truong at left. *(Photo by Karen Pulfer Focht/The Commercial Appeal)*

though she would rather stare at a wall than talk to people. How her mother had a long relationship with a conservative man who didn't believe a girl should go into the world and try to learn. How she spent hours alone in her room, listening to classical music and reading, an attempt to escape from the fate the man wanted for her, that of an ignorant housewife. This man she described as her stepfather had left before her junior year, before our talk at the ice cream shop.

By the time Isaias visited the Memphis University School campus for a Knowledge Bowl tournament later in October, his romance with Magaly had become obvious. Magaly played on the Knowledge Bowl team, too, and in the courtyard between games, Isaias held his arm around her for long moments. She and Isaias chatted with each other online, sometimes writing backward messages. Later in the year, Isaias carried the massive double bass she played. He bought her a dress. In school, he sometimes caressed her face with the back of his hand.

...

Isaias and Magaly, two children of Mexican immigrants, almost always spoke with one another in English.

Perhaps that would surprise people like the scholar Samuel P. Huntington, author of a famous 2009 essay called "The Hispanic Challenge." He warned that immigration might effectively split the United States into two countries and cultures, one English-speaking, one Spanish-speaking. Huntington argued that Hispanic immigration, particularly from Mexico, differed greatly from other immigration waves. "The size, persistence, and concentration of Hispanic immigration tends to perpetuate the use of Spanish through successive generations."[2]

Some Kingsbury students had just arrived from Mexico, didn't speak English well, and took English classes for foreigners. Yet other developments would suggest Huntington was wrong. By 2013, more than two-thirds of U.S. Hispanics reported speaking English proficiently, a trend that reflected an increasing number of Hispanic children born in this country and a slowdown in immigration.

One of the most well-known Spanish-language media personalities was Univision news anchor Jorge Ramos, who told NPR in 2012 that his own children didn't watch his newscasts. "They get their information in English," Ramos said. "Their friends don't watch me. Their generation is not watching us in Spanish. So we have to do something." Univision joined ABC to launch Fusion, a network for English-speaking Hispanics. The network later shifted focus to young people of all ethnicities.

Though Isaias and Dennis maintained their ability to speak Spanish, their younger brother Dustin, born in the United States, didn't speak much Spanish at all, nor did many of his friends. Isaias would remark on this later—how strange it was to meet kids with Mexican names like Rogelio and Jose, none of whom spoke good Spanish. Though speaking good English would lead to success in American society, the lack of a common language between children and parents sometimes hindered normal relationships. "It is not uncommon to overhear discussions in which parents and children switch back and forth between languages and completely miss one another's intent," researchers Carola and Marcelo Suárez-Orozco wrote in 2001. And kids sometimes used language skills to deceive parents. "A thirteen-year-old Mexican boy admitted to us that he had told his parents that the *F* on his report card stood for 'fabulous.'" Sometimes the deception was more serious—a Hispanic officer with the Memphis police told me that because the second generation's main language was English, some parents didn't realize their children were involved in gangs. "Parents aren't even aware of what's happening, even when it's in front of them."

Isaias' mother Cristina said that when she spoke with Dustin, it was usually to express maternal love. If Dustin needed to speak with her about something more serious—a school matter, for instance—she got Isaias to interpret.

· · ·

Churches dotted the neighborhood around Kingsbury High School, and one of them, Iglesia Bella Vista, put on a one-day soccer clinic for boys and girls as part of its outreach efforts.

Many volunteers had come to the Streets Ministries community center to help, including a teenager with a handsome face, large ears and a V-shaped, muscular torso, like a welterweight boxer. He was Rigo Navarro, the best goalie on Kingsbury's soccer team. When the time came for the kids to practice their new shooting skills, Rigo let them try to kick goals past him, and for the little ones, he dropped to his knees so they'd have a chance.

Rigo lived near Isaias and considered him a friend, but they weren't close. Rigo had dated Mariana Hernandez for a time, but that had ended a while ago.

Several days after the soccer clinic I visited Rigo's house, one of the most beautiful I'd seen in the neighborhood. Pink roses bloomed near the entrance. An ample porch housed an upright piano and birdcages with chirping zebra finches, cockatiels and little quails pecking around the bottom.

Rigo Navarro. *(Photo by Karen Pulfer Focht/The Commercial Appeal)*

Rigo came from a big family and had many nieces and nephews, and toys, including a child-sized plastic kitchen, were scattered on the porch.

Rigo introduced me to his father, Rosalio Navarro, who was 59 and graying, and had the same large ears as Rigo. We settled on the porch, and Rigo's father told me that 17-year-old Rigo was his baby, the youngest of his nine children. The oldest were in their 30s.

Rosalio Navarro had grown up in Tequila, the city in Mexico's Jalisco state that was known for producing liquor, and he'd worked for many years in the grinding, low-paid job of harvesting and hauling the agave plants used to make the drink. As Rigo's father talked about growing up so poor that he didn't have shoes, Rigo played with an iPhone.

As a young man, Mr. Navarro entered the United States illegally to work, and for years he traveled back and forth to his home in Mexico. His wife remained at home and bore him several children. When the 1986 amnesty arrived, he got his green card in Fresno, California.

He eventually attained citizenship and applied for papers for other members of his family, including Rigo, whom family members had brought to the United States illegally when he was seven.

Certain immigration procedures had to be done at U.S. consulates outside the country. The immigration process required a teenaged Rigo and one of his brothers to spend several scary weeks in Ciudad Juarez, a Mexican border city that at the time was one of the world's most violent places. At the end of it, though, Rigo got his green card, a coveted document that let him work indefinitely in America and would also make him eligible for federal student aid for college.

Rigo worked construction and sometimes as a waiter at catered events. He loved soccer. Kingsbury fielded a strong team and had a shot at winning the state title in the spring, and Rigo hoped his success as goalie would help him win an athletic scholarship to go to college—none of his five older brothers or three older sisters had studied at the university level. He also thought about joining the military and becoming a helicopter pilot, then perhaps a chef. Or if he went to college, he might join ROTC.

Rigo's father earned about $500 per week in a construction job and sometimes brought in extra through side work. Rigo's mother rarely worked outside the home. Rigo's father said he couldn't help his son pay for college. "I pay for the house, I pay for the light and all this, and I always end up with nothing."

Rosalio Navarro told me that when he grew up in Mexico, his family had so little money that he went to school without notebooks and pencils. During recess, he used to sneak into the classroom, find another student's pencil and break off a piece to use. He told his parents he didn't want to go to school anymore, and they said he didn't have to. So he dropped out and started working.

He was in third grade.

Now Mr. Navarro had trouble understanding Kingsbury's attempts to explain the higher education system to parents. In late October, the school put on an evening session in the library about the college admissions and financial aid process. The session was almost entirely in English. Principal Fuller would later say he couldn't remember why the school hadn't made arrangements for an interpreter that night. Rigo's father came, and afterward I asked him what he thought. "I don't think much about it, because I don't understand much of what they're saying," he said in Spanish. He said he'd asked Rigo to pay close attention.

Mr. Navarro's problems at the college session pointed to a broader issue. Immigrant parents often didn't have enough English skills and literacy to help their children engage with education, even in preschool. Programs that helped adults build those skills were facing funding cuts. One example was a federal Department of Education program called Even Start, which aimed to teach literacy to less-educated parents while encouraging them to become full partners in their children's education. About half of participating parents were Hispanic. But Even Start faced bad evaluations, funding was eliminated in 2011, and similar programs were generally "under-resourced and disjointed in their delivery," a Migration Policy Institute report said. In many cases, schools across the United States had serious difficulty communicating with immigrant parents.[3]

As I left Rigo's home that evening early in the fall, his father noticed a pencil lying on the porch. Perhaps one of the young children in the family had dropped it there. He held up the yellow pencil. "After all that I suffered—now they're just thrown around!"

After that, I drove straight to a college recruiting event at a Memphis hotel, where representatives of Harvard and several other ultra-selective schools took turns going to the podium. Each one described their institution as a sort of academic Disneyland. You can study whatever you want! It's totally open-ended and everyone's brilliant! At Duke you could even study lemurs.

"We like to joke that the student-to-palm-tree ratio is four to one," the recruiter from Stanford University in California said, adding that, of course, adults would want to visit their kids at college. "I highly recommend the vineyards of Napa. Parents?"

I thought of Rigo's dad. It was absurd to imagine that Rigo would even think of applying to Stanford, that his academic record would be strong enough to get in, or that his parents would spend hundreds of dollars to fly across the country to visit him and drink wine. The recruiter's comment reminded me of the chasm of education, wealth and social wherewithal that separated many children of Hispanic immigrants from their better-off peers.

In his senior year, Rigo struggled with a knee injury that threatened his athletic performance. But an even more important threat to Rigo's future was his shaky academic record. He'd missed much of eleventh grade and failed English 3. Now, in his senior year, he would take English 3 and English 4, both with Philip Tuminaro.

Rigo said that this year, he'd have to focus on school. "My future depends on it."

Could Rigo keep his grades up? Would he choose to join the military? Could he become the first in his family to go to college? Would he emerge as a star soccer player and help take his team to the state title? Right now, his future was entirely open.

• • •

That fall, Rigo filled out a form in his seventh-period English class, taught by Mr. Tuminaro and a young assistant teacher, Corey VanHuystee. The first question on the form was "How many books did you read this year?" Like many other students in the class, Rigo wrote "one."

"Say 'hey' if the last book you read was only because someone told you to read it," the assistant teacher said. "Hey," Rigo said, along with some others. "I don't like reading," he said after class. "I usually have a tough time pronouncing words and understanding words that I don't know." But he liked some Greek mythology books with illustrations that he'd read in the ninth grade.

Through the course of the year, Mr. Tuminaro and Mr. VanHuystee tried different strategies to improve the reading level of their students. For a while, they gave them extremely difficult passages to read, in the hopes that they'd learn more by struggling through. But even at the end of the year, some students continued to make basic mistakes in reading and writing, like forgetting to capitalize the first words in sentences. "They shouldn't have reached twelfth grade not being able to read," Mr. Tuminaro said. "It's partially their fault and partially the system's fault."

Despite Rigo's professed lack of interest in reading, Mr. Tuminaro considered him a bright, promising student. And either way, the teacher believed in helping people improve from where they were. Yes, many of the kids read poorly. "But that's why we're here," Mr. Tuminaro said. "If they all understood, we'd be out of a job."

Mr. Tuminaro was a slender, olive-skinned 28-year-old from Poughkeepsie, New York. His mother had come from Bolivia, and his father was Italian-American. Many other teachers had landed at Kingsbury through Teach for America or the program that brought Mr. Tuminaro, Memphis Teacher Residency. Mr. Tuminaro said his faith in God kept him going. "He brought me here and the work is hard, but I really, really do love what I do. Really love some of these students."

Mr. Tuminaro believed in living where he taught, and he and his wife rented a house near the school. One time he drove me around the neighborhood and pointed to a fence where homeowners were fighting a long-standing battle with people spraying gang graffiti. They'd paint the fence, then the taggers would come and deface it again. On another street, Mr. Tuminaro mentioned that someone had been shot in the leg there and had survived. "He ended up being the kid that mowed my lawn for a while later on." Mr. Tuminaro stopped to get fuel at a gas station and had to raise his voice as he spoke with the clerk over the pounding reggaeton music. Continuing our tour, he pointed out Jerry's Sno Cones, an iconic business painted in bright colors that had launched in 1974, back when the neighborhood was still mostly white and working class.

The neighborhood did have some things going for it, Mr. Tuminaro said. Many immigrant families were still intact. But some families led unstable lives.

One day that fall, Mr. Tuminaro tried to call all the parents in his class to deliver progress reports. Reaching parents was no easy task at Kingsbury, since kids often moved from place to place and phones were disconnected. He made the kids who'd come to school that day write down contact information on popsicle sticks that he could use later in drawings to choose random students for class activities. He made calls at the back of the room, sometimes switching to Spanish.

"Do you know who he's staying with?" Mr. Tuminaro said into the receiver, using English this time.

"No idea?" he continued. "Okay. Have you talked to the school's guidance counselor about this?"

The student had disappeared—not disappeared as in kidnapped, but refusing to tell his mom where he was staying. Mr. Tuminaro could relate; as a teenager, he'd often gotten in trouble with his mother and, as a result, had to stay with friends for a while.

The seventh-period English 4 class proved a discipline challenge, too, with students slacking off and talking out of turn. To get the group under control, Mr. Tuminaro and Mr. VanHuystee made a project of working out a sort of contract between themselves and the class. They called it "How we roll," and they made lists of what the teachers expected from students and what the students expected from teachers.

One student undermined the spirit of the thing by scribbling a sarcastic phrase on a board at the side of the room: "How we roll, modafuckas."

But Rigo was among the students who gave a constructive suggestion for how teachers should treat kids.

"Not to give up on us," Rigo said.

"Don't give up on us," Mr. VanHuystee said and wrote it on the board.

· · ·

It might be easy to write off Kingsbury students as hopeless. But even as students in Mr. Tuminaro's class struggled with the fundamentals of reading they should have learned years earlier, students in Jihad Haidar's AP Chemistry class answered questions like this:

10.0 g of acetic acid (CH_3CO_2H) reacts with 10.0 g of lead (II) hydroxide to form . . . lead (II) acetate ($Pb(CH_3CO_2)_2$) and water. Which reactant is in excess? How many grams of it will remain after the reaction goes to completion? How many grams of lead (II) acetate will form?

Compared to the problems that came later in the year, that question from a class worksheet was easy. Students like Magaly Cruz, Mariana Hernandez, Estevon Odria, Franklin Paz Arita and Adam Truong dealt with material so difficult that I didn't come close to understanding it, and I was an adult with a college degree.

If watching the English 4 class left me dismayed at what some Kingsbury kids couldn't do, watching AP Chemistry left me astonished at what others could.

Thirty years old, with dark brown skin, black hair and a round face like a cherub, Jihad Haidar was born in Lebanon in 1982 at a time when Israeli jets were bombing the country. Because he led the soccer team, everyone called him Coach Haidar.

At 17, he'd come to America to study and made extra money working in convenience stores. He was Muslim and was married to a Christian woman from the area. He said he didn't practice his faith very much, but he still fasted and did his best to help the poor and volunteer in the community. The word *jihad*—his first name—could be translated as "holy war," but it also meant struggling to live correctly. "So, for example, if you work hard to feed your family, that's called a form of *jihad*," Coach Haidar said. He was well liked among the Kingsbury staff and as a teacher and coach, he set big goals. He urged the soccer players to go for the state championship in their division. They'd come in second twice. Now he was teaching Advanced Placement Chemistry for the first time, and his students would take a tough national exam in May that would give them a shot at college credit. The test was so hard that barely half of students in the country managed to pass. In the hallway one day, another teacher had told Coach Haidar that he hoped one of the students would make a three, the lowest passing score. But a three wasn't enough for Coach Haidar. He wanted his students to make fours and fives, the highest marks possible.

Doing this was hard without supplies. Coach Haidar said he'd been waiting for weeks for the district to send him books and lab kits for his AP

Chemistry class. He'd been using other written materials and paying for lab supplies out of his own pocket. In September, he said he would give the district one week. If nothing showed up, he'd go to the district officials and ask them the obvious question: Do you want this class to continue or not?

The lab kits finally arrived on October 10. The books arrived on October 15. The school year was well over two months old.

...

Isaias continued his college search. One day that October he took a seat in a classroom next to his friend Daniel Nix, ready to listen to Brandon Chapman, the tall African-American recruiter visiting Kingsbury from Middle Tennessee State University.

If Harvard was an exclusive French restaurant with white tablecloths, Middle Tennessee State was fast food. And indeed, Mr. Chapman started his talk by telling the group of Kingsbury kids that the university's student union had a new Popeye's Chicken franchise. The students responded with approving laughter and murmurs.

"I know y'all like Popeye's," said the recruiter, who wore glasses and a shirt and tie. He went on: the student union offered a Panda Express, a taco bar, a potato bar, Dunkin' Donuts and the new Blue Raider Grill, which was like Chili's. "All included in your meal plan at MTSU!"

He told them more about the university: it had just completed a $147 million science building, it enrolled 25,000 students, and it automatically accepted anyone who met basic grade point average and test score criteria.

For a student like Isaias, MTSU's admissions standards were easy. The cost was another story: $14,000 a year. But the recruiter said the students could get help through a Tennessee HOPE Scholarship funded by the state lottery. However, Isaias and other kids with immigration problems couldn't get this scholarship. Ms. Loeffler, the school counselor, asked how MTSU dealt with immigration status.

"Undocumented status is still a touchy subject with all schools in the state of Tennessee," Mr. Chapman said. "At MTSU because of the policies, you're going to be considered out of state. So it's an extra $10,000 that you're looking at as a cost."

Mr. Chapman said the university president hated this. "MTSU's stance is it's not fair, it's not right. They graduated from a high school in Tennessee, they should be able to have in-state status. However, there are 'powers that be' above us that will not allow us to give them in-state tuition." Isaias showed no reaction. But he had a question. "Where is MTSU?"

"Where is MTSU? It's in Murfreesboro. Which, depending on how you drive, is three or four hours away from Memphis."

Mr. Chapman took more questions and finished with an invitation: MTSU would bring its "True Blue Tour" recruiting event to Memphis later that month. The university president and representatives from all the university's divisions would come, and he said the Kingsbury students should come, too.

The meeting broke up, and Ms. Loeffler brought Isaias to talk to the recruiter. Someone mentioned his ACT score of 29. The big man put his arm around Isaias and told him he could win a scholarship. "For you, it would be everything."

"Are you serious?" Isaias asked.

Mr. Chapman pointed to a brochure. "This full amount right here will be covered. So it now becomes a viable option to you because of a score like this." He gave Isaias a business card, patted him on the back and promised to work out a deal.

"Great!" Isaias said. "That's really good to hear."

And Mr. Chapman said that if Isaias made it to the recruiting event on October 24, he would personally introduce him to the university president and vice president. "We can't let this kid slip through our hands because of a situation we have no control over."

Several factors made Isaias an attractive candidate for MTSU and other schools. He could bring diversity to MTSU's majority white campus, where Hispanics made up only 4 percent of the student body. But more important, he had an unusually high test score.

Recruiters for Ivy League schools said that they considered the whole applicant through essays, grades and recommendations. They said standardized tests represented only part of the equation. State universities in Tennessee made no such claim. The admissions process boiled down to grade point average and ACT scores. Competitive universities outside the South, like Harvard, had historically preferred another test, the SAT. But most Memphis students didn't apply to those schools, and few took the SAT. The ACT was what counted, and it counted for a lot.

A high ACT score could mean automatic admission and thousands of dollars in scholarship money, even if the student had a shaky grade point average. ACT scores were so important that Principal Fuller made them part of his daily mantra on the announcements. "All of our children strive to make 30s on the ACTs!" In September, Estevon Odria, the student who was striving to go to an elite school, scored a 31 on his latest test. The school announced it on the marquee outside:

E ODRIA

30 ON ACT

Which was one point lower than he'd actually scored, but perhaps the idea was that he'd passed the threshold of 30. At Kingsbury, the median ACT score had floated around 16 for years. Roughly 80 percent of students nationwide did better. Even strong Kingsbury students sometimes struggled on the test. That's why when the recruiter met Isaias, he reacted as though he'd found a shiny nugget of gold.

October 24 arrived. The Middle Tennessee State recruiters brought their traveling show to a banquet hall in Germantown, a wealthy Memphis suburb.

They prepared exhibit spaces for the university's major departments, including the music recording industry program that had excited Isaias. Students and parents trickled in and began filling plates with food: chicken on skewers, triangles of pita bread with dip, fudge squares. Isaias had said earlier that he planned to come to the event around 5:00 p.m. But that hour had passed, and he hadn't arrived.

The students and parents settled into rows of chairs as recruiters began to talk about the school. A white woman named Lisa Johnson who worked in sales management for the drug company Pfizer took the microphone and told the audience that her son had just enrolled at MTSU. She'd taken him to see the campus over and over: on the weekend, during the week, on spring break. Now she was an empty nester.

"So making this decision for him was pretty big for me." She caught herself. "*Us* making this decision was pretty big."

Immigrant parents often couldn't do this sort of work for children. The mentors at school were helping Isaias on his journey to college, but they couldn't offer as much attention as a parent would. His parents' ignorance of the system meant that in many ways, he was on his own. The college admissions process required children of immigrants to think like responsible adults, projecting themselves years into the future and imagining the college graduates they could become. But much of the time, they didn't act like responsible adults. They acted like kids.

Across Memphis, students the same age as Isaias were blowing opportunities to win thousands of dollars. A woman named Kaci Murley helped organize the tnAchieves program, which offered scholarships worth up to $3,000 to help high school students attend community colleges and trade schools. She said nearly every high school student who applied won a scholarship automatically. But they had to attend meetings. The problem: the students just didn't come. As of January 2013, roughly half the students across the city who had applied had already forfeited their chance. At Kingsbury, 82 had applied, and 11 came to the mandatory meeting.

And now at the Middle Tennessee State recruiting event, about 20 minutes remained before 7:00 p.m., when the big blue traveling show would pack up and leave. The recruiter who had put his arm around Isaias after the meeting at Kingsbury stood near the door, ready to greet anyone who came through. The tables were still full of food. The leader of the audio recording program waited, ready to talk. The university president hadn't come after all, but several other high-level officials had.

And Isaias was still nowhere to be seen.

Chapter Four

...

A DECK OF CARDS

Isaias finally walked through the door shortly before the recruiting event ended.

He spoke briefly with a representative of the music recording program that interested him, then walked over to the financial aid table, introduced himself and explained his situation. "But the problem is right now I'm undocumented and I'm going through the Deferred Action process. And I want to know if I do want to apply, how would I apply? As an international student or out of state? If I do get Deferred Action, would that change anything? Would it be hard? How could I get scholarships?"

The president had only announced the Deferred Action program a few months before. Many university staffers rarely dealt with immigrant students, and in this case, they didn't know the answers.

But soon Mr. Chapman, the recruiter, reappeared and introduced Isaias to a wiry white man in a suit, David Schmidt. Mr. Schmidt was the vice president of international affairs. Even though Isaias had lived in the United States since 2003, the university would handle him as a foreign student.

"If you apply, there are ways we can work with your situation," Mr. Schmidt told Isaias. "What I would recommend is no matter what your

situation, do not let that prohibit you from pursuing what you want to do."
He wrote out his e-mail address and gave it to Isaias.

"We'll take it step by step, okay?"

They said goodbye, and Isaias got some grapes from the banquet table.
Isaias told me he hadn't asked his parents to come since he figured they'd
likely ask just as many questions as he would. And if he was the one
that really wanted to go to college, he should come and not bother them
with it.

Isaias said he came late because something had lasted longer than he
thought it would. He wouldn't elaborate, saying only that it was private.
Late or not, the conversation with Mr. Schmidt made him happy. "It's very
encouraging to hear that I could contact him directly and we'd be able to
work through the case. I like that," Isaias said, pausing to eat. "These are
good grapes."

As Isaias and most other Kingsbury students considered colleges
close to home, Estevon Odria looked at schools farther away, drawing on
advice from mentors with Memphis PREP, the nonprofit that had sent
him to Phillips Exeter in the summer.

One of Estevon's strongest supporters was the school librarian and
writing teacher Marion Mathis. She'd developed a close relationship
with Estevon when she taught him in eleventh grade and wrote glowing
recommendation letters for him. In one letter, she called Estevon "a quiet yet
fun-loving genius" and "the student I have waited to teach for twenty years."

Tufts University in Massachusetts and Bates College in Maine flew
Estevon to visit their campuses and attend recruiting programs for minority
students. He wasn't impressed with Bates. "It was very cold," he said in
chemistry class one day. "And they had too many lobsters."

A third school flew him to campus that fall for a diversity weekend: Carnegie Mellon University in Pittsburgh. Estevon wanted to go there more
than anywhere else. He had learned about the school from a mentor at
Memphis PREP. *U.S. News and World Report* ranked the university twenty-
third nationally, only slightly below the most elite schools. Estevon saw
Carnegie Mellon as competitive, but he thought he might get in. "People

tell me to go to like Harvard or Yale, an Ivy League school, but I don't want to do that." Those were basically liberal arts colleges, and he wanted to study technology.

Estevon completed an application to the Carnegie Mellon engineering school and did it "early decision," meaning that if he was accepted, he would go. The engineering college accepted only one in five applicants. He couldn't count on getting in.

At Kingsbury, Estevon's ACT test score of 31 was so exceptional that school officials had boasted about it on the marquee outside. At Carnegie Mellon, a 31 was the median, which meant half of admitted students scored higher. In the university's engineering college, fully a quarter of admitted students had scored a perfect 800 on the math section of the other national test, the SAT.

Estevon didn't have a scanner or printer at home, so Ms. Mathis let him use the equipment at her house not far from the high school. He completed applications to New York University Polytechnic School of Engineering; Georgia Tech; the University of Tennessee, Knoxville; Vanderbilt University in Nashville; the University of Texas at Austin; University of California–Berkeley; University of California–Los Angeles; and Rensselaer Polytechnic Institute in Troy, New York.[1]

This process generated much paperwork for the adults around Estevon. He needed recommendation letters and family financial records, and he asked for them again and again. "My son stays on it. He's determined," his mother, Nadine, said months later. "He's gonna call you until you get it sent over, e-mailed. 'Did you do it? Did you do it? Are you gonna do it?'"

Estevon completed his Carnegie Mellon application ahead of the early decision deadline. But he knew just how strong the other applicants were. And he told his grandparents he doubted he'd get in.

. . .

Mariana Hernandez visited a college campus that November and had a chance to observe a biology class. The professor said something that surprised her. "We forgot to pray," she said. "Let's pray real quick."

The professor sang the word "Alleluia," stretching the word into multiple syllables, then sang "Give a high five to the one next to ya!" The students began exchanging high fives, two hands at once. She repeated the words and ended with a prayer. "Father bless us, give us a good day. Amen." Soon the professor was teaching a lesson about how DNA is transcribed into RNA inside a cell.

Mariana and dozens of other high school students were attending an all-day recruiting event at Christian Brothers University, a small Catholic campus in Memphis. The city schools were off for Veterans Day, but the university remained open, which gave Mariana a chance to visit while classes were in session. Two other Kingsbury students had come with her— her boyfriend, Adam Truong, and their friend Tommy Nguyen.

The lighthearted song might suggest a lack of seriousness, but the university had a reputation for delivering a solid education. Its six-year graduation rate was 60 percent, better than many other schools in the area.

The college was founded by the De La Salle Christian Brothers, a religious order that believed in educating young people, particularly the poor. In Memphis, that meant enrolling African-Americans and others who might be first in their family to go to college. The school had enrolled its first black student in 1960, and minorities and international students now made up roughly 44 percent of its total enrollment of 1,600. Even though it was a Catholic college, it enrolled students of many faiths, and some Muslim girls with *hijab* head coverings moved through the campus of modest brick buildings and covered walkways. Mariana thought the prayer and singing were odd—she felt as if she were in church.

But overall, the class gave Mariana a positive impression. "The lady was nice. It was a small classroom. Knew what they were talking about." Mariana and the others knew Christian Brothers students, including Tommy's girlfriend, and they'd spent time on the campus. Mariana had participated in a Streets Ministries summer program that exposed her to college life, and she was taking advanced courses. Compared to many Kingsbury students, she and the others knew a lot about college and were well positioned to go. When another college recruiter visited Kingsbury High that same month, a girl asked a question that showed she had little conception of college life: "They have a bathroom in the dorm, right?"

Later that afternoon, Mariana, Adam and Tommy met with an admissions counselor and reviewed their files. The three of them did this as a group, without their parents.

Tommy's mom usually worked from 8:00 a.m. to 7:30 p.m. at a nail salon, and his dad worked at a warehouse in a night maintenance job and slept during the day. Mariana said, "My dad's very liberal. He's like 'You don't need my help. I'm not going to college. You are. You do it.'"

Adam's mother worked in a nail salon, too. He later said she wanted him to go to college, but she didn't keep up with the details. She didn't understand nuances such as the difference between prestigious private schools and lesser-known public schools, and if Adam asked her to sign a document as part of the college application process, she wrote her signature without understanding what she'd agreed to. It had been this way much of his life: from an early age, Adam and his older sister had acted as interpreters and guides for their parents, immigrants from Vietnam who didn't speak English. The children paid bills and dealt with the mortgage, utilities and the phone company. The responsibility made Adam and his sister grow up fast. So did their family's troubles.

Adam told me he was born in Beaumont, Texas, a small city by the Gulf of Mexico. His father spent months at a time working on commercial shrimp boats. Adam said shrimpers sometimes dealt with the boredom of the long trips by using drugs, and that his dad used cocaine and crack. Adam said that once when his father wanted to apply for a factory job, he made Adam pee in a bag so he'd have clean urine for a drug test.

Both Adam and his sister Ashley remember that their parents began to argue, and that the arguments became increasingly frightening—Ashley remembers one fight in which her parents trashed the living room, throwing pictures on the floor, glass breaking. Adam developed the habit of using video games to escape this environment—but the fights were so intense he couldn't ignore them. "We witnessed a lot of things during the time."

Adam's grandmother on his mom's side visited from Vietnam. After one very bad fight between Adam's parents, she convinced her daughter to leave the marriage. Adam's mother appeared at her children's school in the middle of the day, packed the children's things and told them they were moving to Tennessee, where distant relatives lived.

"It all happened so fast," Adam said. "We didn't know how to take it. Me and my sister cried and that's about it. We didn't know how it was going to be leaving my dad and stuff." He would remember the date—October 26, 2006. He was 11 years old. He and his sister quickly found themselves in a new city, Memphis.

Adam said his father was so shocked by the departure of his wife and children that he changed his life and stopped using drugs. He later reestablished his relationship with his children and sent them money. They began going on trips to see him.

The family's difficulties continued in Memphis. Adam said his mother used to gamble, and sometimes the kids didn't have enough money to buy pencils. In 2015, Adam told me his mother had stopped gambling.

I don't speak Vietnamese, but I wanted to talk with Adam's parents through an interpreter and hear their side. Adam asked them about this possibility and told me shortly before I completed this book that they'd both declined to be interviewed. Adam said his father worked all the time in a gas station and was dealing with two recent deaths in the family and that his mother was busy, too.

Adam acknowledged that his parents had helped him and his sister in an important way: they had pushed their children to work hard and make good grades in their elementary school years, and the children maintained that habit through middle school and high school.

The children also saw the long and hard hours their parents worked. To Adam, his dad and other relatives seemed unhappy. He didn't want to end up like them.

. . .

December 2012:
Five months before graduation

A few weeks after Mariana and the others visited Christian Brothers, Isaias climbed on board a big tour bus that stood parked in front of Kingsbury High in the predawn darkness.

A moment later, the bus pulled out into the sleeping streets. Shortly before 10:00 a.m., the bus arrived in a Murfreesboro district of big box stores and a shopping mall. The driver steered the bus into Middle Tennessee State University's campus, a sprawling collection of big modern buildings. The kids climbed out and walked into the student union, a spacious new building with the feel of an airport.

Admissions staffers brought the group to the parliamentary room, where the student council held its sessions. It was a high-ceilinged space with tiered rows of seats and microphones, and the students immediately started hitting buttons and speaking into them. The MTSU counselors reviewed the admissions requirements again, then took the group on a campus tour.

Magaly had stayed back in Memphis—as an eleventh grader, she only took part in a few of the college search activities that so often occupied Isaias and his twelfth-grade classmates. It seemed strange to see Isaias without Magaly. They had been spending so much time together lately that I had almost begun to think of them as a unit.

After the tour, the Kingsbury students ate lunch and killed time in the campus bookstore. Isaias' friend Daniel Nix tried on an MTSU baseball cap, putting it on sideways. "Hey, now you look like white trash!" Isaias joked.

Soon it was time to return to Memphis. The visit had consisted of an admissions talk, the campus tour, and lunch. The students hadn't done any of the things that more actively involved parents might have arranged for their children. Isaias hadn't sat down one-on-one with a recruiter, visited the recording studios, spoken with students or watched any classes.

On the bus ride home, Isaias shared his thoughts on the visit. "It's nice. It's very pretty. It looks—I don't know. Very interesting. Very appealing."

The bus rolled on to Memphis.

The semester was speeding to an end. A couple of days later, Isaias and Magaly directed other kids in a school play with a script they'd written. They had tried to mimic an old silent film with titles explaining the action. But the projector by the stage didn't work properly, and the scene became a confusing pantomime that had something to do with a girl opening her presents on Christmas morning. As Isaias later put it, "We just looked like idiots running around with the screen down and nothing on it."

In Philip Tuminaro's seventh-period English class for seniors, guidance counselor Brooke Loeffler arrived for a special talk on college applications.

"I'm kind of afraid to ask this question, but how many people have requested a transcript?"

Six hands went up. A bad result. "This group is really behind on college applications, so let me go over what you need to do," she said. She told them about the FAFSA, the Free Application for Federal Student Aid that they'd start filling out in January. And she said they'd better start studying.

"You have 210 seniors in your class right now." Could the seniors guess how many of them had been flagged by teachers as possibly failing?

The students started calling out numbers.

"Ninety!"

"Two hundred!"

"I know I'm one of them," a girl muttered.

"Ninety-eight," Ms. Loeffler said. "Half of your class at this point may not graduate because they are not coming to school or doing their work."

She offered to talk with them individually, either later or right then. Several students lined up to talk with her in the classroom.

Other students chattered so loudly that they drowned out the afternoon announcements.

At a faculty meeting, Mr. Fuller and other staffers gave the teachers instructions for semester grades: if the student hasn't done all the required work, put an "I" for "incomplete" in some cases. And whatever you do, don't put any grade below a 60. On a scale of one to 100, a 60 was a failing grade, but it still implied that the student had done more than half the required work. "We're going to give them the maximum opportunity to pass these classes," Mr. Fuller said.

. . .

On the morning of Christmas Eve, Estevon logged on to his computer and read that he'd been accepted to Carnegie Mellon. He couldn't believe it. "Because my test scores were horrible for that school."

Estevon was probably overstating it, but the scores that made him a standout at Kingsbury were only middling for Carnegie Mellon. He shared the good news with Marion Mathis, the teacher and librarian. "I'm relieved," Ms. Mathis said. "He's driven me crazy!" She laughed, and Estevon laughed, too. I was talking with them in the living room of her house, a place decorated with gargoyle statues and golden-framed portraits that showed dogs and orangutans dressed in human clothing. This house had become Estevon's base of operations as he completed countless applications for colleges and outside grants.

"He's relentless," Ms. Mathis said. "I do admire that about him. If he needs help with something, he is so persistent. He never gives up. And that's how he made it there."

Ms. Mathis wasn't the only person helping Estevon. Among the others was Bitsy Kasselberg, a counselor with the organization Memphis PREP. She met Estevon at the public library several times to help him finalize his application for the Gates Millennium Scholars Program, which required multiple essays. This program for minority students was funded by a grant of more than $1 billion from the charitable foundation led by Bill Gates and his wife, Melinda.

At the time of the grant in 1999, the billionaire had to defend himself against criticism that the new program excluded white students. He told *The New York Times* that some minority groups were woefully underrepresented in the high-tech industry and on many university campuses.

"Nobody can deny that there is a huge gap, particularly in these key areas, for minority students, and the financial barriers are a substantial element in that," he said.[2]

Estevon wouldn't know for months if he'd get the scholarship.

Carnegie Mellon still hadn't given Estevon a formal financial aid offer. But he'd received an estimate, and he was confident he could afford to go. He thought of his father and the significance of the Christmas Eve date. "Because 24 was the day, the anniversary of his death. I think it's just a coincidence, but it's interesting."

. . .

On Christmas Eve, the members of the Ramos family drank *ensalada de Nochebuena*, a traditional punch made with ingredients including sugarcane, beets, the tuber called jicama, oranges and peanuts. Magaly and her mother visited the Ramos family's house and Magaly gave Isaias a nice digital watch, some pajamas and a book called *Stick* that showed great moments in history, art and film, illustrated with stick figures. Isaias bought Magaly fuzzy pajamas and a blanket.

In his room over winter break, Isaias shuffled and reshuffled a deck of cards as he told me how he and Magaly tried to go out the year before, but it hadn't worked, how they'd come back to school this year and he'd felt kind of scared to restart the relationship, but now they were together. "I think there was no other way it could have happened," he said. "It had to happen." The cards snapped against his fingers. In the next semester of high school, fate would continue to deliver surprises, just like those hidden within the deck of cards.

Chapter Five

...

HORSE TO WATER

January 2013:
Four months before graduation

A WHITE FROST CLUNG to the boxlike brick houses across the street from the school on January 15, and the weather report predicted sleet and freezing rain. The school system might cancel classes and send everyone home.

But Isaias still arrived at his financial aid appointment at Patricia Henderson's office, a little glassed-in box inside a larger room by the school's front door. Ms. Henderson was 57, a white grandmother of five, and she had grown up in Waukegan, Illinois, a Chicago suburb. She wore her hair in a silver-blond mane that stuck out several inches from the sides of her head.

For the next several months, Ms. Henderson would hold one-on-one meetings like this with Kingsbury students, a process that could win the kids tens of thousands of dollars. The federal Pell Grant for low-income students was worth up to $5,550 that year—free money that students didn't have to pay back—and it was just one of several federal aid programs available.

Isaias took a seat, and Ms. Henderson asked, "What is your assigned social?"

"Here's what I got," Isaias said, opening a binder and handing her a stiff piece of paper. "I actually got this in the mail yesterday."

She inspected the blue Social Security card, still attached to a larger sheet that bore Isaias' address. The card was stamped with the words "VALID FOR WORK ONLY WITH DHS AUTHORIZATION."

Isaias' application to the Deferred Action program had succeeded. Until the previous year, it would have been all but impossible for someone like Isaias to receive a real Social Security card and the right to work legally within the United States. Now he had both the Social Security card and a two-year renewable work permit. And later that year, these documents enabled him to take a road test and get a Tennessee driver's license, valid as long as the work permit was. His days of driving without a license would end.

In the cubicle, Ms. Henderson told Isaias that she doubted he would qualify for federal financial aid. But she didn't fully understand the president's new immigration program. "Let's just do it all, like you're gonna get

(Photo by Daniel Connolly)

it. And let's just see what happens." Her red-manicured fingernails clicked against the keys.

They worked through the lengthy process of typing information about Isaias' family members and their income. Ms. Henderson said that because Isaias' parents didn't have Social Security numbers, his father would have to sign a form and mail it to an address in Mt. Vernon, Illinois.

"Man, this is complicated!" Isaias said. Ms. Henderson laughed heartily. Then the counselor pulled up a page on a federal website that showed a picture of a smiling Hispanic man with a crew cut. Isaias read aloud. "Many non-U.S. Citizens qualify for federal student aid. If you fall in one of the categories below, you are considered an 'eligible non-citizen.'" He continued reading. "U.S. national. No. U.S. permanent resident. No. You have an arrival-departure record I-94. I don't. Victims of human trafficking… If you are a battered immigrant qualified alien…"

Ms. Henderson interjected: "I haven't seen any of your bruises." She laughed and Isaias laughed, too, quickly. Isaias kept reading and reached the end of the list. The website didn't mention Deferred Action for Childhood Arrivals, the president's new program.

"See?" Ms. Henderson said.

"Wow. That's some crap," said Isaias. He leaned back in the chair, one hand behind his head, the same gesture he had used when he was losing at Knowledge Bowl.

They completed the electronic FAFSA form, and a message appeared on the laptop screen. "Because you are neither a citizen nor eligible non-citizen, you are not eligible for federal student aid."

Ms. Henderson told Isaias he should talk with his immigration lawyer. "What do you have to do to become a permanent resident?" Isaias didn't respond, but under the law, he could do little. The Deferred Action program offered the two-year renewable work permit and nothing more.

Ms. Henderson quickly gave Isaias another assignment. "My next step for you is to call MTSU in the next couple of days and say, 'Okay, I did my financial aid, I'm not qualifying because I just got my assigned Social

Security number. And so, what do I do next? I need money to go to your school and I want to go to your school.'"

"Okay," Isaias said.

They were almost done. "You're just a prime example of a great student," she said. "That's all there is to it. I just wish I had better news for you." He thanked her, and she wrapped him in a big hug. "Oh, Isaias. You're welcome, sweetie."

Isaias had expected bad news. But he felt a bit disappointed to hear it out loud.

. . .

That same week, Isaias and Magaly went to Jacklyn Martin's classroom after school to help set up the next month's black history program and organize a performance of the school play *Trifles*, a murder mystery.

Afterward, in the upstairs hallway, Isaias opened his Knowledge Bowl satchel and showed me the letters he'd just received in the mail. One letter began, "Congratulations and Welcome to MTSU, Isaias!" He'd been granted "honors admission" status, and the university had sent along information about required immunizations.

The University of Memphis had sent a similar acceptance letter, along with a certificate that read "Eligible for Scholarship!" in big letters. No details, but the message cheered Isaias. For the past few weeks, since New Year's, he'd been "all hazy" about college. He couldn't say why.

Later in the school year, he told me he didn't have a calendar to keep track of deadlines. "I tried putting stuff on my phone, but I don't like my phone either. So I just try to keep it in my head, but I forget a lot. But it works."

Now, in the hallway, he said, "For one point, I had even completely gotten college out of my mind. I was just going through life pretty happy." The letters encouraged him to think about college again.

He said he wanted to go. "Even if I try to get it out of my mind, it would be really cool to go to college. If I can get it paid for, I'll fly through."

I asked Magaly what she thought. "I'm happy I guess?" She paused. "I mean, I don't know. I can't rule his world. Like 'go to college for me.' I'm fine with it."

I said I was just curious. "It's a weird question," she said.

I left them and went downstairs, where I ran into a group of people gathered near the front door of the school. Something was going on. "Estevon said it was seven shots that he heard," Patricia Henderson said.

I walked outside and saw a commotion down North Graham Street to my right, by the Streets Ministries community center. A group of police cars had pulled to the curb, a man sat in the back of a cruiser, and an adult administrator from Streets was arguing with an angry girl.

Confusion reigned. I quickly learned the basics: a fight had escalated and a man who apparently wasn't a Kingsbury student had started firing wildly but hadn't hit anyone. Police would arrest and charge several people. I saw Estevon in the crowd, and he confirmed he'd been close to the shooting. "Just gunshots and everything. I didn't run. I just walked over there." Dressed in a black hooded sweatshirt and with a wisp of mustache and goatee, Estevon seemed unaffected. "I'm not surprised. I just don't care, really."

Another person who'd been close to the gunfire was Raul Delgado, a senior and a student leader. Raul was born in Nicaragua, and his black mustache, beard and strong eyebrows gave him an intense look, like Che Guevara. He was so comfortable approaching adults as equals that one time that year he came to a faculty meeting and gave an update on the international club he led. Raul said he had seen the shooter but hadn't been directly in the line of fire, so he didn't worry. "I mean, it's kind of normal, too."

Memphis has long been one of the most violent cities in the country. Shootings are so common that when I became a newspaper intern in 2001, editors coached me to write about gunfire only if someone died, and then usually very briefly. A nonfatal shooting only counted in unusual circumstances—if a child was shot, for instance, or if the number of people wounded was unusually high. Five people with nonfatal gunshot wounds would merit a mention, two people shot might not.

The city's crime rate was actually dropping, and the school building itself was usually quite safe, aside from fistfights. But the gunfire illustrated the day-to-day perils that Kingsbury students like Estevon lived with. It was a long way from here to Carnegie Mellon.

...

February 2013:
Three months before graduation

The Baltimore Ravens beat the San Francisco 49ers in the Super Bowl. Afterward, Patricia Henderson bought a cake with plastic football decorations for a marked-down price of $6.99.

She transformed a school conference room into something that looked like a children's birthday party, decorating the table with conical hats, little kazoo trumpets, and noisemakers that unrolled with a *pffi!* She hung signs on the wall that said "HAPPY NEW YEAR." That was a bit of a stretch because the date was February 4, but it was, in fact, the first meeting that year for the group of high-achieving kids she called the Super All-Stars. To join, the students had to have grade point averages of at least 3.75. She organized parties and took them on fun trips—in November, for instance, they'd gone to see a local appearance by Blue Man Group, the troupe of actors and musicians who performed mutely in blue makeup.

Classes had ended for the day, and students began to arrive. Cousins Tommy Nguyen and Tri Nguyen put on the conical hats, which made them look like wizards.

Leonard Duarte walked in next. A U.S. citizen child of Mexican immigrants, Leonard was tall, wore glasses and held a high rank within the school's JROTC program, and he was likely to graduate as valedictorian. In AP Chemistry class, he rarely spoke, and in slow moments he sometimes drew fantastical creatures on graph paper, all wings and horns and sharp edges. Now he asked, "What's with the hats?"

Ms. Henderson created a party atmosphere for a serious purpose. These students were scheduled to graduate in mid-May, in just over three months, and this meeting was a crucial chance to check their progress toward college.

Each student gave a report on college applications. Isaias said he'd applied to the University of Memphis, Middle Tennessee State University, and Christian Brothers. "And what is your number-one school that you really want to go to?" Ms. Henderson asked.

"I think I'm going to actually end up going to U of M," he said.

"Over MTSU."

"Mmm-hmm."

"Can you share with us why?"

"I can be close to my family. It's cheaper. They have sent me more money in scholarships. And it's not that bad. I mean, it was my second choice."

Isaias and his brother Dennis had talked about it in snippets the previous week while watching TV and playing video games. Money was a big factor. Academic scholarship letters had arrived: MTSU had offered Isaias $4,000 per year. The U of M offered $5,500 per year.

But unauthorized immigrant students like Isaias would pay the out-of-state tuition rate, which at each college totaled more than $20,000 per year. So it looked like the scholarships wouldn't be enough.

However, David Schmidt from Middle Tennessee State had sent an e-mail with more good news:

Dear Isaias:

Good Morning. Because you have your Social Security card and work permit you are now eligible for in-state tuition. This is something new which we just enacted at MTSU. I verified this last night with our domestic admission representative.

Isaias hadn't asked the University of Memphis, but that institution was controlled by the same state board as MTSU; assuming that the U of M also granted him in-state tuition, with the scholarship, Isaias could pay less than $2,000 per year. And he could live at home.

Tri, Tommy, and Jason Doan said they planned to go to the University of Memphis, too. Then Ms. Henderson turned to Estevon.

"All right, Estevon, what is yours?"

"UT-Knoxville for free."

Tri interrupted. "You're going to UT-Knox?!"

"Yeah."

"What happened to Carnegie?"

"That's if I can get enough financial aid from them."

Ms. Henderson interjected. "Tell them how much Carnegie Mellon is."

Estevon said tuition was $45,000 per year. The university listed a slightly higher price on its website, nearly $47,000 per year, with fees, room, board, books and other costs bringing the total price to $62,000.

Even with a big financial aid package, Estevon said he'd have to take out loans, and he didn't want to. Tri said he should. "But you're going to such a good school! You're gonna pay it off in no time!"

"It doesn't matter," Estevon said flatly. Estevon wanted to go to graduate school without the burden of student loans.

"Yeah, he has a point there," Tommy said. Isaias said he would do what Estevon was doing.

When college prices rose to the astronomical Carnegie Mellon levels, even a financial aid package that covered most of the costs could leave a family with thousands of dollars to pay. Patricia Henderson knew that for a poor family, even $1,000 represented a big burden.

She questioned whether students could land a job that paid well enough to cover college loan payments on top of all their other expenses, like a car payment and rent, and she strongly recommended that students avoid debt. As she saw it, if Estevon could avoid loans by choosing UT-Knoxville, he should do it.

She encouraged students with strong grades and test scores to apply to the nation's best universities. But for other students, especially those who would otherwise have to go into debt, she recommended low-cost schools like Southwest Tennessee Community College.

Southwest served as the default option for many Kingsbury students. It cost relatively little and admitted everyone who met minimum standards. But it came with a downside: almost no one graduated.

The completion rate for students who'd started in the fall of 2010 stood at just 6 percent, worse than any other public college or university in the state.[1] Another 9 percent managed to transfer to other schools. Many freshman students arrived at Southwest unprepared for college work and had to take remedial classes. They were often the first in their families to go to college; they faced financial problems, lacked support, and dropped out.

The state government had passed a new law that tied funding to students' progress—if students didn't earn credits and advance toward completion, the college would lose money. Because of the new criteria and several other factors, Southwest's state funding would drop from $38 million in 2008–2009 to $25 million in 2014–2015.

Southwest staffers were trying to raise the graduation rate. In 2015, I spoke with Dr. Cynthia Calhoun, an executive in charge of those efforts, and she described several recent changes. Among them: The college had created an "early alert" system in which professors reported students who were absent or tardy so they could be referred to tutoring or other interventions. A new center on campus offered individual coaching as well as workshops on subjects such as time management and math anxiety. New rules required students to see an advisor before they registered for classes— previously, talks with an advisor were recommended, but not mandatory.

The graduation rate at Middle Tennessee State was better, but still not stellar: 46 percent within six years. At the University of Memphis, it was 43 percent. Rhodes College, perhaps the best private college in the area, had a graduation rate of 81 percent.[2]

Wasn't Ms. Henderson concerned about the low graduation rate at Southwest? Not really. As she saw it, the low graduation rate reflected not the quality of the school, but rather the poor preparation of the incoming students. She said the Memphis City Schools tended to push kids to graduation regardless of their true skill levels, and unlike schools such as Kingsbury, the community college wouldn't give students countless chances to turn in work they should have finished weeks earlier. If they failed, they failed, and for some students, this came as a rude shock.

For Ms. Henderson, college was what the students made it. Students could go to Southwest, become discouraged, and fail. Or they could start hustling, taking advantage of supports like free tutoring.

Isaias and many of Kingsbury's other leading students aimed for the University of Memphis, which more privileged kids would consider a safety school at best.

Of course, hardly anyone at Kingsbury even used terms like "safety school" and "reach school," since almost no students played the privileged youth's game of applying to selective colleges. In the senior class, Estevon Odria was essentially the only one who'd tried it, and now he appeared to be scaling back his ambitions.

The National Bureau of Economic Research studied the college choices of kids much like the ones at the "New Year's" party at Kingsbury: students with low incomes and high test scores. They concluded that the vast majority of these students didn't apply to any selective colleges.[3]

The researchers called this a costly error. Selective colleges wanted qualified low-income students who could add diversity to mostly white campuses; the colleges often gave them generous financial aid, and the students tended to graduate.

Did it really matter whether students went to a selective college like Carnegie Mellon or to a school like Southwest Tennessee Community College? According to researchers at Georgetown University, the answer was yes.

"If I'm the parent of a kid who's at risk of not graduating, I want them to go to the most selective college possible," said Anthony P. Carnevale, director of Georgetown's Center on Education and the Workforce. "Because it's most likely that they'll get a lot of parenting at the college. And the college will not let them leave."

Selective colleges competed with other institutions to show an impressive graduation rate, and administrators didn't want students to drop out and disappoint parents paying huge sums for tuition, Mr. Carnevale said. Selective colleges typically spent more money on their students than less-selective schools and offered much more tutoring, counseling and other support. If students failed to come to class, someone would likely notice and intervene. An array of on-campus activities built a strong culture that likewise attached students to school.

A student with an SAT score that was average or above average had a high probability of graduating from one of the nation's 468 most selective colleges, Mr. Carnevale concluded. If the *same student* chose an open-access college like Southwest that admitted everyone, the odds of completion dropped dramatically. For students who had scored an above-average 1,200 on the SAT, for instance, the graduation rates were 87 percent at selective colleges—at open-access colleges they were only 58 percent.[4]

So why didn't more students from minority and low-income backgrounds apply to selective colleges?

The National Bureau of Economic Research authors pointed to several possible reasons. One was lack of connections—the students were unlikely to meet a teacher or older student who had attended a selective college. The recruiting tactics of selective colleges played a role, too: they often sent recruiters to high-quality public schools that were known for educating large numbers of high-achieving low-income students, and the recruiters often chose to look for these students close to the college campus. Recruiters might never meet the bright but impoverished students scattered throughout the nation's other high schools in cities like Memphis.

Mr. Carnevale offered another reason low-income kids would pick less prestigious schools: they felt comfortable there. The white upper-middle-class environment at selective colleges often made minority kids from low-income backgrounds feel out of place. In the long run, though, a minority student who could push through the difficult transition to a selective college would likely succeed, Mr. Carnevale and a fellow researcher wrote in 2013: "African-Americans and Hispanics clearly benefit by going to selective institutions even when their test scores are substantially below the institutional averages at those schools." The Georgetown researchers concluded that each year, thousands of African-American and Hispanic kids who could have graduated from college didn't do so.

That said, not every selective college was prepared to give low-income students a break.

Universities had begun adjusting financial aid packages and giving low-income students worse deals than they used to, according to a 2014 analysis by *The Dallas Morning News.* The universities were instead spending money on "merit" scholarships that would draw academically strong students from middle- and high-income families who could pay part of the tuition bill and help the universities' finances.[5]

So the Georgetown experts said that going to a selective college was generally a good idea for low-income students, but *The Dallas Morning News* analysis suggested that they might not be able to afford to go—or they might have to borrow money to do it.

By 2015, more than 41 million Americans owed more than $1.2 trillion in student loan debt. The median student debt burden rose from about $13,000 in 2007 to nearly $20,000 in 2014.[6]

One in four borrowers was either behind on payments or had defaulted, a government agency estimated. Those who fell behind could face unpleasant surprises: aggressive phone calls, garnished wages, or a federal tax refund that never showed up because a debt collector intercepted it, said Chad Van Horn, an attorney focusing on bankruptcy and debt resettlement in Fort Lauderdale, Florida. All of this led to stressful lives. "People never think about the psychological effect of carrying debt," he said.

The national student debt picture looked bleak, but a Brookings Institution review of the data made some interesting findings. Many of the people who defaulted on student loans had gone to for-profit colleges and other nonselective institutions. Graduates of these schools often had weak educational outcomes and had trouble finding jobs. "In contrast, most borrowers at four-year public and private non-profit institutions had relatively low rates of default, solid earnings, and steady employment rates," the Brookings report said.[7]

Mr. Carnevale, the Georgetown expert, said that many students made the mistake of taking out too many loans. But disadvantaged students often made the opposite mistake: taking out too *few* loans and instead paying for school by working long hours, which made them less likely to graduate.

Because earnings varied greatly by major, taking out loans could very well make sense, particularly for a high-paying field. "If you're going to be an engineer, you can afford the loans," he said.

Though Carnegie Mellon was certainly a far better choice than Southwest Tennessee Community College, the choice was less clear-cut between Carnegie Mellon and the University of Tennessee, Knoxville, a state flagship school.

An engineering major who graduated from either school would be likely to have good earnings prospects, Carnevale said, but Carnegie Mellon probably had an edge in prestige, better hiring connections to large companies, more per-student spending, higher placement in graduate school, and a higher graduation rate. (At UT, 66 percent of students who began in fall 2006 graduated within six years compared to 87 percent at Carnegie Mellon.)

Someone who planned to go to graduate school might save money by doing the undergraduate years at UT and spending heavily on an expensive graduate program later, Mr. Carnevale said. "If you're just going to get a BA, all things being equal, go to Carnegie Mellon."

. . .

At the New Year's party, Ms. Henderson said the students needed to think about the long-term financial consequences of their choices. "You've got to start thinking in these terms, though, do you see what I'm saying?"

One of the students made a flippant comment: "So should I buy a stripper now . . . or later and pay her back?"

"Oh God, help me," Ms. Henderson said.

The University of Memphis wasn't a top school, but barring disasters, Isaias appeared set to enroll at a college, something no one in his immediate family had done. His path to this moment had not been easy. He had earned good grades in school for years and scored unusually well on his standardized tests. To get an ID, he drove to the closest Mexican consulate, two hours away in Little Rock, Arkansas. He'd gone through the time-consuming and expensive process of applying for the Deferred Action program and getting a Social Security card.

Most importantly, he had talked of quitting but hadn't.

After the meeting between Patricia Henderson and the top students, I wrote a note to my family and friends: "None of this is quite settled yet, but things are looking better for Isaias than they have in months."

As I would soon learn, I was wrong. Isaias' understanding of his own situation was wrong, too. Even the university officials who had spoken with Isaias were wrong. Massive barriers still stood between Isaias and a college education. Despite everything that university officials had said, the State of Tennessee still viewed Isaias as an unauthorized immigrant who could not qualify for in-state tuition or most scholarships. His path to college would be far, far harder than anyone expected.

And even before Isaias learned these harsh facts, his old doubts returned, and he told people he wasn't going to college.

. . .

Mariana Hernandez and Adam Truong broke up, and Adam took it hard. On a college trip in February, Adam looked so depressed that Patricia Henderson put an arm around him and asked, "What's wrong with you today?"

They were on the campus of Victory University, a small college near the high school. In the auditorium, the tour guide said a young Elvis Presley had attended services there, back when the building was a church.

Adam and the others were shown the modest biology lab and the small, cramped library, its shelves stocked with titles like *The Interpreter's Bible* and *All the Children of the Bible*. A student newspaper, *Voice of Virtue*, carried stories about a book written by one of the university's biblical scholars as well as the new dormitories, the startup honors program and a brand-new student government.

Victory University had once been Crichton College, a nonprofit Christian liberal arts school that was founded in the 1940s. Crichton ran into

financial trouble, and in February 2009, a for-profit company called Sig-
nificantPsychology LLC announced that it had bought the institution.
The company would later change the school's name to Victory.

The man behind the deal was Michael Clifford, a well-known figure
within the world of for-profit colleges. He was featured in the 2010 PBS
Frontline documentary "College, Inc." A musician and former drug user
who had never gone to college, Mr. Clifford said his life changed when he
became a born-again Christian. He later got involved in higher education—
more specifically, buying colleges.

"From his headquarters in the sleepy beach community of Del Mar,
California, Clifford is building an empire," the documentary's narrator
said. "He invests in failing universities and injects them with large
amounts of capital. When they go public, he can make a bundle of money
in the process."

For-profit schools had operated in the United States for decades. Most
were local businesses that offered basic career training, said Kevin Kinser,
a professor at the University at Albany and an expert on the industry.

But in Arizona, the University of Phoenix created a new model when it
launched in the 1970s: a publicly traded, highly visible company that spread
nationwide and offered degrees that competed directly with other universities. In 1992, the government banned these schools from paying their
recruiters based on the number of students they brought in. The government feared that the colleges were recruiting unqualified students who
couldn't graduate and couldn't pay back federal loans.

In 2002, the administration of George W. Bush loosened the rules, allowing colleges to give recruiters bonus payments once again, under what
were known as "safe harbor" provisions. Recruiters could get extra pay
twice a year as long as that pay was not based solely on the number of
students they brought in. Student counts rose fast. Across the country, for-
profit institutions enrolled more than 2 million people in 2010, 10 percent
of the total college-going population and more than eight times the number they had enrolled in 1995.

But the *Frontline* documentary laid out troubling facts: Students at for-profit universities dropped out at higher rates than did students at other universities.[8] Graduates from these schools usually carried far more debt than other graduates, and they were more likely to default.[9] In some cases, they struggled to repay debts because they'd gone through a bad college program, and no one would hire them. Victory University fit the bigger for-profit pattern of low graduation rates and dependence on federal student loans. In the 2011–2012 fiscal year, for instance, 100 percent of incoming freshmen received federal student loans, and the graduation rate was only 13 percent. In June 2012, shortly before Isaias began his senior year, an accreditation agency put Victory on warning status. The reason: financial instability. The university needed injections of outside cash to stay alive, the agency wrote. "That sponsorship to date appears to be $8.6 million, and the institution acknowledges that more capital infusion will be needed," the letter said. "Achievement of enrollment goals is yet to materialize." The university's financial problems weren't widely known in Memphis. When the Kingsbury students visited Victory University that day in February, there was little—other than the obvious limitations of the tiny campus—to suggest that it might not be a solid choice.

Neither Adam nor Mariana would enroll at Victory University. They would remain friends after the breakup, though they weren't as close as they'd been before.

• • •

February also marked Black History Month. At Kingsbury, two students played leading roles in organizing the school's cultural program: Isaias and Raul Delgado, both of whom were Hispanic. Isaias recognized this put them in an odd position. "I mean, we can't pretend to know, since a lot of us are not African-American, we don't know exactly what it is to be African-American," he said at one organizational meeting. "But we should at least be respectful of it, be educational, and try to get a message out." He argued that the students should set a serious tone in the cultural program to reflect the unfortunate elements of the black experience. "It hasn't been as happy as others."

Race relations at Kingsbury High weren't always so understanding. In late January, someone smashed the windows of three vehicles in the school parking lot and stole a stereo and other items. As one Hispanic student cleaned up the glass, he angrily said what he'd do if he caught the thief. "I ain't breaking that nigger's window. I'm breaking that nigger's arm." He had no way of knowing the criminal's color, but his assumption reflected broader tensions.

Outside the school, gang members frequently targeted Hispanic immigrants for robberies at gunpoint. Immigrants often carried cash, and robbers apparently believed that widespread illegal immigration status and lack of English made victims less likely to go to police. Many of the robbers were black.

Robberies of Hispanic immigrants became so common that by 2007, then–county prosecutor Bill Gibbons was trying to encourage unauthorized immigrants to testify by issuing crime victims a special card they could show if agents picked them up on immigration charges. After the financial crisis of 2007–2008, robberies against Hispanics dropped, perhaps because criminals no longer saw them as victims flush with cash. Still, the pattern of black criminals targeting Hispanic immigrants persisted on a smaller scale, and the robberies sometimes ended with victims shot dead. Some other immigrants responded with open racism. For their part, some African-Americans resented that employers at times favored Hispanic immigrants—this was particularly true in the warehouse sector, where the two groups vied for the same low-paid jobs.

Within the school, I never heard of racially motivated fights. Yet I noticed a pattern in the cafeteria sometimes: black students gathered at certain tables, while multiethnic groups of Hispanic, Asian and white students clustered around other tables.

A similar pattern emerged in the school's honors and advanced placement classrooms: Hispanic, Asian and white students were more likely than African-Americans to take hard classes.

Consider chemistry, a course that was required for graduation. In the standard-level chemistry sections, black students made up 58 percent of the total. In honors, they made up 28 percent of students, and in advanced placement, the hardest level, only one of the 25 students was African-American. That year at Kingsbury, Isaias was one of five Hispanic students in the top ten, along with three students of Vietnamese descent; one of Middle Eastern origin, Ibrahim Elayan; and one African-American girl, Breanna Thomas, the Knowledge Bowl participant.

No white students cracked the top ten.

White and black families that had money were fleeing inner-city neighborhoods like the ones around Kingsbury, and the white and black families that remained in the area were often troubled. Whites at Kingsbury had very low graduation rates. Only 52 percent of white students graduated in the class before that of Isaias, compared to 64 percent of African-Americans and 62 percent of Hispanics. The principal remembered one white student at another school saying something like, "'Oh man, y'all just think I'm some redneck from Nutbush,'" referring to a neighborhood near Kingsbury High. Mr. Fuller thought some white students in the area had internalized a negative view of themselves.

By contrast, I concluded that for immigrant families escaping third world poverty, the Kingsbury neighborhood represented a step up. The adults in these families had shown unusual ambition and risk-taking by leaving their home countries, and in many cases they passed on at least some of this drive to their children. And immigrant families were often stable. In Tennessee, Hispanic youths were more likely than African-Americans to come from two-parent families—64 percent compared to 75 percent for white children and 33 percent for black children.[10]

Despite occasional conflicts, in general, students of different backgrounds got along at Kingsbury. Raul Delgado said he'd been robbed by masked teenagers in tenth grade, and he believed they were African-American—he could see their hands and hear their voices. Yet he said he didn't hold it against all black people. "Even if it was a white person I wouldn't hold a grudge against them or anything, 'cause not all people are the same."

The day of the black history assembly came, and late in the program,

Isaias connected his smartphone to the sound board in the auditorium. As the black-and-white footage from Martin Luther King, Jr.'s "I Have a Dream" speech rolled on the phone's little screen, the audio boomed over the speakers.

Onstage, student Arzell Rodgers matched his lips and gestures to the words, stepping into the role of the man who had been shot dead in Memphis in 1968, at a time when Kingsbury High was still all white.

"I have a dream that my four little children will one day live in a nation where they will not be judged by the color of their skin, but by the content of their character. I have a dream today!"

Magaly stood beside Isaias at the sound board, and when the speech was over, she applauded, and Isaias lifted his hands in the air and did the same.

. . .

March 2013:
Two months before graduation

During a slow moment at school one rainy day, Adam Truong asked Daniel Nix if he knew where Isaias planned to go to college. Daniel gave a quick summary of Isaias' thinking. "That man's like 'I'm going to college. No, I'm not going to college. I'm going to college. No, I'm not going to college.'"

At the New Year's party in February and in the days that followed, Isaias appeared almost certain to attend the University of Memphis. But he had never formally enrolled.

Patricia Henderson organized a small-scale college fair at the Streets Ministries community center near the school. She and other participants hoped to reach the numerous students who had made no plans for the future. Deadlines for selective schools had passed, but the less prestigious institutions that most Kingsbury students were targeting would still accept applications. Even so, the longer they waited, the more opportunities would pass them by. By early February, only about a third of the students had completed an application for federal student aid, even though Ms. Henderson was available to walk them through it.

"We're doing everything but paying them to do what they need to do," guidance counselor Brooke Loeffler said.

The keynote speaker for the college fair, Vincent Lee, took the stage at the main meeting room at Streets, addressing a crowd of students seated at round tables. A tall African-American man in a brown suit, Mr. Lee described how he had grown up with an alcoholic mother and gone on to become a manager with ServiceMaster Corporation. He warned the students that they must take advantage of the opportunities they had now.

"If you don't prepare now, this world outside this school campus and outside of Streets Ministries don't have love for you," he said. "It really doesn't." As he spoke, some students at the round tables didn't bother to turn and face him.

He wrapped up his speech. Ms. Henderson came to the stage next, calling out, "Good morning, everyone! Where are my ambassadors? I need them up here with me for just a moment." The ambassadors were students who had finished their college applications and would help run the day's program. Ms. Henderson had wanted Isaias to act as an ambassador. But when someone asked Isaias on her behalf, he said no.

Isaias knew the college event at Streets would mess up the whole day's schedule, and juniors were taking the ACT, too, which added to the disruption. Screw that, he'd stay home. He spent most of the day watching movies.

Friends came by his house, and Isaias finally went to school in time for the seventh and last period of the day, Jinger Griner's English class. He had to take the course to graduate, and he liked it. Isaias emerged from Ms. Griner's classroom at the end of the school day and found Magaly waiting in the hall, beaming.

They walked to a hallway in another part of the school to practice for a competition called Canstruction in which they'd use food cans to build a sculpture. Isaias took the lead. "Our three rolls have to fit in this, this and this area," he said, gesturing to a space on the floor. When the timed contest took place at the University of Memphis a few days later, the Kingsbury team would build a replica of a Japanese sushi meal. During this practice session, the students busily set about arranging cans of beans and tomatoes—black labels evoked the seaweed wrap around a sushi roll.

Isaias examined the pile of cans they created. "Not bad, actually," he said. "Squint your eyes. Hopefully we get a guy with really bad vision." Then a student came down the hall with a message for him. "Ms. Henderson wants to see you."

Isaias hurried down the hall toward Ms. Henderson's office.

"Isaias!" she said.

"I heard you wanted to see me?"

"I did. Tell me why when they asked you to be an ambassador today, you refused!" she said, her voice rising. "Tell me why you did that! *I* put your name down!"

She had gone out of her way for Isaias, building a relationship with him over a period of months, bringing him to cultural programs and parties and investing tedious hours in helping him with financial aid and college application paperwork. Now he'd rejected a request for help, and it had come from her.

"Oh, Ms. Henderson. I didn't know that," Isaias said. "I'm sorry. I... thing is, I just... I don't know, like, I didn't want to do it."

"*Why* didn't you want to do it? All these colleges were there."

Even though Isaias had received offers of admission from universities, he still needed to finalize the details, especially financial aid, and Ms. Henderson was angry that he'd blown the chance to talk with people who could help.

"I know. I know," Isaias responded. "I guess I didn't think about that. Missed opportunities. I don't know..."

He leaned on the doorway of her cubicle and continued. "I didn't find it that interesting, that appealing. The whole idea of it. I felt like passing on it."

He said he felt bad for disappointing her, and Ms. Henderson softened and said, "Well, if you would have known *I* put your name in, you probably would have done it." She asked Isaias about his immigration status, and he said nothing had changed. Then she asked about his application to the University of Memphis.

"Honestly, I haven't checked," Isaias said. "Actually, can I tell you something? I don't think I want to go to college, period. I don't want to go to college at all."

He began to say that people at school make you think that you *have* to go to college. Ms. Henderson cut him off, saying that not everyone has to go to college—some would be better off going to trade school.

Magaly arrived and joined Isaias outside Ms. Henderson's cubicle, quietly leaning against him. The counselor continued. "What I'm telling you—you are so smart. You would do well at college."

"I'm pretty sure I would."

Ms. Henderson asked what he wanted to do. "Like seriously, what I really seriously want to do is music. I want to be a musician. I want to tour the country."

"You want to be a musician? You do realize most of that is being at the right place at the right time."

"I know."

He explained what was going on in his life: the successful painting business, how his parents planned to move back to Mexico, that he and Dennis would stay in Memphis, and how they might have to raise nine-year-old Dustin on their own.

She asked how he felt about his parents leaving. "I'm actually kind of excited," Isaias said. "Well, I guess not excited. But I'm eager to see myself, 'cause it's such a change." And he said he and Dennis were up to the challenge of caring for their little brother.

She asked what would happen if Dennis got hurt on the job. Isaias said he'd carry on the business himself.

Ms. Henderson said he needed to have a backup plan. "Whether it's going to school, whether it's getting married. You know. Say you marry Magaly and she said, 'You know what? I don't want to work. I want to have kids. Oh my God, now we don't have two incomes coming in.' You know what I'm saying?" She tried to make it sound hypothetical. "That was a scenario. That was a scenario!"

They laughed, but the marriage scenario didn't seem so far-fetched.

Isaias loved Magaly and wasn't self-conscious about showing it. The teen-agers matched one another in brainpower, personality and interests, and it was easy to imagine them staying together for a long time.

Ms. Henderson asked if he saw his immigration status as a stumbling block. Isaias said no, he'd learned from his father's example. "No matter what, you're gonna make it. You're not gonna let yourself go hungry."

Sometime in the days that followed, Ms. Henderson told Isaias she'd like to see him go to college. She recalled saying, "I don't want to say you'd be wasting your brain on painting or roofing, but I would love to see you be-come an engineer. Because you're so smart. There's no telling where that would take you." She didn't mention this that afternoon in her office, though. She said she might want Isaias and his family to do some work at her home and she mentioned that she might take the Super All-Stars to an outdoor performance of *Hamlet*. Isaias was overjoyed.

"I love Shakespeare so much! I've only read *Macbeth* but that just gets you hooked. That would be crazy!" Then he left to pick up his little brother.

(Photo by Karen Pulfer Focht/The Commercial Appeal)

. . .

Isaias' sense of obligation to care for Dustin reflected a broader sense of duty to family that was common among children of immigrants. Researchers with the Pew Hispanic Center interviewed hundreds of young Hispanics for a 2009 report.[11] Nearly three-quarters of Hispanic youths who cut off their education before college cited financial pressure to support a family. About half cited poor English skills, and about four in ten said that they disliked school or believed they didn't need more education for the careers they intended to pursue.

Even as Isaias professed a lack of interest in college, he continued to pursue intellectual activities in the weeks that followed. With paint specks on his glasses from work, Isaias, alongside Magaly and other students, built the sushi sculpture out of food cans at the competition, and they traveled to an out-of-town robotics competition, too.

People who knew Isaias began to speculate about his thinking. Had his immigration status made him give up on college? He told me that unlike some unauthorized immigrant students, he'd long known about his status. "I'd always had this idea that I'm not quite as privileged as other people, like I'm a little less. As a child I did."

When he was younger, it made him think he couldn't do anything. He'd see people buying lottery tickets and think he couldn't do that. He said perhaps some remnant of that young idea had stayed with him and impacted the way he saw college.

"It probably does. But not really. Like, my ultimate decision, no."

I caught up with him one April morning as he walked into the school, and I checked his understanding of the cost of college. He said yes, he believed the U of M would cost him about $2,000 per year.

"It sounds about right. That's what I remember. I would really need very little money for this. I could work in the summer and I would get about $2,000."

We proceeded into the noisy front hallway. "I've always known inside of me, kind of this whole plan for my life, and college was just never part of it. The longer I stay in school, the more my mind gets corrupted." He'd talked about this earlier, how the culture presented college as part of a normal life and how it influenced him. Now, at his locker, he said he didn't agree with that idea. "If you know, or think you know enough to get by without college, you don't need to go and waste your money—or your time, which is even worse. Four years of nothing. I don't know. Time is really valuable to me."

"How would you rather spend your time?" I asked.

"Anything *but* college would be more productive."

Wouldn't he miss intellectual things?

He said he might—he was already missing math and would like to dive into a calculus book. If he ever went to college, he'd study something fun. "Not college because I have to, but because I want to."

Around the same time, I asked Dennis what he'd heard about Isaias' college plans. Dennis said Isaias hadn't said much and that when their parents wanted to know what Isaias was thinking, they asked Dennis what *he* knew. Cristina later explained her reluctance to question Isaias on the subject. "As a mother, you want to get involved, but your children rebel. They tell you not to interfere in their lives."

Dennis figured Isaias would let the family know eventually. And he said Isaias was excited about joining the painting business and expanding it. Dennis wasn't concerned. "Even if he doesn't go to college, it wouldn't be bad news."

While Isaias worked closely with Patricia Henderson on his college applications, another college access organization had launched its efforts within Kingsbury High. It was called Abriendo Puertas, Spanish for "opening doors," and it was the spearhead of an ambitious effort to boost achievement among the city's Hispanics. It had backing from a large coalition of groups, including Memphis mayor A C Wharton.

The Indianapolis-based Lumina Foundation would pay $600,000 over four years to fund mentors. The social service organization Latino Memphis ran the program.

During the first semester of Isaias' senior year, the new effort had barely gotten off the ground at Kingsbury, and an on-site director came and left quickly. During the spring, though, a former English teacher named Jennifer Alejo took over, and the project gained momentum. She was white and had taken her husband's name when she married. Though her work focused on Hispanics, she offered college guidance to any student who wanted it, regardless of ethnicity. Ms. Alejo quickly became one of the leading experts within Kingsbury on the tricky task of getting unauthorized immigrant students to college.

By mid-April, she was hearing troubling news. Universities were telling her that students with immigration problems couldn't qualify for in-state tuition even if they'd qualified for papers under Deferred Action for Childhood Arrivals. I'd seen the messages that MTSU and the University of Memphis had sent Isaias, and they were impossible to misinterpret. Both universities offered Isaias significant scholarship money. An MTSU official had explicitly offered in-state tuition, and it was reasonable to think the University of Memphis would do the same.

To find out what was happening, I called the University of Memphis and arranged a meeting with the admissions director, Betty Huff. Within a few minutes of arriving in her office, I realized that everything that Isaias and I had understood was wrong.

She expressed sympathy for students with immigration problems but said a new state law tied her hands. In 2012, the Tennessee legislature had passed a law called the Eligibility Verification for Entitlements Act that aimed to block unauthorized immigrants from getting certain state benefits, including nonemergency health care.

I found out later that in August 2012, a state attorney had written a memo concluding that unauthorized immigrant students couldn't get in-state tuition. A later legal memo concluded that Deferred Action students were not "lawfully present" and couldn't qualify for any state scholarships. In the eyes of Tennessee, it meant nothing that Isaias had a Social Security card and a federal work permit. He was still in the country illegally.

"We have never told counselors or students that they were going to be eligible for in-state tuition or scholarships if they were DACA," Ms. Huff said. *Yes you did*, I wanted to say. *Isaias showed me the mail the university sent him. You even sent him a certificate that said "Eligible for scholarship!"* But I didn't mention his name, because I feared that I would ruin whatever chance he had.

If Isaias changed his mind and decided to go to the University of Memphis, he'd have to pay more than $20,000 per year. An impossible sum. Ms. Huff didn't like the policy either. "What I don't understand is the attitude that says they're here, but we don't want to educate them. They're here. They're not going anywhere."

I came to realize that the officials at Middle Tennessee State University and the University of Memphis had genuinely wanted to help Isaias. Without meaning to, they had painted a far rosier picture of his prospects than they should have.

I didn't tell Isaias what I had learned. At some point later—it's unclear when—he found out from someone else. For the moment it looked like a moot point, since he'd already decided not to go.

The same day that I spoke with the U of M admissions director in the morning, I set out for the long drive across Tennessee to Chattanooga, where Isaias would participate in a vocational competition in audio recording through an organization called SkillsUSA. The next day, he ran around one of the hotels that hosted the conference, scrambling to put together an audio presentation along with fellow student Tyler Hunt, an African-American boy with dreadlocks. "I don't think anyone's as excited about their project as we are," Isaias said. "Nobody," Tyler responded. They'd win second place out of five teams.

On the night of Isaias' arrival at the conference, he put on a red jacket and ate dinner in a big banquet hall. Students were coming to the front of the room and making speeches, dressed in the same red jackets.

I sat at a different table, looked at Isaias, and thought, "God help this kid." For days, I had wanted to see Isaias change his mind and decide to go to college. Now the state universities seemed hopelessly out of reach.

Over the next few days, the depth of my sadness surprised me. As it turned out, someone else who knew Isaias felt the same way. She would do something about it.

· · ·

For years, states had been fighting over the question of access to higher education for students like Isaias. As the immigration wave of the 1990s and 2000s swept into the country, the issue took on bigger dimensions. A 2009 report by the College Board described the situation: young people who were brought into the United States illegally or on visas that had expired often couldn't receive in-state tuition, couldn't receive federal financial aid, and finally and most importantly, couldn't work legally in this country.[12]

People unfamiliar with immigration law sometimes assumed that these immigrants could fix their status by paying a visit to their local immigration office and filling out a few forms. Wrong. Both children and adults who had entered illegally or who had overstayed visas often lacked any legal route to regularize their status, ever. But the federal government usually didn't enforce immigration law in the interior of the country—powerful businesses didn't want agents to deport their workers—so these people could stay in the United States for years, in a sort of limbo.

Several states, notably Texas and California in 2001, had moved to open the doors to public universities to young people with immigration problems. "The vast majority of states, however, simply do not have any state policies with respect to undocumented immigrant students," the 2009 College Board report said.

The report cited research that said an estimated 65,000 unauthorized immigrant students who had lived in the United States for five years or longer were graduating from high school, and that only an estimated 5 to 10 percent went to college. The College Board called for a federal solution, but it wasn't forthcoming. A bill called the Dream Act would regularize their status, but it failed repeatedly in Congress.

In 2001, Senator Orrin Hatch of Utah became the first to introduce a bill with the Dream Act name. (A similar bill had been introduced in the

House earlier that year.) The Senate bill wrote the word "dream" in capital letters that stood for "Development, Relief and Education for Alien Minors."

The original concept was simple: a young person with immigration problems who had spent years in the United States could earn legal status by going to college. Over time, the proposed requirements changed, but the general idea was the same: good kids with immigration problems could earn some sort of legal status.

The Dream Act concept was still new in August 2002 when *The Denver Post* ran an article about Jesus Apodaca, a 17-year-old who had been brought illegally from Mexico at age 12. He'd been accepted into the computer engineering program at the University of Colorado at Denver, but due to his immigration status, he would have to pay out-of-state tuition of nearly $7,000 per semester.[13] The tone of the article was sympathetic. Yet for some people, the article inspired not sympathy, but red-hot anger.

"Recent media reports about illegal alien Jesus Apodaca, in which he complains about not being able to receive the benefits of legal aliens and citizens, just makes my blood boil," Barbara Paulsen of Colorado Springs wrote in a letter to her local newspaper.[14] "His attitude of just flouting our immigration laws and then whining because he can't get financial aid for schooling is beyond belief…I hope Rep. Tom Tancredo continues his effort to see that this family does not benefit from its illegal activity."

Congressman Tancredo was a vocal opponent of illegal immigration. When he read the article, he phoned immigration authorities and asked what they planned to do about it. (He later denied urging the authorities to deport the Apodacas.) Still, the spectacle became a national story. One of the most powerful men in America was taking on a 17-year-old who'd had no control over his parents' choice to immigrate.

Political analyst James Carville and others attacked the congressman. Yet others saw him as a hero. The illegal immigration system was based on the fiction that the government was really trying to make these immigrants leave. Mr. Tancredo pointed out, loudly and repeatedly, that this wasn't true, and he persisted even as many members of his own Republican Party turned against him.

Meanwhile, the publicity caused huge problems for the Apodaca family. Colorado journalist Helen Thorpe described them in her book *Just Like Us:* television trucks parked outside their home, reporters called incessantly, and people posted ugly things about them on the Internet.[15]

The Apodacas moved out and got an unlisted phone number. A private donor stepped forward and offered to pay Jesus' tuition at the University of Colorado at Boulder. Then the donor pulled out, and Colorado governor Bill Owens asked one of his biggest donors to pay the tuition. Jesus Apodaca went to a different university. The red-hot anger cooled.

Over the years, I wrote many immigration stories that sparked the same furious reaction. Too often, angry readers aimed their vitriol at the powerless people caught in the middle: the immigrants. They asked why the immigrants broke the law, not why the government had created a system that allowed and encouraged the immigrants to break the law.

The Dream Act ultimately triggered hot emotion, not rational thought. For more than a decade, different versions of the bill failed in Congress, again and again, wilting like daffodils on a scorching day. The Deferred Action process that President Obama created in 2012 was a sort of "Dream Act Lite," a temporary protected status that still fell short of real legal recognition.

But as important as immigration status was for students like Isaias, events that spring would convince me that another factor often played an even bigger role in their lives.

Chapter Six

...

MOTIVATION

April 2012:
One month before graduation

AS THE BUS MOVED SOUTH, Isaias and Daniel Nix played a trivia game on a cell phone. "Latvia!" Isaias called out, then spelled it. "L-A-T-V-I-A."

They were taking a field trip to a FedEx hub—not the huge one at the Memphis airport where workers load and unload jets, but a truck hub across the state line in Olive Branch, Mississippi.

For many years, FedEx has been the biggest employer in the Memphis area. The city enjoys a central location, access to the Mississippi River, and major highway and railroad connections to the rest of the country. Even before the creation of FedEx in the 1970s, the city had long served as a distribution center. The goods have ranged from cotton and slaves in the nineteenth century to Chinese-made consumer products in the modern era. By the mid-2000s, cavernous, boxlike warehouses dotted the industrial landscape in the southern section of the city, and workers pulled items from shelves and made minor upgrades for customers—sewing monograms on Williams-Sonoma bedsheets, for instance. Many students had put on their best clothes for this trip because FedEx was hiring.

Margot Aleman from Streets Ministries rode on the bus with the students. Nothing unusual about this—if you attended any Kingsbury High School function and looked around, chances were you'd see Margot. She often hugged kids in the cafeteria as she had on the first day, she went to football games, and later in the year, she even went to the prom. She used her Spanish to interact with parents, calling them and sometimes visiting them at home. And she helped run the Streets Ministries events at the community center near the high school, including dances, small group meetings and parties.

She often tried to improve children's lives in concrete ways, like helping them graduate from high school. Now Margot was paying attention to Isaias.

The bus arrived at the FedEx site, and in a conference room, one of the company's employees asked the students, "How many are going to college?" Hands went up. Isaias didn't raise his.

A recruiter said the company hired a lot of students as package handlers.

"What does a package handler actually do?" someone asked. The answer: package handlers unloaded trucks, then loaded them again, even in blazing-hot weather, and they did it for a starting wage of about $10.50 per hour.

The students left the room for a tour of the package sorting center. Margot walked alongside Isaias and talked with him about college.

"Whatever you think is best for you," she said.

"Yeah," he responded.

"The only reason we pester you guys on college is that it does open a lot of doors. However—however, I know people who have master's degrees and they're unhappy. But overall, a college degree will open up doors."

The group entered a massive high-ceilinged space of blue-painted metal, conveyor belts and concrete floors. Nothing moved at this time of day. As the tour guide began his talk, Margot felt upset. Isaias had just told her he had made up his mind and never really wanted to go to college. "Freakin' genius," she muttered. She spoke not with sarcasm, but sadness.

As the end of the school year drew closer, Isaias' decision to skip college had provoked concern among adults who cared about him, like Patricia

Henderson and Margot Aleman. But otherwise, it hadn't raised a big alarm among the Kingsbury staff, perhaps because many other students were doing far, far worse.

In April, Kingsbury principal Carlos Fuller unexpectedly called the seniors to the school auditorium. The loudspeakers played "Pomp and Circumstance." The students' names were called and they walked across the stage one by one. Isaias walked in this mock graduation, too, and he mimed accepting the diploma and pretended to pose for a picture.

Mr. Fuller celebrated with his students: "I present to you the graduating class of 2013!" Then he suddenly changed his tone. He told the students that many of them might not walk across the stage at the real graduation in a few weeks because they were failing. "I know the hard work I've put in for some of you guys. Begging. Pleading. Do what you got to do to get this diploma." He pleaded again with the students—if you have bad grades, get with your teachers and make up the work.

"Don't quit now!" he thundered from the stage, holding a microphone in his left hand and gesturing with his right. "In your second semester of your senior year, to quit! If you quit now, what do you truly expect to do for the rest of your life? You quit now, you're gonna be a quitter forever!"

Guidance counselor Brooke Loeffler called the names of students who were failing classes. "I need to see all of you." While Isaias and other successful students left, she handed out preliminary grade reports. One boy in the front row said, "I'm failing Tuminaro. Fuck!"

Ms. Loeffler counted a total of 101 kids who were failing one or more classes—roughly half of all seniors. Of those failing, 47 hadn't shown up for the mock graduation ceremony. Clearly, something was going wrong. Dozens of students on the verge of graduation had apparently decided school just wasn't worth it. What was happening?

It was hard to know the life circumstances of every senior. But some students probably had very good reasons to make school a low priority. Staffers said some Kingsbury students were dealing with extreme situations, like homelessness.

Coach Haidar told me about an African-American boy in his chemistry class some years earlier who was sleeping in an abandoned house. "I went to see, and I'm like 'This is where you live?' He's like 'Yeah.'" The teacher remembered the cold air blowing through an open window. The student had run away from home after fighting with his mother, whom Coach Haidar described as crazy. His father wasn't around. Teachers quietly intervened in the student's case, bringing him food and money. He eventually graduated.

Another teacher told me he'd brought a student home to live with him and his girlfriend after the student's mom had thrown him out.

Some students lived in abusive homes. Early in the year, Eduardo Saggiante, the school interpreter, told me a girl was skipping school because her mother's boyfriend was beating the mother and the girl was afraid to leave her alone. The mom also feared deportation. The interpreter said that James Anderson, the fatherly Memphis police officer assigned to Kingsbury, was going to help and that he, Eduardo, wanted to speak with the mother, too, and let her know that Memphis police don't enforce immigration law.

Other circumstances explained the seniors' absences. Immigrant kids got pulled out of school to interpret for parents. Teen mothers had to care for sick babies.

In one case, it appeared that a parent had pressured a teenager to leave school. The case involved a thin, friendly Hispanic eleventh grader who had helped the librarian, Marion Mathis, build the elaborate display she called the Bat Cave.

Visitors could walk into the library, duck through a low door in the wall, and enter a small room suffused with dim green light and the scent of the live trees that decorated a fake graveyard. Dozens of ghoulish objects crammed the space: skeletons, a gargoyle, a space alien in a casket, an electric-powered mummy woman rhythmically rocking a corpse baby.

Ms. Mathis loved monsters and saw them as underdogs. "When I read *Beowulf,* I always pull for Grendel," she said. She found that kids loved monsters, too, especially when the kids came from troubled backgrounds. Before Ms. Mathis taught at Kingsbury, she'd taught at an alternative middle school for boys who had lived in unstable environments all their lives. Some had been raped. Ms. Mathis said writing about monsters helped them work through their feelings. "And they wrote the most beautiful, creative stories." She said the process of building the Bat Cave taught students how to handle a project from start to finish, and that a related essay contest sharpened writing.

The eleventh grader's class essays revealed a tough upbringing, with a father in prison and bouts of hunger. While others missed school, this boy showed up. He told Ms. Mathis he wanted to be a doctor.

In mid-October, the librarian found that the Bat Cave's black plastic ceiling had collapsed, and she sent the teenager text messages asking him to help fix it. He said he might not come to school anymore.

I'm afraid ill have to be home schooled, he wrote in one message. *I'll work in the morning, 6a–4-5 pm and study in the afternoon. My mom can't take all the house expenses by herself* ;(

In another message, he wrote:

No, Mrs. Mathis. I will actually be working full time in the first shift at a company and study in the afternoon. I sure this changes because i will definitely miss school sooo much.

Ms. Mathis knew that in this case, homeschooling could mean no schooling. The next day, she almost cried. "He was such a good student and I know he wanted to go to college."

I never saw him at school again.[1]

For other students, immigration problems killed their motivation to study.

"It messes with your head," said Jose Perez, the senior who wanted to join the Marines but was having difficulty because he'd been brought to the country illegally as an infant. As the year wore on, if he started to feel bad, or unmotivated, he'd simply leave school. Or he'd skip entire days to work construction. Other laborers asked why he bothered to go to school at all if he was just going to end up working with them.

Yet some of the seniors who skipped school didn't face immigration problems. Apathy was widespread throughout the senior class, Ms. Loeffler said. "It's not just with our undocumented students, it's with all of our students."

Rigo Navarro, the soccer goalie, had the legal immigration status that students like Jose Perez craved. Yet he skipped school, too, and now he was in serious academic trouble, failing both of the English courses he needed to graduate.

Earlier in the semester, I'd asked Rigo why he'd missed so many days recently. He gave a long string of explanations, each of which accounted for a few hours or a few days away from school: He'd eaten a big bag of chips and become sick. He'd had a flare-up of costochondritis, a painful condition of the chest wall. His mom didn't drive and didn't speak English, and when she got a new puppy, he had to help her go to the veterinarian's office. He had to take a driver's license test. One of his brothers was having car trouble. Rigo went with him to the junkyard to find a part but lost the key to his own car there. "It took me five hours to find it," Rigo said. Then he went to Arkansas to do an estimate for a fence-building project and missed more hours of school. Oh, and he failed the driver's license test and he'd have to take it again and miss another day of school.

Teachers sometimes grew impatient.

"Are you going to be here more now that you have soccer practice every day?" Corey VanHuystee, the assistant English teacher, asked Rigo back in January.

"Well, I've been sick," Rigo said.

"You've been sick a *lot*," the teacher said in a doubtful tone.

"It's not my fault. I take care of a little baby." (Rigo's big family sometimes pressed him into babysitting duty.)

"Hmm ... I know, but you need to be at school, too."

Rigo wasn't content to live like a typical high school student.

"One of my brothers in Mexico told me that I'm living a very adult life at a very young age," Rigo said. The summer before his senior year, he'd thought about dropping out entirely and sticking with his construction job, where he said he was making between $1,500 and $2,000 per week. But Rigo said his employers told him that if he dropped out of school, he couldn't keep the job.

After graduation, Rigo planned to go back to work for the same company. Down the road, he would study, too, probably drafting. "I don't want to do a four-year college because I know how I am. And I'm gonna be honest. I like money."

Rigo spent money on expensive shirts and luxury-brand belts as well as on cars and trucks. When he went out to eat with a friend, Rigo would usually pay.

Rigo would say later that he understood why adults would doubt his explanations for missing school. The way he was living—the hard work, the expensive clothes—wasn't normal.

Rigo said other factors diminished his will to stay in school. Though deportations were relatively rare in the interior of the country, one of Rigo's older brothers had been deported during Rigo's junior year. Rigo's father said it had happened after police in Arkansas found a small amount of cocaine in the truck the brother was driving, and though Rigo's father said he had denied the cocaine was his, he was deported.

Rigo said that his brother had been a sort of father figure for him, and Rigo had slipped into a depression. Soccer injuries dampened his spirits, too.

Recruiters from the University of Memphis soccer team had spoken with Rigo earlier in his high school career about giving him an athletic scholarship. But Rigo lost contact with the recruiters during his senior year and assumed they were no longer interested. "When I found out I lost my scholarship, I basically gave up," he said much later.

Rigo said that during his senior year, his parents rarely spoke with him about school. "They were like 'He's going to school,' so they think I was doing good," he said later. He felt his parents were too busy to pay him much attention, and he believed other Hispanic kids experienced the same thing. "So [the kids] end up doing whatever other students do, because they're the ones giving the attention to them...I myself tried a few drugs, knowing that it was not the right thing, but my friends were doing it."

Immigrant parents often believed they could help their children by working hard, yet that meant leaving many children unattended, researchers Carola and Marcelo Suárez-Orozco wrote in their 2001 book *Children of Immigration*. And many immigrant parents suffered from anxiety and depression, which made them emotionally unavailable. Parental absence made some children hyper-responsible. In other cases, absent parents resulted in depressed kids who were drawn to alternative family structures such as gangs, the researchers wrote.

Rigo's father said that when he was raising Rigo's older siblings, he'd been so busy earning money that he often had to miss time with them. But he said that by the time Rigo, his youngest, was growing up, the older siblings were contributing to the household income and he had more time, and he made an effort to pay attention to Rigo. He said he often went to watch Rigo's soccer games. "Why? Because I wanted my son to see that I was interested in him."

. . .

That spring, even one of the most supremely motivated students in the senior class was showing signs of apathy. "Estevon, wake up!" Coach Haidar said to the figure slouched forward on the desk. "Let's go!"

This had been happening a lot lately. Estevon would sleep in class, or at least appear to sleep, and the chemistry teacher would tell him to sit up and pay attention. Coach Haidar said he believed Estevon was far more ambitious than he appeared. "He already read the whole book for his test. I guarantee you that. That's the kind of person he is." Estevon's goals were changing. He said he'd withdrawn his application to Carnegie Mellon and was now aiming for Georgia Tech in Atlanta. "My sister lives there and if I get aid I can go there for free," he said.

For Marion Mathis, the teacher and librarian who'd poured her energy into helping Estevon, this was bad news. She thought he was settling for something less than what he really wanted. "My first response was, 'You're going to regret this the rest of your life.'" Estevon was still awaiting results of one of the big grants he'd applied for, the Gates Millennium

Scholars Program. And Ms. Mathis thought his fear of taking loans was irrational—with a good job, he could pay them off easily.

It was only later that Estevon told me what was going on inside his mind. "This year is so much stress. Like you can see the gray hair on my head. I've been stressing out a lot. Like, the second semester, I've been really depressed." As he put it, he was in this "life dilemma," and he and his mother had been arguing. And chemistry class was really, really hard. Estevon said he sometimes had a difficult time showing that he cared. But he did.

This was the downside to really trying. At Kingsbury and schools like it, making an effort meant subjecting yourself to anguish that few others would feel.

In March, Estevon learned he'd been named a finalist for the Gates Millennium Scholars Program. He felt happy. But his anxiety spiked the week before the ultimate winners were announced. He didn't think he would get it. He thought to himself, "Oh my God, if I don't get it, why did I even try?"

. . .

The decision to try or not try appeared pivotal. I wanted to see the government give legal immigration status to students like Mariana, Jose Perez and Isaias. But after spending time at Kingsbury, I knew legal status wasn't an instant cure for all the challenges that young Hispanics faced. Just look at Rigo: he had legal immigration status but didn't come to school. U.S. citizenship didn't necessarily help either. White and African-American U.S.-born students dropped out at Kingsbury, too. I came to the conclusion that one factor often mattered more than immigration status or citizenship: motivation.

Elena Delevega agreed with me. "Clearly, I think so. I think motivation matters more. And I think that if you're driven, you're driven. But again, let's not discount the effect of immigration status, in that if I think that I'll never be able to get a job as anything else other than a maid, I may just lose my motivation."

Born in Mexico, Ms. Delevega was a professor of social work at the University of Memphis. She pointed out that in a neighborhood like the one around Kingsbury High, many young people know little about the world outside. They won't aspire to do anything different from what the people around them are doing. I've heard her argument formulated another way: you can't *be* what you can't *see*.[2]

So she tried to show them what they could be. She arranged for children at Kingsbury Elementary to go on a series of field trips to a local museum that would expose them to math and science and encourage them to pursue degrees in those fields. They got to do things like touch dead sharks.

"I want them to say, 'This is cool, this is possible, and I want it for myself. And it's going to take so much hard work. It doesn't matter if I have to be up 13 hours sitting in front of a stupid computer screen. Because I want this like I've never wanted anything in my life. And I want this more than I want sex and more than I want a car and more than I want drugs. I want this more than I want to lounge around.'"

They have to think it's possible before they'll want it, though. "Because wanting something that is unattainable, it hurts a lot. And we are very good at avoiding pain."

The apathy that I saw at Kingsbury was common across the country, said Daphna Oyserman, a psychologist at the University of Southern California who has dedicated her career to finding ways to boost motivation, especially among black and Hispanic kids.

"I've never been in an inner-city school where there weren't lots of great teachers and where there weren't a whole bunch of resources that were basically missing the mark," she said. Teachers would stay to tutor, and no students would come. The public address system would tell students to get materials for a science project, and they wouldn't do it.

She offered an explanation: school is hard, and students often don't see any reason to push through obstacles. "No one works hard in school because this is the most fun thing and they can't imagine a more fun thing to do. People work hard in school because they imagine how satisfied they'll be when they attain a future self," she said. "Kids often say they want to do well. But 'school is boring, school is stupid.' What they really mean is 'I can think of a better thing to do with my time.' Because when it's hard

I just think, 'Oh well, it's not for me.'" She said that's not how American society talks about athletics.

"We have the 'no pain no gain.' 'Missing all the shots that you don't try to take.' There's all sorts of metaphors in sports. And weirdly, in academics where it really matters, we have no such metaphors. We act as though talent is a thing that descends upon us by the grace of God. And you either are smart or you work hard. No. You get smart by working hard."

Ms. Oyserman tries to teach young people three key ideas: first, that when something is hard, it doesn't mean it's impossible, it means it's important. Second, she tries to teach that academic success is something that's consistent with ethnic or racial identity: for instance, that black and Hispanic kids do well in school.

"If you cue kids to think in that way, that 'Oh, we care about school, I care about being a member of this group,' then kids work harder in school." She said kids who think of themselves as connected to both their group and to the broader society tend to do better, too—for instance, if they think of themselves as not just Mexican, but Mexican-American.

The third key idea she teaches is that the future isn't far away, but intimately connected to the present—as she puts it, "The future is close." She was working with the Lansing, Michigan, school district to set up bank accounts for students to save for college, starting in kindergarten. They couldn't save enough money to cover the whole cost, but she hopes they will start thinking of themselves as people with futures. "So if I'm going to have a future, maybe I should also do my homework now."

In 2015, the U.S. Department of Education asked researchers to submit grant proposals on how to "scale up" psychological interventions to improve motivation.

Ms. Oyserman and colleagues won a $2.7 million grant to develop a computer game that teaches ideas like "If it's hard, it means it's important" and test the game among middle and high school students in Colorado to see if it leads to improvements in outcomes such as grades and attendance.

Many other researchers around the country recognize the importance of student motivation and are trying to identify the best ways to boost it.

As of this writing, there is no consensus on how to do this, and not even a standard language to use. Some speak of "non-cognitive factors," others "grit" or "mindset." I hope the researchers will figure out which motivation interventions really work. If that happens, I'd like to see the government encourage schools to put the interventions into practice on a broad scale. Otherwise, intriguing results might sit unused for years, and thousands of students will slide through their school days in a cloud of apathy. And adults will still be standing in front of high school seniors and begging them to please, please, please do some work.

. . .

Rigo finally found a subject that motivated him. One afternoon in April, he walked to the front of the seventh-period English classroom, looking sharp in a pink dress shirt. "Hello, class, my name is Rigoberto Navarro. My capstone project is on cartels."

Speaking without notes, he launched into a presentation on Mexican drug-trafficking organizations. He flashed images onto the screen: Chapo Guzman, head of the Sinaloa Cartel. Smuggling methods, including a submarine.

Then Rigo warned that he was about to show some gruesome pictures. After a pause, he went on and displayed photos that showed a pile of drugs and a pile of money.

"Have you ever wondered what is between these two pictures? How they turn drugs into tons of money? Here's the answer. Death." Rigo proceeded to display photos of the bloody results of fights between cartels.

One image showed a bullet-riddled pile of corpses, people shot dead at a party. The next images showed horribly mutilated bodies. Rigo said he'd decided to spare the class the video of a guy getting his throat cut with a chainsaw. Mexico's cartels were fighting a bloody war against one another and the government, and Mexico's rule of law was so weak that most homicides weren't even investigated.

Rigo wrapped up. A student asked him why he picked this topic. "As a Hispanic, I care about my country," he said. "This is what happens daily in my country." He also said one of his brothers had dealt drugs. Rigo's father later confirmed this and said the brother had served time in prison for it.

Another question from the class: "Would you ever consider becoming a drug dealer?"

"To be honest, yes, I did," Rigo said in class.

Rigo told me later that a man named Rene used to work for his family and then left. Later, Rene's associates asked Rigo to help them. "And when I was like in need of money, they were like 'Well, I can't lend you money, but I can make you get fast money by taking basically drugs to Jonesboro,'" Rigo said, referring to a town across the river in Arkansas. "And since my brothers were working in Jonesboro, [the men said] it will make it seem like you're just visiting your brothers."

Drug-trafficking organizations prized Memphis for its transportation links just as legitimate companies did. As far back as the 1930s, the city had served as a distribution center for illegal narcotics, and as Mexican drug-trafficking organizations began to dominate the business, they worked in Memphis, too.[3] Money from drug buyers in Memphis and cities like it was shipped to Mexico, where it lined traffickers' pockets and covered costs ranging from bribing officials to hiring torturers.

So did Rigo agree to drive the drugs to Jonesboro?

"I decided not to," he said. "It was so tempting. I won't lie."

He said no for two reasons. One, he didn't have a car. "And two, I was with Mariana back then so I talked to her and she straightened me up. She made me decide between that and her."

Mariana confirmed the conversation, though she said they'd already broken up at that point. "I was very against it. I let him know." She opposed any illegal activity, and she thought it was wrong that anyone would ask an underage person to do such things.

The man Rigo's family knew, 36-year-old Rene Hernandez, was one of four men arrested on April 1 of Rigo's senior year when Memphis police officers raided a house on Reenie Street, about two miles north of Kingsbury High. The newspaper said police found a gun, Xanax pills, $170,000 in cash and marijuana bricks the size of paving stones: 2,100 pounds in all. Rene Hernandez later pleaded guilty and was sentenced to 33 months in federal prison.[4]

To conclude his presentation, Rigo showed the class elaborate dioramas he had built to illustrate the drug-trafficking business. Rigo cared about the issue, and it showed. "Your project is amazing, Rigo," Mr. Tuminaro said.

Even though Rigo had missed so much class, Mr. Tuminaro offered him a chance to redeem himself. He could take oral exams for both English 3 and English 4.

Mr. Tuminaro knew something about giving extra chances to students who'd made mistakes. He only had to look at his own history.

As a teenager growing up in Poughkeepsie, New York, Mr. Tuminaro had thought that what he was learning in school was stupid and boring. He figured out a way to slack off for nine months of the year: he failed his regular classes and went to summer school, which lasted only two months or so and was much easier, since practically all he had to do to get an A was show up.

"Remember, that's the problem with our school system," he said. "Kids don't get punished for failing. School systems and teachers do. They lose their funding, people lose their jobs... So summer school is not a kid's last chance. Summer school is the *school's* last chance."

Around the time Mr. Tuminaro slogged to the end of high school, he began feeling disgusted with himself. "I'm about to face the world—I'm not prepared for it and I'm a bum, you know?" He started reading the Bible and committed himself to Jesus. He said he needed three attempts for the change to take hold, but it eventually did. A church helped him get into a college by writing a letter that said he had poor grades, but needed a second chance. One thing helped him: he had grown up middle class, and outside of school, he enjoyed reading. So when his second chance came, he was ready.

Mr. Tuminaro's own experience and his years at Kingsbury had made him critical of the current education system. As Mr. Tuminaro saw it, teachers like him spent most of their time dealing with students who didn't want to go to school.

He believed mandatory studies killed motivation. "You're forcing people to sit through four years. They don't know what it's for. They don't know what it's about. They don't think it has anything to do with them. And many of them are incapable of doing it because they don't know the basics."

His solution was radical: make education mandatory through the sixth grade only. After that, make it optional—and make it available only to those who had shown proficiency in basic math, reading and writing. If students didn't have to go to school, they would realize how hard the real world was and *want* to study. And he believed schools should let students focus on what they wanted to learn by letting them choose a major, even in high school.

No one was planning to implement Mr. Tuminaro's radical education reforms, of course, so he worked within the existing system. He said he joined the teaching profession to help students who were falling by the wayside, the ones who hated it and didn't want to learn. Now, despite Mr. Tuminaro's efforts, some of his students still couldn't read. It made him feel he was failing.

One day I mentioned an idea to Mr. Tuminaro: that the students at Kingsbury weren't just dealing with the question of what college to attend or what job to take, but also with the deeper question of the meaning and purpose of their lives.

Mr. Tuminaro agreed and recalled a quote he'd read somewhere: "I think he said, 'As long as a man has a *why*, he can overcome any *how.*'"

As Mr. Tuminaro saw it, he had a *why:* to glorify God. He said that meant loving the students, even when they didn't deserve it, even when they were bad, treating the unworthy as though they were worthy, just as Christ had done for him. "I have a why," he said. "Which allows me to survive this job, which at times seems impossible."

. . .

Rigo could have spent the next several days cramming for the make-or-break tests. Instead, he decided to travel to Florida with one of his brothers to work on a home-remodeling job and talk with an employer who had an

office there. The employer might hire him for the summer on a construction job in Tennessee.

Once again, Rigo would miss several days of school. But he expected
he'd have time to study. "It's gonna be eat, work and study. And when I come
back, I know for sure I'll ace it."

· · ·

That April, Estevon Odria obsessively followed news about the Gates
Millennium Scholars Program on a Facebook page for applicants. A friend
from Nashville won the scholarship, and Estevon felt angry, almost as
though that student had taken Estevon's slot.

Based on the Facebook postings and the timing of the last round of letters announcing finalists, Estevon figured that his envelope would arrive
on Thursday, April 18. The night before, he didn't sleep, drinking coffee
and walking around in circles in his room with the blue walls and the hardwood floor and the crucifix on the dresser.

After school, he grabbed a friend and insisted he come with him to the
mailbox for emotional support. They made their way to the white house
where Estevon lived, near a fence with gang graffiti. From the pictures
online, Estevon knew exactly what an acceptance letter would look like.

He opened the mailbox.

· · ·

On the afternoon of April 19, Isaias was dying of nerves for another reason. In a few hours, he would play keyboard with a new rock band, Los
Psychosis. It would mark the first time he'd joined the band in public. They
would play on the sidewalk during an art festival in midtown Memphis, not
far from the school. Hundreds of people would walk by and hear them for
a few seconds at least, or longer if they stopped and listened.

Dennis had been the first of the Ramos brothers to get into rock music,
and in a way, it had changed the course of his life. He'd always been different from other kids. In middle school, he was bullied, and he looked for a
way to fit in. He gravitated toward a group of boys from Mexico, El Salvador

and Honduras who dressed up like gangsters, brought cigarettes to school, drank and smoked marijuana. Dennis' father remembers him coming home with a pair of saggy, gangster-style shorts. He told Dennis they made him look like a woman, and Dennis didn't want to wear them anymore.

They argued about boundaries. Dennis wanted to go out and party and drive around, and why wouldn't his parents let him? His father remembered telling him, "Go ahead, I won't stop you." But he warned that if one day Dennis landed in jail, he wouldn't bail him out. Jail was more than an abstract possibility. Dennis remembered that one of the other kids had been caught by the police with a gun and was sentenced to house arrest.

Then Dennis joined JROTC and felt proud of the uniform, and he met a new friend named Jonathan, a rock kid from Mexico City. Rock music enjoyed a strong following in Mexico—when Eduardo Saggiante, the school interpreter, was growing up, for instance, he wore black clothes and listened to heavy metal. Mario, Isaias and Dennis' father, had been a fan of Led Zeppelin.

Dennis liked Jonathan, this cool kid who spoke Spanish with a city accent, and he drifted away from the wannabe criminals. Their friendship led Dennis to another rock kid who'd been bullied for being different, Javi Arcega. They started playing together, and Isaias came along to practices and shows. Isaias played the drums in a bar, even though he was only 13 at the time. Javi loved The Cramps, a band that had begun in the 1970s and had recorded in Memphis. The Cramps played a weird mix of rockabilly and punk and wore strange costumes onstage.[5] Javi even got the band's name tattooed on the inside of his right arm.

Javi wanted to play like The Cramps, but Dennis and Isaias didn't. One day the Ramos brothers came over to the practice space, collected their things and left. A few years later, Javi ran into Dennis and his parents at a furniture store, which led to a restart of the friendship and eventually to Javi inviting them to play music together. Javi now was 22, the same age as Dennis, but bony, and a sad look would sometimes come into his dark eyes.

Javi explained the origin of the band's name, Los Psychosis: "Well, psychosis is sort of like a disorder and that's how I feel a lot of the time," he said. "That's how a lot of people feel when they listen to music." He also mentioned the famous Mexican wrestler named Psichosis.

That spring they began practicing together at Javi's house, a duplex where they would walk through a living room full of vinyl records and packages of diapers and climb a ladder into an attic practice space that was decorated with posters of Jose Feliciano and Tav Falco–Panther Burns. They rehearsed a set of songs that Javi had written, playing so loudly that the neighbors sometimes called the police.

Javi's young wife, Stephanie Avila, had recently given birth to their daughter, Melody. Stephanie liked rock music, too, and the baby had been hearing it since she was in the womb. Javi sang and played lead guitar, Dennis played bass, and Isaias played keyboard.

On the afternoon of the show, Dennis steered his tan pickup truck with the Darwin fish onto Broad Avenue, an industrial neighborhood a short distance from Kingsbury High. The neighborhood was coming to life again as a center for the visual arts. Small galleries and shops lined the street, and the arts festival was already getting into full swing as the band members began placing their equipment in a narrow sidewalk space between the front of the Broadway Pizza shop and the parked cars.

They stretched a handmade banner spelling out the words "Los Psychosis" on the wall outside the shop and found an empty paint can to collect tips.

"If they ask, we're Polish," Isaias said.

Javi the lead singer agreed. "We just spend a lot of time in the sun."

The fourth member of the band was Tommy Fletcher, a 35-year-old drummer with tattoos on his upper arms. One tattoo showed the Grim Reaper and the words "Some die young." Tonight, Tommy was wearing a black t-shirt that had a picture of a gun and the words "Welcome to Memphis. Duck Mother Fucker." Tommy was white and said they should introduce themselves as "vegetable soup." "Three beans and a cracker from Memphis, Tennessee."

As the sun set behind a nearby water tower, they began their first set, making the concrete sidewalk shake. Tommy's sticks flew on the drums with professional fury. Isaias threw chords into the keyboard and Dennis rocked slightly as he played bass. Javi sang about bluesman Robert Johnson at the crossroads: "Papa Legba knows me well and is gonna take my soul away / away, away, away, away to misery."

Herb Levy, who had taught Isaias in biology the year before, stopped and watched, and his little son dropped money into the paint bucket. One woman walked out of the pizza shop with her fingers in her ears. Most people simply passed by. But the music drew some punk rock fans, several of them white and fortyish, and they stopped and listened, rapt.

Night fell and a group of new fans stuck around for the band's next set. For the second time that evening, the band played "Violent Sunset," a song with a slow oom-pah-pah beat, like in *norteña* music. "Take me by your scaly hands!" Javi sang as he strummed the electric guitar. "Take me to Cairo and show me your sorrow. Hidden castles in the moon / We shall be there singing lonely tunes / But now...Now you know where I'll be! At the end of valley—and that's where I'll beeeeeeee..." He drew out the last syllable as Tommy delivered a final drum flurry.

(Photo by Daniel Connolly)

The band neared the end of the set. Javi took a swig of amber liquid from a big bottle, then passed it to Tommy, who did the same. "Okay, one more time before we go," Javi said, his voice reverberating over the microphone. "My name is Javi. This is Dennis. This is 'No Mas' Tomas," he said, pointing to the drummer.

Javi turned to Isaias at the keyboard. "We got Chay on keys. Look at him, he's still wearing his school uniform!" Sure enough, Isaias was wearing tan pants and a white shirt. As the small crowd cheered and laughed, he spread out his arms wide in a shrugging acknowledgment. "This guy right here, he's about to graduate from high school," Javi continued. "Congratulations."

Javi hadn't finished high school himself. He said he'd clashed with his Mexican immigrant parents and they threw him out of the house. He moved to a friend's house and had to get a job. He returned once more to Kingsbury High to turn in his books and quit.

Now Javi began to sing. "Do the late night rock / at a horror house!"

The little knot of punk rock fans loved it and began to dance and whoop again. Javi fed off their energy as he strummed the guitar wildly, climbed onto an amplifier and hit Tommy's cymbal with his head. He lived for moments like this. He earned money washing dishes, busing tables and helping in the kitchen in a sushi restaurant, but he thought about music all the time. He wanted Los Psychosis to become a huge success. As he saw it, music was his only chance to triumph at anything.

And then the show was over. The new fans stayed around for a while, and Javi invited them to come to his house, but it didn't happen. One fan called "Good set, guys" as he left.

The musicians drove to Javi's duplex. His wife, Stephanie, had watched part of the show, and as the band members brought in the amps and instruments, she rocked the baby in a little bouncing chair. "All of you guys look ten feet taller," she said. "You're all excited. High as hell." Tommy passed pieces of equipment up a ladder and through a hole in the ceiling to Isaias, who pulled them into the attic practice space.

Dennis inventoried the contents of the paint bucket: "Hey, Tomas, it's 29 dollars and a quarter." Someone had thrown in a pair of sunglasses. One of the band members rolled the bills into a little cylinder and put a rubber band around it, and the musicians batted their earnings around the room like a toy.

. . .

Kingsbury held an end-of-year ceremony to honor its top students on Class Day, April 26, and in the slack time outside the auditorium before the event began, Jacklyn Martin, the English teacher, spoke with Isaias.

"I've got a band that's playing together," he said.

"How's that going?"

"It's going great. We had, like, three shows and we're already big. We're not big, but we played at the art walk on Broad Avenue."

She said she'd seen the article about him in *Falcon Express*, the school newsletter. School librarian Marion Mathis had written the headline, which played on police jargon for "Be on the lookout": "BOLO: Two Hispanic Males, Armed with ACT Scores!" Isaias and Estevon Odria held the

Walking to Class Day: (from left to right) Juan Avalos, Isaias, Daniel Nix and Ibrahim Elayan. *(Photo by Daniel Connolly)*

school's highest scores on the college entrance test, and the article said both planned to go to college. But now, Isaias told Ms. Martin, his situation had changed. He wasn't going to college after all.

Isaias went off to join his friends, leaving Ms. Martin to process what he had said. She wondered if Isaias really wanted to skip college. She thought he was afraid to hope. And what a waste. With other students dying to go to college, it disturbed her to see Isaias shrug it off. How much of it was an emotional defense mechanism against the possibility that he couldn't go? How much of it was him really being different?

The awards ceremony started, and Isaias got his first prize of the day for his performance in economics. A few minutes later, Ms. Martin went onstage and gave him her own award. "Lastly, I want to acknowledge the captain of our Knowledge Bowl team," she said. "This is one of only two students to get a perfect score on the TCAP writing test last year. This student has also shown exceptional leadership skills with our Kingsbury International Club. That would be Isaias Ramos."

Isaias strode forward again, and the students clapped and whooped as he climbed the steps. Some shouted his name. Moments later, Isaias came back to the stage yet again to accept a prize for participation in the school's Super All-Stars club.

Then it was time for announcements of scholarship awards. Dressed in a black suit and with her mane of coiffed hair sticking out as usual, Ms. Henderson read a long list of names and dollar amounts that colleges and outside organizations had offered them, and the students cheered loudly.

"Daniel Nix—$22,000!"

"Cash Price—$58,000!"

"Breanna Thomas—$104,000!" The cheers grew louder.

"Adam Truong—two hundred..." she began, and the cheers drowned her out. Soon she'd reached the end of the list.

"I had to save the big one for last," Ms. Henderson said. "Estevon Odria—please stand. For the Gates Millennium Scholarship to Carnegie Mellon—for $268,000!"

Huge cheers. Students jumped out of their wooden seats around Estevon. He stood up in his shirt and tie, his dark mustache neatly trimmed and dark hair cropped short, his expression serious.

When Estevon opened the mailbox after school a few days earlier, he saw a letter inside, a wide one. He eagerly clawed the packet out. He cried. He hugged his friend. He rushed into the house and told his grandmother, with her oxygen tube. He told Marion Mathis, and within minutes, Principal Fuller was sharing the news with assistant principal Norah Jones over his handheld radio. "Estevon got a full scholarship, bachelor's and master's at Carnegie Mellon!"

Estevon had withdrawn his Carnegie Mellon application. But he could reverse that step and still go.

Mr. Fuller read the news the next morning over the announcements as Estevon stood next to him at the microphone, shifting from side to side in the white school uniform shirt he'd only have to wear for a few more days.

Estevon was one of only three students named Gates Millennium Scholars within the entire Memphis City Schools system and one of 1,000 winners nationwide. The announcement letter said, "Your accomplishment is especially notable in context of the more than 54,000 students who applied, making this year's the largest and most competitive group of candidates in the program's history."

Technically, the Gates Millennium Scholars Program didn't pay the $268,000 amount that Ms. Henderson had cited at Class Day. The exact amount would depend on the financial aid package Carnegie Mellon offered. But in short, Estevon could go to one of the nation's most prestigious universities without taking out loans.

Now he could even help his grandparents financially later in life. And if he went on to graduate school in a field such as computer science or engineering, the Gates program might help pay for that too.

He said he'd encourage younger students to apply. "It might seem scary at first but I know if I can get it, they can get it."

"Just like, don't give up hope in life, because if you work hard, it's going to get you somewhere. And if I still didn't get this scholarship, I know I would work it out somehow."

The Gates Millennium Scholars Program aimed to help Hispanics and other minorities, yet the scholarship rules required them to be a "citizen, national or legal permanent resident of the United States." That meant students like Isaias couldn't get it. And the scholarship program wouldn't last forever. A spokeswoman told me the program had been designed to fund 20,000 students, and in 2015, it was recruiting the last of them. The Gates program illustrated how a big commitment of dollars to education could change lives. I hope others will follow Bill Gates' example.

At the Class Day ceremony, Estevon Odria's name was last on the list. Patricia Henderson had read all the scholarship winners without mentioning Isaias.

Principal Carlos Fuller took the microphone to address the students once more before dismissal. "Guys, time is short now. We got exams, baccalaureate, graduation rehearsal. And if you forgive me, we gonna throw up the deuces." In other words, we'll say goodbye. The students cheered.

Mr. Fuller continued, mentioning the prize that Isaias had won in the audio production contest in Chattanooga. "He was a silver medalist, second in the state." More cheers. Isaias hadn't expected so much recognition. He had imagined going to Class Day as something like the Oscars award show, something that he would simply watch.

As the students left, Ms. Martin sought out Ms. Henderson, Isaias' college counselor. In the counselor's office, Ms. Martin told her Isaias was the best student she'd ever taught, hands down. She said she'd adopt him if she could. Wasn't there some way he could go to college? Ms. Henderson said she didn't see a solution. The young teacher began to cry.

Chapter Seven

...

INTERVENTION

May 2013:
Final days before graduation

THE CASE OF ISAIAS RAMOS gnawed at the conscience of Margot Aleman, the counselor from Streets Ministries. She had developed her own theory for Isaias' reluctance to go to college: that his parents might want him to work in the family painting and remodeling business. "I don't think his family knows how brilliant this kid is." She'd never met them, and she realized she might be wrong.

Over a period of days, she planned an intervention. She told Isaias she wanted to speak with him and his parents at home, and he agreed. She convinced Isaias' former English teacher and Knowledge Bowl coach Jacklyn Martin to come with her. She'd also bring along Jennifer Alejo, the counselor who specialized in finding scholarships for unauthorized immigrant students.

They set the date for May 15, after Isaias' classes were over.

...

Was college worth it? Was it legitimate for adults to encourage Isaias to go? Across the country, people were questioning the value of higher education.

That skepticism was in sharp contrast to the scene that took place one day in August 2006, when then–Memphis City Schools superintendent Carol Johnson led thousands of employees at the FedExForum basketball arena in a chant: "EVERY CHILD! EVERY DAY! COLLEGE BOUND!" The superintendent said the words in other settings, too, and the school system itself referred to them as a "mantra."[1] As the school system moved toward adopting the phrases as its official slogan, critics attacked the message. "Don't expect me to go out there and say 'every child, every day, college bound,'" school board member Kenneth Whalum, Jr., told a reporter in 2007. "Everybody here knows it's not true." At the time, the district's graduation rate stood at only 66.3 percent—its highest in years.

"I struggle with the message. I do," the superintendent responded. "I am trying to raise the bar. If we don't start, we will never get there."

Mr. Whalum cast the only "no" vote when the school board voted 8–1 to adopt the slogan as its official brand. The system launched an accompanying advertising campaign. A news release clarified that "college bound" didn't necessarily mean a four-year college, "but includes students who attend a two-year community or technical school, a trade school or other fields including the arts and music."

Then in June 2007, the superintendent announced she was leaving Memphis to become head of public schools in Boston. The following year, a new superintendent, Kriner Cash, quietly replaced the "college bound" slogan without a school board vote. Now the slogan was "Breakthrough Leadership. Breakthrough Results."

Around the time Isaias was finishing high school, news stories abounded of "boomerang kids" graduating from universities and moving back in with their parents, burdened with student loan debt and struggling to find work. Some young people were even living in homeless shelters, including many with college credits or work histories, *The New York Times* reported in a

December 2012 story.[2] Workers aged 18 to 24 had the highest unemployment rates of all adults.

Observers at *The Wall Street Journal* and elsewhere began to point to alternative careers in fields like welding, where a determined worker could earn more than $100,000 per year.[3]

Such middle-skilled jobs offered high salaries and seemed to make a lot of sense in the context of Kingsbury. In January, a bus carrying 21 Kingsbury students pulled up outside a drab brown building in downtown Memphis, the local campus of a state trade school called Tennessee Technology Center. Perhaps the biggest evangelist of practical training the Kingsbury students met that day was Ed York, instructor for HVAC, or heating, ventilation and air conditioning. With obvious pride, Mr. York showed the Kingsbury students the old refrigerators and ice machines that his trainees learned to fix. He said every grocery store, convenience store and restaurant needed these machines, and the people who repaired them could earn $20 to $30 per hour. Or students could specialize in repairing walk-in freezers. "They call you, they've got $30,000 worth of food in those walk-in freezers. So when they call you, they don't care what it costs! They just want it fixed. So if you can fix it, you can make a lot of money." Or they could fix air conditioners and run around all summer taking calls, making as much money as they wanted.

For some Kingsbury students, this wasn't their first exposure to a trade. The vocational center near the high school, where Isaias did his audio recording class, also trained students in welding and other hands-on courses like small engine repair and cosmetology.

Now, the HVAC instructor was letting the students imagine what practical training could offer: mastery of a craft, pride, financial independence. And such training could appeal to the many Kingsbury students who didn't care about academics. They wouldn't have to read thick books and write essays. "And it's only a year and a half," guidance counselor Brooke Loeffler said as the tour group left the building. "You don't have to commit a year to remedial classes and another four to five years to get your bachelor's."

Only 32 percent of Americans had a college degree in 2013, according to Census data, and among Hispanics it was 15 percent. Isaias knew few people who'd gone to college. In his family, the only one he could name when we spoke that April was a cousin in Mexico, but Isaias said she hadn't finished. Outside his family, the only friend he could think of who was in college was Tommy Nguyen's girlfriend, a student at Christian Brothers, but now Isaias didn't talk with her much. It's notable that both the people he named were young women—indeed, female high school graduates were more likely to enroll immediately in college than males. The gender gap in college enrollment had increased in the general population and especially among African-Americans and Hispanics.[4]

For Isaias, painting and remodeling in the family business could accomplish much the same as an HVAC job: money, independence, a sense of purpose.

Viewed in this context, his skepticism about college was understandable. Yet one small incident illustrated some of the risks of choosing a career in the family business. Isaias was installing drywall with his father and Dennis in the storeroom of a house one cold day in his senior year when he got a splinter embedded in his hand. He tried sucking it out, and said, *"Ya la rompí"*—I already broke it. Then he took a piece of duct tape, laid it against the splinter embedded in the skin, and tried to pull it out that way.

It was a tiny injury and quickly forgotten, but one that illustrated the risks in the job. He and Dennis sometimes climbed ladders, and a bad fall could lead to injury, medical bills and lost work.

In the Ramos family, only young Dustin, the citizen, had health insurance. For minor ailments, the Ramos family relied on traditional herbal remedies that Mario had learned from his mother. When someone had a more serious illness, they'd pay to visit a for-profit clinic called Healthy Life that catered to Hispanics.[5]

Of course, traditional remedies and clinic visits couldn't always prevent something from going catastrophically wrong on the job. Hispanic laborers had the highest rates of workplace deaths among major ethnic and racial groups, probably because they did dangerous jobs, and they and their bosses sometimes disregarded safety measures.[6]

When Isaias and Magaly toured the library at Rhodes College, they doubtless had no idea that a man had fallen to his death while building it. The college memorialized him with a plaque. It read:

IN MEMORY OF

FRANCISCO JAVIER HERNANDEZ

OF

SAN FRANCISCO DE RINCON, MÉXICO

1958–2004

CARPENTER FOR THE PAUL BARRET, JR. LIBRARY

"EN LA CASA DE MI PADRE MUCHAS MORADAS HAY."

In my father's house there are many dwellings.

A short time after Isaias' senior year, economists from the Federal Reserve of New York took a fresh look at the value of college: Given rising tuition for college, heavy student loan debt, and lower wages for college graduates, did investing in a degree still make sense? In dollar terms, the answer was a clear yes. Workers with a bachelor's degree would, on average, earn far more over the course of their lifetime than those with only a high school diploma—to be precise, $1 million more.[7] The lifetime advantage for those with an associate's degree was smaller, but still significant: $325,000.

Yes, it was true that college graduates had trouble finding good jobs and that their wages had declined. But for less-educated workers, the problems were even worse. The researchers wrote, "Investing in a college degree may be more important than ever before because those who fail to do so are falling further and further behind."

There were some risks. Going to college for a while and dropping out—as almost all Southwest Tennessee Community College students did—generally didn't help students much, the Federal Reserve Bank researchers wrote.

The presence or absence of a college degree was correlated with a wide range of other successes, too. People with bachelor's degrees were far more likely to marry and remain married, and less likely to have children out of wedlock.[8]

People with college degrees also tended to live longer, according to a report from the Centers for Disease Control.[9] For instance, consider a 25-year-old man living in 2006. He could expect to live to 72 if he dropped out of high school, to 76 if he finished, and to 81 if he had a bachelor's degree or higher. A 25-year-old woman who dropped out of high school could expect to live to 77, whereas a college-educated woman could expect to live to 85.

"Highly educated people tend to have healthier behaviors, avoid unhealthy ones and have more access to medical care when they need it," the report's lead author said, adding that poor people sometimes live in communities with less access to healthy foods and places to exercise.

And this is to say nothing of the other benefits of higher education: its value in preparing people to participate in a democracy, or the intellectual joy of understanding the world and learning new things—a joy that Isaias appeared far more likely to experience than would most of his peers.

• • •

That May, Isaias' father Mario discussed the value of college, too, relating a recent case he'd heard from back home in Santa Maria Asunción.

"We know a girl who studied political science and had problems when she finished. They're paying her 1,500 pesos every 15 days." That was about $125. "Imagine," Mario said. "That's ridiculous."

He and Cristina were talking with Mariana Hernandez's parents at a special banquet that Kingsbury was hosting to honor the senior class's top ten graduates. Isaias and his parents arrived late, and Isaias explained that they'd had to work. They had all dressed up for the occasion, and they took seats at a table with the Hernandez family. The parents had never met before, and they talked about their jobs and the climate and populations of their hometowns in Mexico, and Mario shared the story about the college graduate they knew.

Each student was allowed to bring guests, but only Isaias, Mariana,

Ibrahim Elayan and Breanna Thomas had brought a parent. Leonard Duarte, the valedictorian, came alone. So did Juan Avalos. Estevon Odria came with Marion Mathis, the librarian and teacher who had helped him with his applications. Tommy Nguyen brought his girlfriend. Jason Doan didn't come.

Adam Truong was accompanied by his sister, but not his mother. Adam later said it didn't bother him that his mother didn't come to these events. He thought she wanted to be there, but she needed to earn money at the nail salon. She did come a few days later, when he graduated second in his class.

They finished eating, the ceremony started, and the English teacher, Jinger Griner, invited the students up one by one, gave them a plaque and said a few words about each of them. When it was Estevon's turn, he held up the plaque so it partially covered his face, and Principal Fuller smiled as Ms. Griner described Estevon's college success that year.

"So I'm very excited for Estevon," she said. "And I hope he doesn't forget Kingsbury."

"I won't. I'll e-mail you," Estevon said.

"You'll e-mail me?"

"I'll send you some soup."

If Ms. Griner had been in her classroom, she might have added this comment to her running list of Estevon's odd sayings. But now she simply said, "Some soup? Okay. Good job, Estevon!" Everyone laughed and applauded.

. . .

A few nights later, Isaias and the band pounded out "Late Night Rockin'" again, the song that had closed out the show at Broad Avenue in April. Only this time, almost no one was listening. They were playing in a mostly empty, dimly lit bar called Murphy's on a Thursday night, opening for the group Coma in Algiers, which had come from Austin, Texas.

The set ended into sudden dead silence. Through the smoky, neon-lit air, Tommy the drummer called out to a man in the bar. "Don't worry, we'll be the audience in just a minute." The man replied, "We'll be the band."

"I don't know where everybody went, man," Tommy said. The band members started packing up their equipment and carrying it outside. Isaias thought it was their best-sounding show to date. He marveled that the members of Coma in Algiers had come from so far away. "Those guys are from Texas! That's crazy." Isaias wanted to stay and told Dennis, "Let's be the audience." Dennis was reluctant. "I got to go to work tomorrow."

"Just for a second at least," Isaias said. "I'm going in."

He went back inside and took a seat at a table facing the stage. Dennis followed and took a seat at the bar. Tomorrow, Isaias would go to Kingsbury High School for the last time. As a senior, he had the right to wrap up school a few days earlier than everyone else, and he would take care of final details. And that would be it. No more Kingsbury High—and for that matter, no more school, period.

As we sat there in the bar, I asked Isaias how he felt. "I don't know. I feel like I'm going to miss it. I don't know when else I'm going to go to an institution of knowledge like that." He said he realized that many people who'd been part of his life wouldn't be there anymore. Onstage, the members of Coma in Algiers began to warm up.

Isaias said he would miss his biology class from last year. He would miss calculus. Maybe he'd catch glimpses of it from Magaly's learning, but he wouldn't study it himself. He wouldn't read literature in class. "I loved *Macbeth* when we read it, absolutely loved it. One of my favorite stories." Then he thought of people. "I'm gonna miss Ms. Wilks. I'm gonna miss Ms. Martin. Ms. Dowda. Mr. Levy. Ms. Griner. It's just sad."

I had never seen Isaias cry, but now he seemed close. "Even though I'm not going anywhere, it still feels like I'm going to be so far away. Like no matter what, I'm never going to be there anymore. I'm not gonna be there again." He paused. "It's a happy sad."

Around the end of the year, the students in the Advanced Placement Chemistry class took their national test. The tests were scored from one through five. A score of three or better could get them college credit.

The results came back months later, during the summer. Unfortunately, none of the students earned better than a two—not even Magaly Cruz, Mariana Hernandez, Leonard Duarte or Adam Truong. Several of them, like Estevon Odria, had scored high on their other standardized tests.

Coach Haidar was surprised. "They came out feeling good about it. 'Test seems easy to us.'" Still, he took it in stride. It was his first year teaching Advanced Placement Chemistry, and he figured it would take three to five years to really get the program going. And he thought the course would still help the students in college chemistry.

"When they go to school, to college and sit in the class, they're gonna shake their heads. 'We've done all this.' So it's not a loss in the long run."

When the last day of twelfth grade arrived, Jamal Jones was still trying to figure out what he would do next. He was a quiet African-American boy with glasses who liked rock bands like Nirvana. He couldn't get into rap because, as he saw it, it just didn't make sense. He said people at another school had picked on him, but it didn't happen as much at Kingsbury.

He said his friends were "overachiever people" and they'd sometimes make mean comments about his struggles. "It's hard talking to them about it because they tend to put me down," he told Patricia Henderson as he sat in her cubicle.

He told her he'd scored a 14 on the ACT, a low mark that was largely attributable to his problems in math. His father had died at age 22, his mother had dropped out of school when she got pregnant with him, and he stayed with his grandmother.

They talked some more, and Ms. Henderson suggested he go to Tennessee Technology Center or Southwest. Jamal had told me he liked music but saw majoring in that area as a risk. He'd taken a survey I'd passed out a couple of days before in the English classes—I'd asked a few basic questions on what the students planned to do after graduation. Jamal wrote that he'd go to Tennessee Tech. Asked about work plans, he wrote, "Simple manual labor or whatever my degree can get me."

A total of 111 students answered my survey. The biggest group—41 percent—said they planned to go to technical school or community college. The second-largest group—36 percent—said they planned to go to the University of Memphis or another four-year college. Some of the students going to two-year or four-year colleges expressed interest in the military as well.

Six percent said they planned to forgo college and join the military immediately. Another six percent said they were considering both two-year and four-year options. I didn't ask if the students had already applied and been accepted to college or to the military, so I can't say if their intentions represented firm plans or vague dreams.

Ten percent of the students said they had no immediate plans to go to college or join the military.

One girl wrote that after graduation she would "have a long vacation." Under college plans she wrote, "I don't know." Under work plans, "I don't know." A boy wrote: "I have no clue right now... Just work intill I find something I like to do."

More than 100 seniors on the official roster didn't answer the survey at all. Even if the sample wasn't perfect, one theme came through clearly in the responses: many showed academic weakness. When I passed out the sheets, several students hadn't brought pens or pencils to class, and I let them borrow mine. Many made basic errors in writing, like not putting periods at the ends of sentences. One misspelled "Tennessee," the name of the state he lived in.

• • •

Some people believed that one way to avoid big academic weaknesses among high school seniors was to intervene years earlier, when they were small children. The younger the student at the time of intervention, the bigger the long-term impact, argued James J. Heckman, a Nobel Prize–winning economist.

Big gaps in skills open up very early between advantaged and disadvantaged groups in the United States, Heckman said. He argued that good preschools can raise both academic performance and "soft skills" like perseverance, attention, self-confidence and motivation, thus leading to long-term improvements in schooling, crime rates, workforce productivity and reduction of teenage pregnancy.

"Skill begets skill; motivation begets motivation," he wrote in a presentation.[10] "If a child is not motivated and stimulated to learn and engage early on in life, the more likely it is that when the child becomes an adult, it will fail in social and economic life."

"The longer society waits to intervene in the life cycle of a disadvantaged child, the more costly it is to remediate disadvantage."

Spending money on Pell Grants to help low-income kids afford college is less effective than early childhood training that sets them up to succeed in life, he argued.

Advocates for Hispanic children also pointed to preschool education as a priority. "If I had a magic wand, I would make sure that every Hispanic student had access to a high-quality early learning program in their community," Alejandra Ceja from the White House Initiative on Educational Excellence for Hispanics told me. Deborah Santiago with the group *Excelencia* in Education likewise called for increased spending on early childhood education.

Hispanic children were the least likely of all major ethnic groups to attend preschool. Only 52 percent of Hispanic children aged three to six went to an early childhood program in 2012, compared to 63 percent of non-Hispanic white children and 68 percent of black children. Hispanic children were also the least likely to have the skills needed for kindergarten—for instance, recognizing all the letters of the alphabet and writing their first name. That said, they generally showed good skills in areas such as self-control and solving problems without fighting. And the proportion of Hispanic children in early childhood programs was trending upward.[11]

. . .

In the audio recording class on his last day of school, Isaias took a final exam in the studio, a wood-paneled space. As the other students continued to work on the test, he turned in his exam to teacher Corey A. Davis, who began grading it immediately and promptly told him he'd scored a 97. "Good job, Isaias. Very good."

All too soon, the class was over, and Mr. Davis handed his business card to Isaias, pointing out his cell phone number and e-mail address on the back. "Call if you need anything." He told Isaias to feel free to come back any time.

When that afternoon's announcements started inside the main high school building, students began to shout. Mohammad Toutio leaped to a shelflike space on top of the lockers and sat there for a moment; someone else threw a handful of torn-up scraps of paper in the air, and they drifted down like confetti. Isaias said he'd tried to leave a reminder of himself at Kingsbury. "I wrote in my locker. Kind of just my name and date."

· · ·

Classes continued for students in grades nine, ten and eleven, and the next week, Rigo came back to school for his make-or-break exam for Mr. Tuminaro's twelfth-grade English class. I spoke with him shortly before he took it. "I studied maybe 30 minutes a day," he said. "Maybe. Since I left to Florida." He laughed and looked away. "I procrastinated a little bit."

That afternoon, Rigo went to Mr. Tuminaro's classroom on the second floor for the test. The teacher sat at his own desk at the back of the room. Rigo took a seat at another desk turned around to face him. Mr. Tuminaro asked questions about grammar, then about the themes in literature they'd read, such as *Lord of the Flies* and *1984*, then research methods. Each time Rigo answered a question, Mr. Tuminaro made a tally mark on a sheet of scrap paper.

Soon, the tally of wrong answers grew past the mathematical point of no return. Rigo had failed.

They sat silently for a moment. Mr. Tuminaro felt sad. He'd reached the same situation with a lot of kids. Sometimes they'd rush out crying or say "I hate you!" But Rigo took it well. They talked about summer school.

The conversation left Mr. Tuminaro feeling better. "As long as he can get to summer school, he's going to be fine. He's very, very talented. Very smart."

· · ·

May 15 arrived, and Isaias waited in his bedroom for Margot and the other visitors who would try to change his path.

Outside, Dennis was using a bright orange cloth to polish his pickup truck when he saw Margot Aleman's old Toyota Corolla turn into the quiet street, and he motioned for her to pull into the driveway. "You can park here!" Margot climbed out, along with Jennifer Alejo, the counselor from Latino Memphis, as well as Jacklyn Martin, the English teacher and Knowledge Bowl coach.

Dennis brought them through the front door and to the living room, where his parents waited. There was a flurry of introductions and greetings.

Isaias emerged from a back room, seemingly in a good mood. "Hi, Margot!" More introductions—though Ms. Alejo had worked in the school for several months, Isaias had never met her.

"You guys want to come into the kitchen?" he asked. He fetched a piano bench from the keyboard in his room. Isaias and his parents and the visitors took spots around the table, under the plaque of Jesus that Cristina had carried across the Arizona desert in her backpack.

Dennis stayed out of the kitchen.

Though the introductions had been friendly, everyone seemed a bit on edge. The visitors would use soft words, but they could not hide the blunt message that they questioned Isaias' decisions, and no one could predict how he would take it.[12] And they might even find themselves in direct conflict with his parents. Because Isaias' parents understood very little English, Margot would have to interpret for the other two women.

"We love this boy a lot," Margot began in Spanish. Mario replied, "We do, too!" Everyone laughed, and Margot realized that what she'd just said might suggest the visitors loved Isaias more than his own parents did. "No one's going to win," she said quickly. "If anyone loves him, it's you." Switching between languages, she continued. "We believe in him. He's a very,

very, very intelligent boy." She pulled out a copy of his transcript. Isaias was surprised she'd brought it. "Really?" he said. She showed his parents his grade point average of 3.6 unweighted, 4.3 when the average was weighted to give extra points for harder classes. And she explained that he'd scored very well on an important exam, the ACT, a 29. *"Eso es ridículamente alto,"* she said—an awkward rendering of an English phrase: That's ridiculously high.

Isaias maintained a serious expression.

Ms. Martin spoke up next, addressing Isaias' parents, whom she'd never met before this night. "First of all, I just want to say that I have complete respect for Isaias and for you as well," she began, and waited for Margot to interpret. "My purpose is not to make anyone decide anything or persuade. It's simply to discuss some options."

She had wanted to meet Isaias' parents for a long time and tell them how special he was, but it had never happened, and she felt intimidated because she didn't speak Spanish. Now the meeting was happening in their home, at a crucial moment in Isaias' life, with all eyes on him.

Ms. Martin told Mario and Cristina that she'd never met another student who wrote as well as Isaias, not even students she taught at the university. She said Isaias once wrote a paper so good that another teacher thought he must have plagiarized it.

She paused again as Margot interpreted. "I also think it's important to say I don't believe that everyone should go to college. My brother, for example, never did well in school and didn't like school, and so I don't think college was for him." Another pause. "However, I think that Isaias has so much potential that I strongly believe he would excel in college.

"And not just for a job or because it's the right thing to do or to get a degree, but because I think that you would be able to expand and learn and meet so many neat people." Isaias nodded.

Cristina sat with eyes down, uncharacteristically quiet, looking serious. Now it was Jennifer Alejo's turn. She mentioned Victory University, the for-profit Christian school not far away. She said Isaias could study at night and work during the day with his family.

They brought out a folder of Victory recruiting materials, and Margot pointed to a photo of a young woman, a current Victory student on a scholarship. "I don't know if you ever met her."

"Oh, Bianca, yeah," Isaias said. "I never met her personally, but I know her." Bianca Tudon had graduated from Kingsbury in 2009, the same year as Dennis. She'd finished second in her class, and the principal still had her vivid painting of blues musician B. B. King hanging in his office. She had also been brought illegally from Mexico as a young child and couldn't get in-state tuition at public universities. After high school, she went to work cleaning houses with her mother, earning about $30 per day, then went to work as a secretary in a law firm. Bianca's father heard a recruiter talk about Victory on Spanish-language radio and encouraged her to apply. She'd enrolled the previous year.

Margot said that even at this late date, Isaias had such strong test scores that he could win scholarship money at Victory.

"All he has to do is apply. And this is thousands and thousands and thousands and thousands of dollars. This university is here, about ten minutes from here," Margot said. She showed them the list of majors the school offered, including business administration.

Cristina spoke softly to Isaias. *Esto está muy bueno.* This is very good.

"Mm-hmm," Isaias murmured.

A few moments later, Mario finally spoke up. "In fact, I've been excited for a long time about having a son in the university," he said in his soft, gentle voice. "We're from a family of *campesinos*, humble, and we didn't have great opportunities. We had to work like donkeys."

Mario said Isaias had told him a few weeks earlier that he'd decided not to attend college: "It hit me like a splash of water." He said they'd come home and talked about it as a family. "I told him that I'd made many mistakes in my life and I'm not going to make a mistake with you. You're going to decide." He would support Isaias either way.

Ms. Martin said she felt exactly the same. "I would be proud of you, Isaias, no matter what you did. Honestly, I'm just proud to know you." Ms.

Alejo said Isaias should act fast, though, since his high school scores would go stale after a few years.

Cristina turned to Isaias. *"¿Tú que piensas?"* What do you think?

"Estoy escuchando." I'm listening.

A clock ticked in the background. They talked some more. Ms. Martin asked Isaias if he felt pressured, and he indicated he didn't.

"Okay, good. I really want you to know this is not about pressuring you. I even joked like this is a college intervention. It's not like that. It's just that we want you to know that you have options, and we want to make sure that you look at your options before you make a decision. That's all."

Margot spoke up again. "I want to ask him a question. *Y la pregunta es, ¿cuál es tu razón por no ir al colegio?"*

Isaias responded, "Okay, well, the question you asked is like 'Why don't I want to go to college.' I've already told this to my parents so I guess I can say it in English."

"Like…the reason—I guess it's a big, complicated reason," he said.

(Photo by Karen Pulfer Focht/The Commercial Appeal)

"But, like, most importantly, I ask myself, 'Why am I going? What am I going to do there? Is it the place for me?'"

He said he had two choices right now. He could work, save money, start buying houses and renting them out. "Invest in the stock market, why not?" Or he could spend years studying and start again at the bottom of a company. And did he truly want to become a conformist wage slave?

"People who say that money is no matter to them, that they don't care about money, but they still get up in the morning to pay their bills, like they look forward to their paycheck so they can buy a Snickers bar or go somewhere, or go downtown . . . Like, do I want to be part of that? I really don't."

One by one, everyone around the table made a case for college. Margot said a business degree could open doors. Ms. Alejo said a degree could lead to personal connections. Ms. Martin offered a different perspective. "I think you raised a lot of valid points, kind of like being a slave to your hourly day. I mean, I get that. But to be fair, if you were renting houses, like a lot of your argument for not going to college was financial. You know. Renting houses, and then I can rent another house to get a paycheck. You know, like, it's similar."

"It's similar," Isaias agreed.

She said he was missing something important. "I told you this before. I didn't go to college to get a job or to get money. I went to college because I liked learning. And I loved it. I loved it so much that I might even go back and get a Ph.D. because I read so much and I was exposed to philosophy and different languages and I got the first person ever who beat me at chess. And those experiences you can't always trade in."

Isaias' father fiddled quietly with a carpenter's pencil, a flat, blue thing. Margot turned to Cristina. *"¿Cómo se siente usted, señora?"* How do you feel, señora?

Cristina responded, "I felt awful when he told me 'I don't want to go to school anymore' after he'd told me so many times that he was going to go."

She breathed out softly, then turned to Isaias again, and said he shouldn't think education would stand in the way of his dreams. "It could help you and make things easier. We ignorant people don't know anything, and you do."

His father weighed in, too. "At first we were afraid we wouldn't be able to cover the costs. How am I going to pay? Even so, I told him that if you decide, we'll have to do it." He said he'd seen Isaias stay up all night doing homework and knew his capacity. "I know he can do it, and everything's in him. Right now, if it were up to me, I would grab him by the ears and throw him in the university."

Margot said she'd spoken with Adriana Garza, the recruiter at Victory. If Isaias wanted to win a scholarship, he would have to apply immediately. Margot told Isaias' parents she'd go with them if they wanted to speak with Ms. Garza the next day.

Mario said, "Right now let us talk with Isaias, see what he thinks and we'll call you immediately." From another room, the low sound of Dennis playing bass drifted into the kitchen. For Isaias' father, the visit from the teachers marked a rare moment in America in which someone had reached out and tried to help them. "Thank you for coming and thank you for worrying about him," Mario said. "I've been worried about him, too."

Then the visitors left.

Afterward, Jacklyn Martin felt worried. She knew that Isaias rejected the concept of God just as he rejected college. How would an atheist fit in at a Christian school like Victory? And how would this sometimes rebellious 18-year-old respond to the pressure of the intervention? Isaias had stayed silent for so much of the visit. She texted me.

He's not going to go, is he?

Chapter Eight

...

BIANCA THE GUIDE

AFTER THE VISITORS LEFT, Isaias retreated to his room.[1] The sky outside was dark as he used his smartphone to send a Facebook message to Bianca Tudon, the student whose picture appeared in the Victory University brochure.

Hello. You really don't know me. My name is Isaias Ramos.

He reminded her he was Dennis' brother, then said he needed advice about Victory. *I'm really trying to weigh all my options, and I can't really afford to waste too much time in my life.*

About half an hour later, his cell phone sounded with a musical *Zing!* A little photo of Bianca popped onto the screen, with a message. *Hey. Yes I remember you. I just saw you at Jerry's Sno Cones lol. Anyway, yes I will tell you all I know.*

She told him he'd have to take a religion class, that the classes were small and challenging, that she recommended honors courses, that teachers were willing to work with students one-on-one, that the food was okay, the student center was tiny, and the library was small, too.

Isaias lay facedown on his bed as they exchanged more messages. He said he hadn't noticed her at the frozen treat stand. He wrote: *I suppose I'm interested in a business degree or something similar. What are you majoring in? Do you know anything about the "business" department of Victory? Do your classes interfere much with work? it would be awesome if you let me see some of your syllabi. Things like campus size and food don't bother me. I would definitely go for honors courses if you think it would help. And I don't get sore about religion, so that class won't be a problem. It's great that you're pointing all of this out to me, I truly appreciate it. I suppose the biggest obstacle then would be money. If the question doesn't bother you, How did you afford it?*

Zing! Bianca replied: *I got a scholarship. Must have a 3.5 GPA on transcript and above a 23 or 25 to qualify for the Trinity Honors Scholarship.*

The numbers referred to ACT scores. She continued:

It will pay for everything except books. That is where Dr. Hostutler comes in. He is a History teacher at Victory but he is also the founder of the Trinity Scholarship.

Isaias wrote: *Wow cool, do you know when he works? Maybe I could go visit him. I really wasn't planning on going to college and so I didn't apply yet or anything, but this looks like a really good option. I'll see if I can apply and do all of that, and if I get the Trinity Scholarship then that will be awesome. I suppose the books are a concern, but a small one. How does the schedule fit you?*

It was already nearly 11:00 p.m., but they kept sending messages. Bianca had said she'd put him in touch with a friend who was studying business. She wrote: *I had never considered Victory University but I am very grateful to be there now. I am getting a decent education for free. And the lady that signed me up told me that I was wasting my life lol. that pretty much pushed me into signing up....*

Isaias tapped out another message: *I think you're absolutely right about getting decent education. That's my biggest concern, right up there with costs. I would not want to waste anyone's time and money if I don't get back what I put [in].*

More messages, then it was past 11:00 p.m. Isaias sent one more, thanking her. *Zing!* She wrote back: *no problem. no worries. I am glad to help*
> *goodnight*

The next day, Margot Aleman sent a text message to everyone who'd been at Isaias' house the night before.

Isaias Ramos is going to college!!! I am taking him to Victory today at 3:30 pm!! Thank you!!!!

Jacklyn Martin texted too. *I'm SO FREAKING happy.* :-)

But the visit to Victory brought no guarantees. Isaias still had to earn the scholarship, and the following day—24 hours before Kingsbury's graduation—he pulled out a composition book and began jotting notes for an application essay. He typed the essay on the family computer. "My parents have always been hard workers, and they never wanted that same fate for my brothers and I," he wrote. "My father always wanted a university education for me. Money has always been tight with us, and it is one of the reasons for my application to Victory. Victory University is one of the few institutions willing to help students like me, us students from a foreign background and a middle-class family. It's difficult to explain how grateful I am for just having a shot at a free education. . . . I never wanted to be a burden on my parents, and I never wanted to lay the responsibility of a college tuition on them, which is why I am striving to receive the Presidential Scholarship. However, this decision to attend Victory University is not my parents'; it is my own.

"Learning has always been a passion of mine. I am absolutely in love with learning and expanding my mind beyond my comfort zone."

Jacklyn Martin would read the essay later and see it as evidence that her hunch about Isaias was true—he did want to attend college but did not want to risk disappointment.

• • •

Around the same time, other Kingsbury seniors were doing makeup work in a last-ditch attempt to graduate. Sometimes the sessions went late into the night.

"Mr. Fuller gonna try real hard *not* to fail you," the principal said, referring to himself in the third person. "But what some of the kids will tell you—if you're graduating on a Saturday, you've probably been with me all night Friday." He said he insisted that in these sessions, the students actually do the work, and do it right.

On the Saturday afternoon of the graduation ceremony, a dark brown horse pulled a carriage down the street past the crowd of Kingsbury students outside the grand old Orpheum Theater in downtown Memphis.[2] The annual Memphis in May barbecue contest was taking place just down the street. Foot traffic was heavy, bottles of water were on sale for $1, and old trolleys rumbled by from time to time, bells clanging.

Isaias joined other students lining up in a room, out of view. The Ramos family members found places in the red velvet seats. I asked Dennis what he thought of the counselors' visit earlier that week. "I wasn't impressed really because I have seen things like that before," he said. "And a lot of people came and talked to me and offered me help but because I didn't have any form of identification, they couldn't help me really. So I wasn't impressed."

Dennis said the family wanted to buy houses, renovate them, rent them out or resell them. He said they'd just put in an application to buy another house in the neighborhood for $11,000. "We want to invest, we want to become strong as a family. And we just don't need a degree for that. We just don't." If he ever went back to school, it would be for fun, for the love of learning. "Not because I need the education. Rather that I want it."

I had heard almost the exact words before—from Isaias. As the big brother, Dennis had played a profound role in shaping Isaias' character, from his atheism to his taste in music. And unlike Isaias' parents, he wasn't showing the same support for his education.

As Dennis spoke, the school orchestra struck up "Pomp and Circumstance." *Dah-dah-da da daaa daaa.* Magaly, dressed in her black orchestra t-shirt, was playing the big double bass. The audience members stood up as the graduates began walking onto the stage, wearing robes and mortarboards in maroon, the Kingsbury color, with white scarf-like stoles. As a top ten student, Isaias took a place in the front row of the brightly lit stage, smiling. Leonard Duarte, the valedictorian, looked straight ahead as the others filed in and took seats behind them.

The student orchestra switched to the national anthem. In the audience, Dennis, Mario and Cristina held their hands over their hearts. Mario told Dustin to do the same.

Then came speeches, and Isaias and the other students walked across

(Photo by Karen Pulfer Focht/The Commercial Appeal)

the stage and shook hands with Mr. Fuller one by one. The families in the audience ignored the warnings to hold their applause and shouted for their kids.

The last student crossed the stage, the graduates began to cheer, and Mr. Fuller began to pump his fists. Some students threw their hats into the air. "Don't lose your hats yet, children," he said, and told them to calm down.

"This has been a challenging yet rewarding group," he said, adding that he'd make them follow policy until the very last second. "For some of my children, we had to work the last second of the last day to get here. But we're here."

The students cheered. Mr. Fuller finished by repeating some of the catchphrases he used on the morning announcements each day.

"Surround yourself with..."

"Positive people!" the students shouted.

"Every decision you make will have a negative or..."

"Positive consequence!"

"Whether it is positive or negative depends on..."

"*You!*"

"So please make good..."

"*Decisions!*"

"I told you these kids were smart, because they come from the school of scholars and .."

"*Champions!*"

"Where every day is 90-60..."

"*Thirty!*" they shouted, recognizing the reference to the test score goals.

"At this time..." Mr. Fuller began, and the cheers drowned out his instructions. Isaias turned the tassel on his cap, threw the hat into the air and whooped, his face joyous.

It was around this time that Estevon Odria began crying with a frightening intensity. Later, he couldn't really explain his overwhelming reaction. "Because I'm sad, but I'm happy. I was emotional...'cause this year's been crazy. Because it's crazy, a lot of stuff going on. Just crazy."

After the ceremony, the Ramos family caught up with Isaias in the crowd outside the Orpheum Theater, and Mario took several pictures. He handed me his cell phone so I could take a picture of all five of them. Their expressions were serious, just as they had been in Walmart roughly a decade earlier.

Margot Aleman found Isaias, too, wrapped him in a hug, and held him for a long time. And then Isaias found Magaly. They embraced on the sidewalk and ran off together through the hazy air, toward the Mississippi River.

• • •

In the days after graduation, Rigo the goalie and the rest of the Kingsbury soccer team traveled to Murfreesboro for the state championship tournament. They'd lost many games in mid-season, but now they were winning, and they fought their way to the title game for schools their size. On a sunny day on a green field, Kingsbury's multicultural squad in maroon jerseys faced Christian Academy of Knoxville, a mostly white team in white jerseys. In the first half, a player from the other team scored against Rigo. Then Kingsbury player Aro Nebk, who came from Sudan, was thrown out of the game. The official reason: foul language directed at a referee. Aro said he'd cursed in frustration when another player stepped on his foot, but he said he hadn't directed the curse at the referee. Aro got a red card, which meant that for the rest of the game, Kingsbury had to play with ten players rather than the normal eleven.

At halftime the Kingsbury players looked badly discouraged, their bodies slumped. Jose Perez, the JROTC leader and soccer player who longed to become a Marine, tried to fire them up. "Come on, guys! It matters so much more to us."

The second half began, and another shot got past Rigo, putting Kingsbury down 2–0. But Rigo kept playing hard. When one opposing player threatened to score, Rigo ran forward and blocked the player's path to the goal. The opponent kicked the ball right into Rigo's body, and it bounced off harmlessly. Kingsbury player Tony Marquez shot a goal late in the second half, bringing the score to 2–1. "This has to be the turning point!" player Franklin Paz Arita yelled. But Kingsbury's follow-up attacks came to nothing.

A siren went off—*woo-woo-woo!* Time was up. The players from the other team exploded in giddy, whooping celebration. The Kingsbury players sank into deeper misery. Jose sobbed and wiped away tears, not bothering to hide them. He would never play a high school soccer game again. Nor would Rigo, who came off the field with a leg injury, limping and grimacing, helped by an assistant coach. Principal Fuller had traveled to the game, and now he quietly consoled the players with handshakes and embraces.

For the third year in a row, Kingsbury's soccer team had to settle for second place. The athletes didn't care that they'd played against some of the strongest teams in the state and had proven themselves among the best. The only thing that mattered was that when they made it to the final game, they lost.

Early in the year, Rigo had faced numerous questions. Would he keep his grades up? Would he go into the military? Would he go to college? Would he win the soccer championship?

Now, in the waning days of May, all those questions had been answered, and the answer to each was the same.

No.

More than two years later, I asked Rigo why he'd failed to graduate with his class. "Mainly my loss of concentration," he said. He was 20 when we spoke again and said he was trying to offer advice to a younger nephew who was skipping school much like he had, a nephew who would say things like, "School is not for me, and I'm not for school."

Rigo wanted something different for his nephew because his own end of high school was a source of embarrassment. "Because whenever people ask me about my school, I usually tell them I graduated with my class. And I feel ashamed of myself because I didn't. I should have, but I didn't. And I don't want him to feel the same thing as I did."

Rigo told me that after failing the exam with Mr. Tuminaro, he'd gone to summer school, taken the two English courses again and passed. But he still needed one more credit for a personal finance course. He said that in 2015, he finally completed his diploma at Gateway, the Christian school that served as a backup option for so many students in the neighborhood. Through it all, Rigo had worked. He was now earning $15 per hour on a carpentry crew led by two of his brothers.

Rigo's father told me that in the months after the end of high school, his son hid the real reasons why he hadn't yet received his diploma. "He told me a lot of things that weren't so," Mr. Navarro said, explaining that it was easy to keep the truth from him because he couldn't speak or read English. Rigo's dad finally went to the school and spoke with someone through an interpreter. "And there, they told me all the problems that Rigo had." For his part, Rigo said he wasn't trying to hide the truth from his father. "I was a bit mad and I didn't want to talk about the problem."

Mr. Navarro had only made it as far as third grade, and he wanted to see Rigo go much further. He told Rigo that if he studied, he could get a really good job, maybe in nursing, or as an accountant or a school-teacher or dentist. Rigo's father described these jobs as *cosas sencillas*— simple things—apparently underestimating how much time they would really take to learn.

Mr. Navarro wondered if he'd made the right choices. He'd taken his sons to work with him in construction, and he'd paid them, and then they'd liked the money and didn't want to go to school anymore. "Maybe I didn't know how to guide my children," he said.

Mr. Navarro said he'd told Rigo that he'd lived in America and worked so hard all these years so that his nine children could go to school, so they could eat, so they could have everything. He recalled telling Rigo, "But if you don't want to go to school anymore, I don't have anything else to do here because you're the youngest. And I'll go to Mexico." As a 62-year-old naturalized citizen, Mr. Navarro was already collecting a small Social Security retirement payment as he continued to work in construction, and the payment would go far in a low-cost country like Mexico. He also imagined working in a business that one of Rigo's brothers was considering launching there: renting small boats to tourists who wanted a fun day on the water. Mr. Navarro and his wife were planning a temporary trip back to their old home in Tequila, Mexico, and he was trying to convince her to move back permanently.

For his part, Rigo was considering three options. First, he could keep working in Memphis and perhaps take a more senior role within the brothers' carpentry business. Second, he could join the U.S. military. Or third, he could go to Mexico and work in his brother's proposed boat business.

His brother would manage the boat company and study at the same time, and maybe Rigo could help with the business and study, too. Plus he could spend a lot of time at the beach! Rigo laughed, and said, "So it would work out as a great job." He seemed intrigued with this last idea, of going to the old country to start something new.

Many possibilities had slipped away from the teenaged Rigo, but now perhaps he would choose an opportunity, grab it and hold it tightly as it pulled him into the years ahead.

• • •

Rigo wasn't the only student who failed to graduate with the Kingsbury class of 2013. In October of that academic year, the school roster had listed

224 seniors. By graduation day, that number had dwindled to 171, representing attrition of nearly a quarter of the senior class. Moreover, the guidance staff had told me that not every student who walked across the stage would really graduate. At least 40 seniors were waiting for the results of state end-of-course exams that could affect their final grades.

The math became complex. Months would pass before the state published the final graduation rate for Isaias' class. It was the worst in four years: 55 percent.

As always, the graduation rate was an educated guess. If the administration could show that an absent Kingsbury student had enrolled elsewhere, the student would be taken off the list of dropouts. Kingsbury administrators tried to locate missing students, but this was especially difficult if the student had moved back to the family's home country. Or an absent student might have enrolled and started paying tuition down the street at Gateway, the Christian school, and not told Kingsbury. Mr. Fuller said that after Isaias' senior year, he started giving students an incentive to inform the school that they'd transferred: "If you can come up and give me some Gateway paperwork, I'll give you $5 for your gas."

Even if you assumed that some missing Kingsbury students had earned a diploma somewhere else, a 55 percent graduation rate was still quite low, and well below that year's goal of 67 percent.

Mr. Fuller had said his own survival in his job depended in part on improving the graduation rate. Despite the bad results for the 2013 class, Mr. Fuller said later that the school system didn't come down hard on him. "Fact of the matter was, they kind of backed off on that a little bit. Now, *we* didn't," he said, meaning the Kingsbury leadership team. "But it was just so difficult to move the graduation rate."

He said Kingsbury was in a tough neighborhood with tough demographics. He recalled the story of a tall white kid from a troubled family who decided in the second semester of his senior year to stop coming to school. "He was adamant. 'I just no longer want to do this.'" White students had the worst graduation rate of all ethnic groups in Isaias' senior class:

45 percent, compared to 55 percent for Hispanics, 58 percent for African-Americans, and 73 percent for Asians.

Mr. Fuller left Kingsbury in 2014 for reasons unrelated to the graduation rate. When I spoke with him the following year, he was working as a principal at Forrest City Junior High in Arkansas. He said that school was struggling, but he embraced the challenge. "And I love Kingsbury," he said. "Still love it. Still bleed maroon. Put a lot of hard work into Kingsbury. Lot of hard work into Kingsbury. And we turned the corner. We made gains."

Though Kingsbury missed its graduation rate goal in 2013, it met its state test score objectives that year on subjects including Algebra 1, Algebra 2, English 2 and English 3. For example, the school's goal for Algebra 1 was that 47 percent would test proficient or advanced. The proportion of students who actually did it was five points higher, 52 percent. In Algebra 2, the goal was that 10 percent would test proficient or advanced, and 16 percent actually did.

Modest progress, yes, but progress all the same.

The new principal at Kingsbury High was Terry Ross, a big, broad-shouldered 43-year-old whom everyone called Dr. Ross. He said he aimed to increase the graduation rate, improve attendance, reduce suspensions and increase community engagement.

Eduardo Saggiante, the interpreter, had moved away after Isaias' senior year. Another Spanish interpreter now worked at the school, and Dr. Ross said he was going to hire a second to go "on offense": monitoring grades, making phone calls, tracking down missing kids and finding ways to intervene. And he planned to hire a third person to help with tutoring. Two new Hispanic teachers had joined the staff. "I'm trying to make an intentional effort to get more personnel in the school who look like the students," said Dr. Ross, who is African-American.

Hispanics made up a greater and greater proportion of the student population at Kingsbury High—48.7 percent on the day we spoke in October 2015. Kingsbury would almost certainly make Memphis history as the first majority Hispanic high school in the area. "It matters here because if we can get it right here, then we can get it right across the country," Dr. Ross said. He paraphrased the quote from Martin Luther King, Jr., who said injustice anywhere is a threat to justice everywhere. If you treated one person wrong, that created a ripple effect. But Dr. Ross said if you tried to do the right thing for a whole group of people—for Hispanic students, for instance—that would cause a ripple effect as well, a positive one.

By the summer of 2013, the bulk of my time within Kingsbury High was over. I was about to follow the Ramos family's story to a new, very different place.

Chapter Nine

...

A FUNERAL IN MEXICO

Late June 2013:
About one month after graduation

THE PLANE'S JET ENGINES droned. My seatmate, an elderly woman with glasses and a cane, asked me to help her fill out the visa entry card she'd give the officials in Mexico. *"No sé escribir,"* she said. I don't know how to write.

More than a month had passed since Isaias graduated, and I was traveling to Santa Maria Asunción, the Ramos family's hometown in Mexico. I wanted to learn about their lives there, and they readily agreed to help.

They showed me recent images of their old house on Google Street View: in their absence, the house had been partially converted into a tire shop. Mario and Cristina prepared gifts for me to deliver to their relatives, mostly t-shirts in plastic wrap with names written on scraps of paper pinned to them: a tan shirt for Blankita Chica, a pink one for Emma Celeste, and so on. They wrote out a list of names and addresses of their friends and family members and used Facebook and phone calls to let them know I was coming.

Isaias' future remained uncertain. He had completed his application to

Victory University but hadn't heard back about the scholarship. One June night, Isaias said he'd thought about calling the staffers at Victory but didn't look forward to it. If the university accepted him, great. If not, well, at least he had tried. He didn't mention the idea of asking for help from Margot Aleman or his other supporters at school.

On the plane, the passenger who didn't know how to write handed her passport to me, a stranger. I wrote her name, Ofelia Yanes, and her date of birth in 1946 on the immigration form. I gave the form back to her and she signed it, copying the signature from her passport.

She lived in Lubbock, Texas, cooked in a restaurant, and was visiting family members back home in Mexico. Her green card allowed her to travel, and she was about to meet a daughter she hadn't seen in four years. She hadn't made it beyond second grade in Mexico, but she told me some of her grandchildren were now enrolled in college.

Her story echoed the ones I had heard at Kingsbury and reminded me that what was happening there was happening across the country as the children of immigrants made their way in the world.

Mexico was still seeing horrific drug-related violence. Fortunately, I wouldn't be traveling alone: I would work with Dominic Bracco II, a young American photographer now living in Mexico City who had already spent years working in some of the country's roughest areas.

Cristina had far more serious worries than I did. Her sister Gregoria, who lived in Santa Maria Asunción, had terminal cancer. She hadn't eaten solid food for days.

Gregoria was 51, a married mother of five whom Cristina would remember later as the older sister who moved away when Cristina was still young. When Gregoria had her babies, Cristina would go to her house and help with chores like washing dishes. At Christmas, Gregoria would come to the family's old house on the hill with gifts of bread and fruit so her brothers and sisters would have something to enjoy for the holiday.

They'd talked on the phone recently, Gregoria wishing Cristina luck, then mentioning a child who wanted to come to the United States. Cristina didn't want to get involved. And that was the last time they would ever speak.

Gregoria would die soon, and it would mark the second time that Cristina had lost a sister. A little over six years earlier, another one of Cristina's sisters, Antonia, was walking or standing near the main road through town. A microbus had just dropped off passengers, and the bus driver pulled out in front of a large white truck cab that was traveling without a trailer. The truck driver swerved off the road to avoid hitting the microbus, but instead hit Antonia, killing her instantly.[1]

Antonia was in her early thirties and left three small children.

Cristina and Antonia had been so close as girls that they not only slept together, but shared all their clothes, even underwear. Antonia suffered from rashes and would tell Cristina "Scratch me!" and Cristina would, every night. They would shut themselves in a room and share all their secrets. They dreamed of growing up and becoming grandmothers together. Antonia cried when Cristina got married because she feared she would leave her.

And the last time Antonia talked with Cristina on the phone, she scolded her, saying she shouldn't have gone to America. Then Antonia was dead, remembered by a white wooden cross at the side of the road.

Cristina hadn't gone back for Antonia's funeral. She hadn't gone back when her father died in 2010. And now with Gregoria dying, she still made no plans to return. The brothers and sisters in Mexico couldn't understand Cristina. "We're dying," they would say to her on the phone. "And you won't come."

"They think I'm made of stone," Cristina said. Not so—she felt the same pain as the others did, but she didn't let it show. That wouldn't achieve anything.

If Cristina visited Mexico, she could find herself locked out of the United States forever and separated from her family in Memphis. Neither she nor Mario had a legal right to return to the United States; Dennis and Isaias with their Deferred Action paperwork could only get permission to leave and return under special circumstances.[2] In addition, illegal border crossings had become even more risky. When the Ramos family crossed in 2003, about 9,800 Border Patrol agents were assigned to cover the southern border. A decade later, the number had nearly doubled, to 18,600. In the same time period, the Border Patrol's budget rose to $3.5 billion, an increase of more than 80 percent, adjusted for inflation. The increase was even more dramatic if you compared 2013's Border Patrol budget to that from 1990—adjusted for inflation, the United States was now spending more than seven times as much.[3]

For most of American history, border security had been weak. The Border Patrol wasn't even created until 1924, and for decades afterward, Mexican migrants could easily cross back and forth over the lightly protected 2,000-mile-long border for seasonal jobs in agriculture.

But over the decades, the politics of immigration had prompted the federal government to pour more money into border security. When the public demanded that the government *do something* about illegal immigration, spending money on border security was what politicians did. Researchers concluded that between 2009 and 2014, more Mexicans left the United States than came in.[4] But calls for greater border security continued. And of course, strengthening border security did nothing to address the fact that millions of unauthorized immigrants still lived and worked in America.

The country's immigration enforcement was like a coconut: solid on the outside, milky and soft on the inside. Anyone who got through the tightening gauntlet of security at the border faced little chance of getting caught later.

This led to bizarre contrasts. Even as Congress threw hundreds of millions of dollars at border security, the Internal Revenue Service urged immigrants to file income tax returns even if they lived in the United States illegally—and many unauthorized immigrants filed the documents. Real estate professionals in Memphis happily made home loans to unauthorized immigrants. I spoke in 2006 with one of the people involved, Bob Byrd, chairman and CEO of a Memphis-area financial institution called the Bank of Bartlett.[5]

"We're doing this because we think it's right," he said. "We're doing this because it's legal. And we're doing this because it's profitable."

He said the Memphis-area bank had arranged between $12 million and $14 million in home loans for immigrants who lacked a Social Security number. Many immigrants in this category had come illegally or over-stayed visas. None of the loan recipients had defaulted or been deported, and Mr. Byrd considered it unlikely that it would happen. "For the life of me, I can't remember the report of a deportation in recent times."

Years later, advocates for immigrants demanded that President Obama do more to help them and mocked him as the "deporter in chief," pointing to statistics that showed rising numbers of expulsions. Yet when the *Los Angeles Times* looked closely at the deportation numbers in 2014, they found that most of the expulsions were for people arrested within 100 miles of the border—in general, people who had just recently crossed. Deporta-tions of people in non-border areas, like the Ramos family in Memphis, had actually dropped from 237,941 in Obama's first year to 133,551 in 2013, and most of those deported from the interior in 2013 came to the attention of immigration authorities after criminal convictions.[6]

"If you are a run-of-the-mill immigrant here illegally, your odds of getting deported are close to zero—it's just highly unlikely to happen," said John Sandweg, who had served as acting director of Immigration and Customs Enforcement. He told the *Los Angeles Times* that even when im-migration officials wanted to deport someone who had already settled in the country, doing so was "virtually impossible" because of a lengthy back-log in the immigration courts.

Unauthorized immigrants like Cristina were relatively secure if they stayed where they were—but if they tried to leave the United States, visit Mexico, and come back, they not only would have to contend with the Border Patrol and the sometimes deadly desert heat, they also would risk run-ins with the border zone's many criminals. Some criminals simply preyed on migrants, robbing or raping them at gunpoint. Other criminals ran organized smuggling rings and worked for the migrants—supposedly.

Consider the story of Elizabeth Bonilla, the mother of Dante Bonilla, a classmate of Isaias'. In 2002, she'd come to America to work and to flee a violent relationship, leaving her three boys behind with her mother in

Mexico. She met a better man in Memphis, had a baby girl with him, and when her mother was dying in 2007, she went back to Mexico to fetch the boys.

That left the problem of getting back across the border. She hired a smuggler named Victor, whom she remembered as a big man with light skin and an evil face. Elizabeth agreed to pay Victor a transport price of $1,700 per person, or $6,800 for all four of them.

Their first attempt to cross failed, and Victor helped them try again. They succeeded, but when they arrived in Houston, Victor demanded more money for his extra trouble: $1,000 apiece, or $4,000 total. Elizabeth didn't have the money but said she could send it later. Then Victor brought her alone to an upper room in a house and put a pistol to her head.

She remembered him telling her that he wasn't playing. That he would kill her, kill the children, put their bodies in bags, and no one would know what happened to her. That until she paid, he would keep the children.

Elizabeth cried, begged and tried to reason with him. If she couldn't pay the debt for the crossing, how could she pay him to feed three boys?

She remembered him telling her that she was right. He would keep just one boy.

So she called her husband in Memphis, who drove to Houston to pick up Elizabeth and her two youngest sons. The oldest, 12-year-old Dante, stayed behind with Victor.

In Memphis, Elizabeth and her husband sold almost everything they owned, even their beds. They worked long hours, stopped paying rent and were evicted from an apartment. Elizabeth told her story to a Spanish-language radio host, who shared it on the air. Some listeners called her a bad mother. Others donated cash. All the while, Victor called her cell phone to spit curses and threats. She said he demanded the money and threatened to kill Dante, cut him into pieces and throw them away. He said if he saw any police around the house, he'd kill Dante immediately.

Elizabeth and her husband sent money for three months until, finally, Victor told Elizabeth to come alone to an Arkansas gas station. He was transporting a vanload of migrants and would deliver Dante.

He kept his word. The boy was alive and mostly well. Victor had kept him locked in his house for a while before giving him to a female associate, who in turn gave him to a family that treated him decently and let him play outside with their children. Dante said he was never abused, and he didn't know about the death threats until he heard his mother tell the story years later.

Regret still ate at Elizabeth Bonilla. She said ignorance and fear stopped her from going to the authorities—in hindsight, a huge mistake. She carried a photo in her purse of what Dante looked like the day she got him back: haggard and in need of a haircut. It served as her personal reminder that she must never allow anything or anyone to hurt her children. She told them to seize all the opportunities they had in this country. Look at what it took to get them here.

Samuel P. Huntington wrote in 2009 that Mexican immigrants would not assimilate into America because Mexico was right next door. Mexican immigrants could remain in intimate contact with their families, friends and hometowns, unlike other immigrants whose home countries lay across wide oceans. They would retain their Mexican identity for a long time—perhaps for generations.[7]

But for people like Cristina, Mexico might as well have been as far away as Australia. And though Cristina still didn't quite fit into American society—she didn't speak English, for instance—each death in her family snipped a strand from the cord of connections that bound her to her home.

Cristina wanted papers: not full-blown citizenship, but something like a travel pass, a document that would let her cross the border and return. But the politics of the day made that impossible, so Cristina clung more tightly to her husband and sons in Memphis. They were all she had.

Millions of people lived in a similar predicament. As illegal immigration slowed down, unauthorized immigrants were more and more likely to have lived in the United States for many years. Demographers estimated that as of 2013, there were 11.3 million unauthorized immigrants living in the United States, and that they had been there for a median of 13 years—meaning half had lived there longer. Many had U.S.-born children.[8]

. . .

Below us, the suburbs of Mexico City crawled into view, a vast expanse of buildings sprawling into the distance in the sun and smog. The plane descended. When the wheels finally touched the runway, Ofelia Yanes, my seatmate, said, *"Dios mío. Gracias."* My God. Thank you.

At Mexican immigration, the official at the desk asked me one question. *"¿De dónde llegas?"* Where are you coming from? *"De los Estados Unidos."* From the United States.

He stamped my passport and I was in. When I came back to America a few days later, the process proved nearly as easy. My U.S. passport served as a magic ticket.

I met Dominic, the photographer, for the first time at the Thrifty car rental spot by the massive international airport. Over the next few days, he showed an ability to quickly understand other people's feelings, and I trusted him. He knew when to take a picture and when to put the camera away.

Dominic drove the rented vehicle through Mexico City traffic, a mess of fast-merging cars and trucks that went on for many frightening miles. In time, the city gave way to the countryside. We arrived at Tulancingo, a big town, and checked into our comfortable high-end hotel. Then we took the road out of town, past green hills, prickly pear cacti, agaves that looked like giant versions of an aloe vera plant you'd see on a windowsill, and a street vendor holding up a newspaper with the headline "Young Professional Woman Disappeared." Shops had been constructed haphazardly along the main road, with unpaved gravel areas for parking.

Within minutes we arrived in Santa Maria Asunción, and along the main road we found the house that Mario and Cristina had left behind. Black tires were arranged in decorative patterns in the bare dirt of the front yard. A handwritten sign on a wall advertised oil changes, and dogs wandered about.

Various relatives had used the house since the Ramos family left. For the past five years it had been occupied by one of Cristina's nieces, 36-year-old Maria Ines Castro Vargas, along with her husband and their two sons. Cristina had told them we were coming, but Maria Ines seemed nervous. Still, she let us in and showed us the house.

It was arranged around a central courtyard with trees and a big, rusty satellite dish that Maria Ines was using that day to dry her family's jeans and socks. She said she'd been doing laundry when we arrived since the water ran only on Thursday and she had to use it when it became available. The roof was made of corrugated metal and held down with the weight of bricks and tires.

After we'd talked for a while, Maria Ines began to relax around us, the strangers. She pointed out a closed door that led to other rooms, explaining that the Ramos family had locked up their belongings inside. She didn't have a key. But she mentioned that one of the walls to the closed area had begun to fall down, and her family had put up some blocks to replace it. Those blocks were loose. She said if we wanted, we could take some blocks out and look inside.

So, standing in the courtyard, we removed blocks in the storeroom wall until we created a hole big enough to peer through. I put my face close to the opening and felt cool air flow out, like from a cave. In the dim light I saw shapes: a toy truck, a top, a child's dinosaur lying on its side, and two dusty bicycles. Isaias and Dennis had locked these toys away so they could play with them when they came back. Now it was far too late for that.

We put the blocks back in the wall, entombing the toys again.

• • •

Throughout our time in Santa Maria Asunción, I traded text messages with Isaias. He asked us to take a lot of photos of his old house, and we did. Because the Ramos family had paved the way for us and continued to make phone calls on our behalf from the United States, we found open doors everywhere. People served us delicious home-cooked meals of blue corn tacos, pozole with big pieces of hominy, and sweet flan.

I shared much of this with Isaias. *That sounds great*, he wrote in one text message. *I am kind of envious haha*. He asked when we would visit his uncle Alberto in Tepaltzingo, the village where his mother had grown up.

On the third day of our visit to Hidalgo state, we drove up a steep hill from Santa Maria Asunción to Cristina's village.

We found Uncle Alberto's house, and he greeted us in crisply pleated slacks and a white dress shirt. He was 50 and worked as a driver for a businessman in Mexico City, where he sometimes shared a tiny apartment with another man, but this house on the hill was his home. He introduced us to one of his sisters, Maria Candelaria, age 52, who had come to meet us.

We had already spent hours talking with friends and relatives of the Ramos family, but no one could remember anything like a going-away party before they emigrated to America. When I spoke with Uncle Alberto and Maria Candelaria, it became clear why: Mario and Cristina had vanished without saying goodbye.

Family members heard from Cristina a few days after she disappeared, when she called a *caseta*, a sort of public telephone that everyone in the village used. An employee from the *caseta* business found Cristina's family in the village. Cristina arranged to call the *caseta* back at a specific time, and someone from her family came and took the call. And that was how her brothers and sisters learned she had left for America.

Cristina's mother had died years earlier, but her father, Pedro Vargas, remained in Santa Maria Asunción. Until his last days, he had hoped his daughter and her family would come back, said Emma Celeste Castro Vargas, a 23-year-old cousin of Dennis and Isaias who'd often played with them when she was a girl.

She recalled that as her grandfather Pedro lay dying, his mind drifted back to his grandchildren Isaias and Dennis. She remembered him saying, "Did you talk to Chay and Denny? They're running around outside and their mom's going to scold them. Tell them to come in."

She told him, "Isaias isn't here anymore, Grandpa." Pedro Vargas died in November 2010, having never seen his daughter and her children again.

All these years later, the sudden disappearance of Cristina and her husband and children still bothered Uncle Alberto. Perhaps Cristina didn't owe it to her brothers and sisters to tell them she was leaving, but as he saw it, parents were a different story.

"Look, we've always acted independently," Mario explained to me later. "We've almost always preferred not to share our plans with other people. I speak with her," he said, indicating Cristina, "and we decide with the boys, with Dennis and Isaias and now Dustin. But we don't tell other people."

Cristina offered another reason for not saying goodbye. "Sometimes we're afraid that when you talk, people won't let you do things."

"They won't let you grow," Mario added.

That day in Cristina's village, Uncle Alberto and Maria Candelaria seemed torn between the impulse to criticize Cristina and the desire to forgive her and wish her well.

Maria Candelaria said, "Thinking it over, it was the best decision she could have made. At first I thought she'd acted very, very ungratefully or definitely didn't feel anything for us, her family. But I reached the conclusion that she had left here at a young age," she said, referring to Cristina's time working in the big town during middle school. "And she didn't feel the same way as the rest of us who were always together." Maria Candelaria went on to talk about Antonia's death when she was hit by the truck. "[Cristina] called and said, 'I'm sorry. I'm with you.' It's not the same as living it, seeing it, to be so far away and say 'I'm sorry.'"

Alberto spoke up. "My papa died and it was the same thing. She gives us a call, and that's it." Then Maria Candelaria swung back to the compassionate side. "She did it to seek other goals for her children, and what a good thing." Uncle Alberto agreed. "Hopefully everything will go well for her, and on that side they'll reach all the goals that they want. Because separating from a family, from your customs, from your roots—for nothing—I think it's pretty difficult. But if they reach the objective for which they went, go ahead."

They said Cristina still called and talked about coming back. Maria Candelaria said, "We're losing hope of seeing her again…And my other sister's going through agony right now. She won't see her again. It could be any one of us tomorrow."

Later we took a walk with Uncle Alberto, and he pointed to a house. He said the parents were simple workers, but they'd managed to send their children to college. One son had become an architect, a daughter had become a lawyer, and another son was studying civil engineering. His argument: you could improve your children's lives without leaving home.

Uncle Alberto had a point. It seemed that everywhere we went in Santa Maria Asunción, we met young people who had gone to college. One of them was 22-year-old Blanca Vargas Martinez, nicknamed "Blankita Chica," or "Blankita Hija," who had recently graduated from a university with a degree in political science and public administration. She'd given up the low-paid job that Mario had mentioned at the Top 10 dinner in May and was now looking for another one.

Another married couple was sending their son named Ever to the university in Puebla with the funds from the cake business they'd built. It was a typical immigrant success story. Well, minus the part about immigrating.

In fact, the mother and cake entrepreneur Maria Isabel Vargas Tellez said the business was what had *stopped* her husband, Alejandro, from leaving the country to go earn money in America, unlike all three of her brothers, who had emigrated to the United States. So far, only one brother had come back.

And Ponchito, the childhood friend of Isaias, was now studying business administration at a university in Tulancingo, the big town. He'd grown up tall. His full name was Oscar Alfonso Barrios Silva, and many people had stopped using the diminutive "-ito" at the end of his nickname. With his glasses, Ponchito—or Poncho—looked as if he could be Isaias' brother.

His family ran a large-scale fruit-selling business. He drove us around town in his parents' van and showed us the places that had figured in the story of Isaias: the creek where they'd caught frogs, an old well, the elementary school playground where Isaias had told Ponchito he'd soon walk across the desert to America. We were talking in the center of town, and I showed Ponchito a cell phone video of Isaias practicing with Los Psychosis and chattering with his bandmates in English. "He's almost unrecognizable," Ponchito said. "He's changed a lot."

Opportunities for young people in Mexico had changed a lot, too. In 1970, when Mario was nine, nearly a third of all Mexicans over the age of 15 had only gone to preschool or kindergarten, or had never gone to school at all. More than a quarter of the population was illiterate. Underlying every story of young Mexican children dropping out of school was poverty: public schools charged various fees, and some parents didn't pay or couldn't pay.

By 2010, the situation had changed dramatically. Only 7 percent of the Mexican population had never gone to school. Fifty-eight percent of the population had completed at least ninth grade, and 17 percent had completed a university degree.[9]

Even the children of the lower middle class started going to universities, something that people like them had never done before, Jaime Ros, a leading Mexican economist, told me later.

He explained that Mexico's economy had expanded rapidly until the early 1980s, when it entered long decades of slow growth. Even so, many Mexicans moved out of poverty and became educated. Why? Ros pointed to the "demographic bonus"—in other words, smaller families.

In the late 1960s, the average Mexican woman gave birth to seven children. But in the 1970s, the government began promoting contraception and smaller families, and birth rates fell dramatically. By 2013, Mexico's birth rate had dropped to 2.2.[10] "That's allowed families also to spend more on their fewer children, allowing them to go through school and college more easily than in the past," Mr. Ros said.

And more Mexicans began living in cities, a trend that went hand in hand with cosmopolitan thinking and smaller families. Concentrated populations also made it easier for the government to provide schooling.

Despite the growing middle class and success stories like those of the cake entrepreneurs, the research organization Coneval estimated that in 2012, nearly half of all Mexicans were still poor.[11]

We met 53-year-old Herlinda Sanchez Licona, who earned a living working at home, using her three sewing machines to stitch together the little pieces of fabric that made up a shirt. "It's laborious. And it's tiring," she said. At busy times she'd stay up all night, which sometimes bothered her children, since three of them slept in the same room where she worked. She said the kids would sometimes complain: "Mama, turn out your light!" If she worked all day, she could finish ten shirts and earn the equivalent of roughly nine dollars.

Perhaps the biggest threat to Mexican society was what Rigo Navarro had described so graphically in his senior class presentation back in Memphis: drug corruption and crime, fueled by American users.

But as we walked with Uncle Alberto in the green hills around his town on the third day of our visit, we saw nothing but tranquil countryside. We spotted a horned toad lizard moving along the dusty soil, which was peppered with sharp black chunks of obsidian. I picked up several of the glassy stones as souvenirs. At a village church that evening, a priest said Mass and called for a special prayer for the health of Gregoria Vargas, the sister of Cristina.

The next morning, Gregoria died.

. . .

I had been planning for months to go to Mexico, and I hadn't expected Gregoria to die while we were in town. Now Dominic and I found ourselves in a strange position: the friends and family members in Mexico naturally saw us almost as emissaries sent by the absent Cristina, who had helped arrange our visit.

We went with the family of Blankita Chica to buy flowers, which we brought to the wake. Uncle Alberto and the others received us graciously.

They held the wake in Gregoria's own home, in a room whose walls were painted pink, and burning candles illuminated the mourners, the white flowers, and the casket with a panel of glass that offered a view of Gregoria's face. A woman sang a slow hymn, and the mourners responded again and again with the chorus.

Rows of chairs had been set up before the casket, and people offered the visitors sweet bread, tamales wrapped in green leaves and hot sugared

Mourners, including Uncle Alberto (second from left), Gregoria's daughter Claudia (at casket) and her other daughter, Paz (right), remember Gregoria at her wake. *(Photo by Dominic Bracco II/Prime)*

lemonade, the drink servers often going two by two, one with a pitcher, one with Styrofoam cups. Some mourners would stay all night. We paid our respects and left, the stars glowing bright above us.

The next day, Gregoria's friends and relatives crowded into the white adobe church at Santa Maria Asunción for her funeral. Many people had to wait outside, some holding umbrellas against the summer sun, and a teenaged boy fainted. A woman called "Alcohol!" and someone rubbed it onto his face to revive him. Dominic helped bring the teenager into the shade, where he recovered. The teenager had green sprigs of herbs tucked behind his ears, as did Blankita and many other mourners. Blankita said the herbs were *ruda*, or rue, as well as *romero*, or rosemary. She had a sprig tucked under her blouse, too. She said people believe that the dead person emits an energy of sadness or pain that other people don't want to absorb, and that the herbs help block it. "It's a protection we have."

Later, the church bells rang, and a group of men carried out Gregoria's maroon casket on their shoulders. Fireworks went off with loud bangs.

(Photo by Dominic Bracco II/Prime)

A group of musicians dressed in black played and walked before the casket, *huapangero*-style with a sawing fiddle and a guitar, and the procession with its umbrellas turned right, toward the main highway, not far from where the truck had killed Antonia years earlier.

People had stopped their vehicles to block traffic, and we walked across the highway and past cornfields to the cemetery, a place with high weeds and tombs that rose into the air like small castles.

Hundreds of people crowded among the graves, some in jeans, some women in old-fashioned clothes that looked like aprons. A breeze blew the umbrellas. Again, people offered refreshments: cookies, chocolate, bottles of water and juice. Swallows flew overhead.

Workers in baseball caps shoveled dirt into the grave as the mourners watched. The musicians sang songs, including a popular tune from years earlier.

Como quisiera que tu vivieras ... the chorus began.

How I wish you were alive.

Later, in a corner of the graveyard, Uncle Alberto asked me to tell

Cristina to call him, and that afternoon I made a phone call to Memphis and relayed the message. I told her I was sorry for her loss, and I stated the obvious: that it was unfair that I could go to her sister's burial and she couldn't. She said *"gracias"* several times. Her voice sounded sad and strained.

Cristina went to work in Memphis that day, as she almost always did. "This country doesn't forgive," she said later, and laughed. Work itself could serve as a sort of therapy. So could talking with her husband. And life had made her strong, determined to move forward. She said if something was in her hands, if she could help, she would. If it was outside her control, she would let it go.

That night I thought about everything that had happened.

Was coming to America worth never seeing your sister again, even when she was dying of cancer? If Ponchito went to college in Mexico and Isaias didn't do the same in America, what did that say about the choice to emigrate?

And what about the millions of people just like Mario and Cristina, people who had ignored the expiration date on their visas or crossed the border illegally? Was it wise for America to create a system that allowed these people to live in the United States for years, but with only limited rights? And was it wise for society to pay little attention to the particular needs of the immigrants' children?

Was *any* of this a good idea?

It was too late for these questions. Mexican immigration had permanently changed both sides of the border. Once an elderly newspaper reader in the Kingsbury neighborhood called me to complain about the Hispanics who had so thoroughly changed the area. She wanted everything to go back to the way it was before. But that was a fantasy.

What was done was done. Business interests, their political allies, and human rights groups would not tolerate a forced mass migration out of the United States.

Isaias and Dennis would never brush the dust off their childhood bicycles and ride them again. The birth of Dustin could not be reversed, nor could the births in America of millions of other children of immigrants—all U.S. citizens.

For Isaias, his family, and the rest of America, the only way out was forward. That meant mining the untapped talent among children of immigrants at places like Kingsbury High and making sure that these children truly became part of America.

Cristina wanted to move forward too. She later told me she'd thought about returning to Santa Maria Asunción and living in the house where Maria Ines lived now. "But that's like wanting to roll back your life ten years," she said. "You can't hide everything that you lived through. That's why it's better that we move forward and seek other places. Get to know people. Now it's too late to go backwards."

Nor did Isaias want to go back to Mexico. In his mind, it was a sort of dreamlike land where everything was perfect. He didn't want to see the real country and spoil the illusion.

On the last day in Santa Maria Asunción, Dominic and I drove through the village and said goodbye to everyone who had helped us. Soon I flew back to the green city where Isaias still awaited his fate.

Chapter Ten

...

VICTORY

Early July 2013:
A month and a half after graduation

Two days after Gregoria's funeral, the members of the Ramos family took a day off and prepared to repaint the outside of their home in Memphis. Then a minivan pulled up.

Out stepped Adriana Garza, the recruiter from Victory University. *¡Felicidades!* she said—Isaias had won the scholarship!

Mario and Cristina were elated. But Isaias showed much less enthusiasm. Ms. Garza had already called Isaias on his cell phone when he was eating breakfast and told him the news. The scholarship covered tuition, and he'd only have to pay for his books. But Isaias hadn't passed the news along to his parents. The only reason Ms. Garza had come to the house was that she'd passed by with her husband, who specialized in selling insurance to the Hispanic market, and when he saw the Hispanic family, he wanted to stop and give them his business card. Then Ms. Garza recognized Isaias.

The muted reaction from Isaias didn't shock the recruiter. Students usually wanted to go to other, more established schools, and Victory meant disappointment. Sometimes she'd beg them to come.

In Isaias, though, Ms. Garza was meeting someone who felt ambivalent not just about this particular university, but about the idea of college itself. Isaias said he didn't know if he'd accept.[1]

. . .

Victory was a for-profit institution, and it was losing money. So why did it let students like Isaias attend for free?

University president Shirley Robinson Pippins said that by giving scholarships to athletes and to high-performing students, Victory boosted its image and made itself a more diverse and attractive environment. That, in turn, would draw students who might otherwise not have applied.

Moreover, Dr. Pippins said she believed in opening opportunities to students who might not get them elsewhere. "That's just something near and dear to my heart and then I think also within the Christian mission of a school like Victory."

Mariana Hernandez had planned to go to Victory University, too. But she said Ms. Garza had told her the school was having financial problems, especially with scholarship money, and that the staffer's own job was in jeopardy because of the issues. So shortly before the first semester started, Mariana enrolled at Mid-South Community College, just across the river in Arkansas. She paid out-of-state tuition, but it was cheaper than the out-of-state rate she'd have to pay at public schools in Tennessee, where she lived.

Mariana's case illustrated that even though students with immigration problems were priced out of some universities, they sometimes found ways to keep studying. But Jose Perez, the student leader in JROTC, wanted to join the military. That was a different story.

Late in his senior year, he'd shaken off his apathy and started coming to school and doing work again. He achieved something no one on his father's side of the family had ever done: he graduated from high school. Over and over, he visited the Marine Corps recruitment office. He said that each time, the recruiter told him he needed documents. Finally, Jose got Deferred Action status, went to the Social Security office and applied for a number. They gave him a paper saying he'd soon get a Social Security card, and he immediately went back to the recruiter and showed him the paper. Jose recalled that the recruiter looked at it and said he still couldn't accept it. This latest rejection shifted something within Jose's mind—he thought he would never get a chance to join. And he was correct. Under a policy still in effect at the time of this writing in 2015, people with Deferred Action status could not join the Marines. Similar restrictions were in effect for other branches of the military.

Jose said that after that last meeting with the recruiter, he went home and cried for nearly the whole day, then the day after. For days after that, he hid in his room.

Everything he'd done in JROTC in high school seemed like a joke, like playing dress-up or playing with Barbie dolls. He remembered putting the old JROTC uniform on the doorknob of his closet and staring at it for a long time. He felt afraid to put it on or touch it because it represented the only connection he still had to the military. He said it took him a month or two to recover from the depression. At the time we spoke in April 2014, he was working in his uncle's remodeling company and sometimes in a Mexican restaurant. He said he kept the room he shared with his girlfriend stuffed with Marine Corps gear, even Marine Corps sheets. He was wearing a Marine Corps t-shirt when we spoke, and he said he still went home every day and looked at the JROTC uniform. "And I'm like, man, it would have been so different if I had been born here."

In November 2015, Jose's Facebook page still prominently displayed a 2012 photo of himself in fatigues, standing next to the Marine recruiter.

• • •

While Jose struggled, Estevon Odria seemed to find a sort of peace in the months before he headed to Carnegie Mellon. In July, he sent a Facebook message to his mother, Nadine. Estevon and Nadine had clashed often. Now he sought to make amends.

"Dear my beloved mother: I am truly sorry and apologize for my disrespectful and spiteful attitude toward you at times," he wrote. "I have realized how much it has hurt you. I want you to know that I forgive and love you with all my heart even if I refuse to communicate with you at times."

Nadine took Estevon out to eat before he went to college, and then they went out to eat again with his grandparents. "The night before he left, we sat there and took pictures and stuff and I told him to answer my phone calls and he hasn't," Nadine said. "He told me I had to e-mail him." She gave a small laugh.

Still, Nadine felt that her decision not to raise him herself had been for the best. He had turned out well. "So I did something right," she said.

I spoke with Estevon by phone in September 2015, just days after he'd begun his third year of college. He said he felt different from most of the people there—but that was okay.

Different how? "I don't know. They just seem very like middle-, upper-class people. Or like, they really haven't gotten much experience of life or something like that." At Carnegie Mellon, he had chosen a hard subject, electrical and computer engineering. He wasn't prepared at first. "What happened was, the first year was horrible," Estevon said.

Estevon took several difficult courses in his first semester, including Fundamentals of Programming and Computer Science, also known as 15-112. Bloomberg news service featured this course in an article headlined "Five of the Best Computer Science Classes in the U.S.—This Is Where the Smartest Coders Cut Their Teeth."[2]

Estevon said homework assignments could take ten hours, and the course also required a major project, such as making a game from scratch. That first semester, Estevon dropped 15-112 without completing it. The first year was so tough that Estevon's grandfather feared he might drop out entirely. Estevon somehow got through the year.

"And then, like, the first semester of my sophomore year was really bad also," Estevon said. He retook 15-112 that fall and passed it. Finally, in the second semester of his sophomore year, Estevon began to get the hang of Carnegie Mellon work. It was his best semester so far.

I asked about his grades. "They're all right," he said. "I mean, it's a pretty tough major and the average GPA is like a 2.8 for my major. So I'll just leave it at that."

Estevon appeared likely to graduate from Carnegie Mellon and to reap financial rewards. Companies fought to recruit the university's students, and recent graduates in his major earned a median starting salary of $86,000. They had gone to work for corporations including Amazon, Facebook, General Motors, Goldman Sachs, Google, Microsoft, Samsung and SpaceX.[3]

Estevon said he was focused on right now and was not thinking much about life after graduation. "I'll just take it as it comes."

. . .

Isaias finally made a decision about college.

On the Fourth of July, the Ramos family finished work early. Cristina made hamburgers with thick chunks of cheddar cheese. The boys ate them fast and retreated to Dennis' room to play video games. Outside, small American flags fluttered in the decorative metal grating of the porch pillars, where Dustin had put them some days earlier.

I had just come back from Mexico, and when I visited that day I gave Mario and Cristina some presents in the kitchen—a plastic container of *mole* cooking spice that their friend Maria the cake entrepreneur had sent them, a decorated roof tile that I had bought from a member of Blankita Chica's family, a plastic-wrapped container of chocolate chunks for drinks, and a little tin of sweets that I had bought in the Mexico City airport. I also showed them some of the pictures I had taken with my cell phone, and I gave them some of the obsidian rocks that I had picked up in Cristina's village on the hill. Cristina recalled how as children, she and other kids had played with these rocks. Dustin, the little brother they called Pato, or Duck, came into the kitchen and saw the rocks. "What is that?" he said in English.

"Se llaman obsidianas," Mario said in Spanish.

"Obsidian?" Dustin answered, in English again.

I went to Dennis' room, where he and Isaias were playing the video game *Battlefield 4.* They paused the game, and Isaias gave his verdict on the Victory University scholarship. "Not bad. I think I'll end up going. It can't hurt, right?" Dennis said he'd like to see Isaias go to school full-time. "And get it over with as soon as possible."

And the day came that fall when Isaias took his backpack and drove off to start classes at Victory. His father watched Isaias with what he called *hormigueo*, a tingling, happy sense of excitement.

Isaias thrived in college. One Sunday in October 2013, five months after graduation, I went to the family's house. Isaias had just come back from work and still wore his white paint-specked pants and white t-shirt with the Porter Paints logo.

Never had he done so much reading, but he liked it, and he was having lots of fun learning. "Especially the religious classes. The religious classes are great sometimes." He showed me the books he was reading, laying them out on the hardwood floor of his bedroom.

They numbered 15 in all, including the classic writing guide *The Elements of Style* as well as a blue-bound Bible that Adriana Garza, the recruiter, had given him. He had read *Foundations of Christian Thought*, which compared Christianity to other world views, including secular humanism, then concluded that Christianity was true. "I think that's the only funny part, that in the end they're all wrong, Christianity's right," said Isaias, who still identified as an atheist. "Otherwise it's a decent book."

But he'd also been assigned secular works, including *Zealot: The Life and Times*

(Photo by Daniel Connolly)

of Jesus of Nazareth, a new book by a Muslim author named Reza Aslan who questioned biblical teaching, examined the historical Jesus and concluded he was a Jewish rebel against the Roman Empire.

Isaias said he wouldn't know if he wanted to stay in college for the long term until he started taking classes for his major, business. He hadn't talked about audio recording for a long time. Right now, he saw himself in a wait-it-out moment. "See what happens. Do your best. Don't ruin your opportunity, 'cause you don't know yet."

A few months later, Victory University shut down.

Chapter Eleven

...

A LOCKED DOOR

March 2014:
Nine months after graduation

THE NEWS THAT VICTORY UNIVERSITY was shutting down hit Isaias hard.

I was working at my desk in the pressroom on the second floor of City Hall in Memphis when my cell phone chimed. Another news reporter, Timberly Moore, had sent me a text message. *Hey! Victory is closing and I know that's where Isaias is supposed to go. Just thought you may want to check on him and possibly write something.*

Closing?

I had finished my leave of absence from *The Commercial Appeal* newspaper, gone back to work, and written a long Sunday article about Isaias. Now people knew about him, and after I was assigned to cover City Hall, even high-ranking government officials sometimes asked how he was doing. Everything looked good: he was living at home, going to Victory University, playing with the band, still dating Magaly and working with his family now and then.

Now this. Reports were all over the local media. The Victory University spokesman seemed just as shocked as everyone else. He said university officials had discussed Victory's financial struggles the day before but hadn't talked about closing. The university would shut down at the end of the semester.

I hadn't spoken with Isaias in weeks. From City Hall, I called his cell phone, and he answered. He and Dennis were buying painting supplies. Had he heard the news? He hadn't. I told him the little I knew. "Wow," he said. "That's incredible. That's crazy." He sounded stunned and said he needed to learn more. "It's a great institution. I like it. I'll see what I can do to help out."

The university president, Shirley Robinson Pippins, offered an explanation that day: the university needed more money, and couldn't find it.[1] She elaborated when I spoke with her more than a year later. She said the school faced serious problems with the technology it used to keep track of items such as the payroll system and online courses. Fixing the technology issues and moving the college forward would take more money than the investors could find. "And you know, I think Michael Clifford and his team were working until the very last day to bring that money in," she said, referring to the school's owner.

The university's sudden collapse reflected a nationwide battle between two powerful forces: a profitable, fast-growing industry of corporate universities that relied heavily on federal student loans, and a federal government that fought to curb the industry's abuses.

Around 2011, the government had eliminated the "safe harbor" provisions under which for-profit university recruiters could earn money based in part on the number of people they convinced to enroll, said Kevin Kinser, the expert on for-profit universities from the University at Albany. Mr. Kinser argued that the rule change led directly to a nationwide slump in enrollment at for-profit universities that would continue for years.

A few days after the Victory University shutdown was announced, I wrote an article that listed the recruiting events that institutions such as LeMoyne-Owen College and Christian Brothers University were offering to Victory University students.[2] Then I e-mailed the article to Isaias to make sure he saw it, adding that Jennifer Alejo, the counselor from the Abriendo Puertas group, would like to speak with him.

Isaias wrote back: "Okay. Thank you very much."

In sending Isaias the article, I was playing a much more active role than I had during my year at Kingsbury, when I had tried to avoid giving the students advice about college. I thought a reporter should document the story, not change it. If I told Isaias or any other student what to do, I would be acting like a sports reporter who tried to advise the quarterback during the game. But now the high school year was over, and I'd already affected Isaias' life by writing about him in the newspaper, which had prompted some people to give him money and brought his family some new clients. I felt less obligation to stick to my "no advice" rule.

Mario Ramos had seen how going to college had changed his second son. Isaias hadn't wanted to go, but once he enrolled, he got excited and worked hard. He was happy. Because Isaias received a full scholarship, he would escape the collapse of Victory University with no debt. Still, when the news came that the school would shut down, it hurt him badly.

Mario wondered if he and Cristina had made a mistake by encouraging Isaias to go to college when he didn't want to. For a while, he felt guilty, but then he decided it wasn't his fault. Cristina said she and Mario had gone through so many changes and harsh setbacks in life that nothing shocked them. But for Isaias, the shutdown of Victory came as a cruel blow, and it hurt his mother to see him suffer.

One day at the breakfast table at home, Cristina asked Isaias what was wrong. He said he couldn't eat and couldn't sleep. He didn't know what he would do. Mario told him to try the other schools, like Christian Brothers or Rhodes, and if that didn't work, Southwest. And as a last resort, he could go to work with them.

Dennis hugged Isaias at the table. Don't be afraid. It's okay. We'll help you no matter what happens. If no school accepts you, come with us and we'll go to work. After that, Isaias calmed down and started eating and focusing on school. In mid-April, Isaias was feeling overwhelmed, managing his remaining Victory schoolwork, the applications to other colleges, and practices with Los Psychosis. He said he had spoken with Christian Brothers recruiters. Jennifer Alejo suggested he try Rhodes College, and he was working on an application. Now he was thinking about civil engineering or computer programming rather than business.

"My parents really wanted me to go to college," he said. "And I guess I understand that. Because it's really risky to just go out into the family business." He said he'd keep trying to go to another university.

The shutdown also affected Adriana Garza, the Victory recruiter who had worked with Isaias during his application and delivered the news of the scholarship acceptance to his parents. Ms. Garza told me that on the day of the shutdown, staffers were asked to go to group meetings with the president. Like Isaias, she was stunned to learn the school would close. "We couldn't believe what she was talking about." Ms. Garza said she spoke up in the meeting. How are you doing this without telling us? Why didn't you let us prepare the students? And what will happen to them?

She wanted to stay and help the students figure out their next steps. But the university was laying off its admissions staff immediately. Soon she was told to hand over her keys and business cell phone and leave. The experience left her saddened and disappointed. "You feel like—used." She lost contact with many students, including Isaias.

The Commercial Appeal newspaper assigned business reporter Jennifer Backer to write follow-up articles on the shutdown. She obtained federal e-mail records that revealed a surprise: at the time Victory University announced its closure, it was facing intense government scrutiny.

It's unclear exactly when and why the inquiry started, but on February 25, 2014, the U.S. Department of Education told the college president by e-mail that inspectors would come to the Victory University campus on March 24 and stay for four days. The government demanded that Victory hand over records related to every aspect of its financial aid operations. Just nine days after the e-mail, the university announced its shutdown. Education department officials saw the sudden shutdown as suspicious, the e-mail correspondence said.

The investigators came to campus anyway and found several discrepancies, including that students had been charged for courses they weren't enrolled in.

The school closed in May. Later, a state regulator concluded that Victory had failed to comply with shutdown procedures. The federal government demanded audits to show what Victory had done with the financial aid dollars. The school didn't provide the audits, which prompted the government to demand that the school pay back money—at first, the government wanted $28.4 million, then later reduced the demand to $8.1 million.[3]

In late 2015, it was still unclear who, if anyone, would pay back the money, and whether the feds would try hard to recover it. When Jennifer Backer and I spoke on a conference call with the owner, Michael Clifford, he distanced himself from Victory, saying he was a passive investor and hadn't been involved in the decision to shut down the school. "Every decision was made by the board of trustees," he said. "I didn't even know about it until after it happened."

The last person to serve as chairman of Victory's board was Beverly C. Robertson, the retired president of the highly regarded National Civil Rights Museum in Memphis. She gave a much different account than that given by Mr. Clifford, saying that decisions by him and other investors forced the shutdown of the school.

She said the news of the federal inspection didn't play a role. Rather, she said Dr. Pippins, the president, realized the school faced a big financial shortfall and that she asked Mr. Clifford and other investors for help.

"But the investors basically came back and said that no, they weren't going to make any additional investments in the college," Ms. Robertson said. She said that left the board no choice but to shut down Victory. "I think people were upset with the investors because they realized that children's futures hung in the balance ... I know the students were upset. That's a given. I can tell you that the staff was crushed. The administration, Dr. Pippins. People were in tears, almost, at the board meeting. It was just a really sad set of circumstances."

In the conference call with us, Mr. Clifford said he didn't even know who was on Victory's board. This surprised me. "Wait, so you're saying you don't know who was on the board of Victory University?" I asked.

"No," he said. "I was not on the board and I never went to a board meeting. I had no interaction with the board."

But he was listed as a board member in the 2009–2010 Victory University catalog. Jennifer Backer found business and personal connections between Mr. Clifford and some board members. When I told Ms. Robertson what he'd said, she laughed. She said Mr. Clifford had, in fact, come to some board meetings.

"Well, I *thought* I saw him at a board meeting," she said sarcastically. "I thought he was there. Maybe it was a figment of my imagination."

The experience at Victory left her questioning the concept of for-profit colleges. If an investor wants to make money, higher education might not be the best way to do it, she said. "Because higher education is costly. You know, even public institutions have a hard time making it."

My colleague and I contacted Mr. Clifford for comment on what Ms. Robertson had said. He wouldn't agree to another phone interview and wrote an e-mail repeating much of what he'd said the first time: "My family did our best to help build something very special in Memphis…but we lost a lot causing real hardship for us. And I spoke with you because you sounded honest." Now he said he was suspicious of us.

Across the United States, more for-profit schools were collapsing. Multiple federal actions forced for-profit chain Corinthian Colleges to begin closing campuses. The company finally declared bankruptcy in April 2015 and closed 28 campuses nationwide on a day's notice, leaving an estimated 16,000 students struggling through the same shock Isaias and others had experienced.[4]

The nation's biggest for-profit university chain, the University of Phoenix, saw its enrollment, profits and stock value plunge as federal pressure continued.

Many people reached out to Isaias after Victory shut down, including Margot Aleman, the Streets Ministries counselor who had led the last-minute intervention at his house. In March, she told me Isaias hadn't been returning her calls and that she found it a bit hurtful.

Then Isaias stopped returning my calls, too. When his girlfriend

Magaly graduated as Kingsbury valedictorian in May 2014, I went to the ceremony, knowing he'd almost certainly be there. But in the crowd, I couldn't find him.

A few weeks later, Javi Arcega the rock musician sent me an invitation on Facebook to watch Los Psychosis play another show at Murphy's, the same smoky, dimly lit bar where the band had played on the night before Isaias' last day of high school.

I hadn't heard from Isaias in about two months, but when I texted him and Dennis about the show time, he wrote back. *Hey Daniel. Sorry I haven't been able to reply sooner,* he began, and gave me the show details. He later said he'd seen my messages but sometimes forgot to answer—he wasn't trying to push me away.

So that's how I ended up at a picnic table outside the bar, talking with Isaias and Dennis. It was a Monday night in mid-June 2014, more than a year after Isaias had graduated from high school and more than a month since Victory had shut down. I asked Isaias what was going on.

"Well, since my parents are moving to Mexico—" Isaias began.

Dennis interjected. "We're trying to convince them *not* to move."

Isaias continued. "But the idea right now is that they will. Sometime during the winter."

On the subject of his own future, he said, "I was thinking I *can*, but I don't think it would be pretty if I went right back to school. Having to take Dustin to middle school, Dennis going to work. It just seems like it would be rough. We got a pretty good thing going, Dennis and I together working."

Isaias told me what he'd been doing since April: dealing with the chaotic shutdown of Victory, confusion over how to get transcripts, long lines at the business office. On the last day of the semester, he had to turn in a take-home final exam for his math class. When Isaias arrived at the building, the security guard, a man he knew, told him students couldn't go in. Isaias eventually met the instructor outside the building and handed over the exam.

He said Jennifer Alejo had tried to help him. "I guess I never got to use her help." He said he felt he couldn't really ask Abriendo Puertas to help him unless he participated in the group's activities, and he'd never really had time for that.

That night outside Murphy's, Isaias said work was occupying his mind as the painting business took on more and more projects. Christian Brothers made Isaias an offer of $18,000 in scholarships, but tuition cost about $29,000. Isaias told me he'd completed his application to Rhodes College but wasn't sure if his professors had turned in their letters of recommendation. He'd never heard from the college. "I guess I could have been keeping up. I didn't."

Isaias' close friend Daniel Nix had exchanged group messages with Isaias around this time, along with Juan Avalos and Ibrahim Elayan. Daniel later said Isaias was concerned about money. "It kind of sucks that he didn't go . . . but it's going to be on his terms. We can't make him."

Jennifer Alejo later told me a new college scholarship possibility had developed at Christian Brothers University during the summer, and she wanted Isaias to go for it. Ms. Alejo had called Isaias, texted him, e-mailed, and asked Magaly to relay messages. But Isaias didn't reply.

Ms. Alejo didn't know what Isaias was thinking, but she had a guess. You get your hopes up, you go to a school, you finally accept that it can happen. And when that's stripped from you, it can damage your faith and motivation to try to go anywhere else.

Eventually, Isaias' silence left the counselor with no choice. She moved on and worked with the students who wanted college more.

That June night at Murphy's, Isaias said Victory's closing still bothered him. "It was sad. It would have been nice to go there. College was tough. I enjoyed it. I mean, I don't mind going. I wouldn't mind going back."

Inside the bar, a guitar began to strum and a woman began to sing, country-style.

I thought Isaias was letting his shot at college slip away. I suggested he call Rhodes and ask for the status of his application. I told him I thought I'd be remiss if I didn't say that—but that it was his life. "Okay," Isaias said.

Soon he said he'd like to go into the bar. "I don't want to be an asshole."

It would be rude for him to ignore the show, especially since he'd play later and would appreciate the other band's support.

Isaias walked inside, where the lead singer, a soul-baring presence on the tiny stage, was giving a far better show than anyone should expect to see at a dive bar on a Monday night. But as Isaias' own story demonstrated, you find potential everywhere.

Isaias moved toward the music.

Chapter Twelve

...

DUSTIN'S DESTINY

October 2014:
One year and five months after graduation

ONE EVENING, Mario and Cristina were talking in their kitchen with their old friend Paulina Badillo Garcia, the woman with long, curly dark hair who had worked for them in their sewing shop in Santa Maria Asunción and sheltered them when they first arrived in Memphis. Paulina had brought her seven-month-old baby son, and Cristina played with him, cheerful and laughing. Now the baby's mother cradled the infant as they spoke, and Mario and Cristina let slip that they were going back to Mexico.

"Soon?" Paulina asked, surprised.

"Yes, in a month or two," Mario said.

"Seriously?" Paulina asked.

"Yes!"

They hadn't told many people. "Yes, we're going now," Mario said. "We want to go live in Santa Maria, the beach. Cristina says Chile. We don't know yet." They had thought about applying for immigration visas to several different countries, like Argentina, Germany, Italy and Spain. They would see which country accepted them first, then go there.

"We'll go on another adventure," Mario said. "We'll see what happens. I don't want to die in Memphis. I don't want to die in the same place."

Another reason drove them to consider going back to Mexico. They still owned property there, the old house and some other parcels, and they could sell it, but they believed they'd have to do so in person. They also feared losing ownership of the property and wanted to handle the transaction sooner rather than later.

They planned to leave around January and were counting down their last days in Memphis. Cristina said people sometimes questioned her actions. Why did she plant trees in the yard if she was about to leave? She said she wanted to keep working until the last moment, just as she had in the beginning.

"And the boy?" Paulina asked, meaning Dustin. "Is he going with you?"

"No, he'll stay," Mario said.

"We'll send for him," Cristina said. "Later. When I'm doing well and I see that there's not crime. That's what we're afraid of."

They talked about a Mexican tradition: if you're about to leave on a journey, your mother blesses you and says, "May God be with you." Now it would be reversed: instead of the parents saying this to their children, the children, Dennis and Isaias, would say this to their parents.

Isaias and Dennis said they had come to terms with their parents' departure. "Yeah, I just accept it, you know?" Isaias said. "Not angry."

If Mario and Cristina returned to Mexico, it might take them years to come back to Memphis, and it might ultimately prove impossible to do it legally.

Mario said friends of Mariana Hernandez's parents had asked him why they were going. Weren't they afraid of losing everything they had? He said he told them no, he wasn't. "I can find a new world. A new story, something new to tell. A new life."

They would start from scratch, carrying only the basics on the airplane home, just some clothes and a toothbrush. "And your soap," Cristina told her husband. "So you don't stink." He laughed. But the prospect of leaving also bothered Cristina. She and Mario told Paulina about a strange dream she'd had: that her husband had thrown out everything from the house in Santa Maria that he didn't like, and that only a vacant lot remained. And then in the dream, Cristina talked with God, telling him she was afraid of the good, easy life because it becomes a habit, and habits can kill you. "We're a little anxious," Cristina told Paulina at the table. And she and Mario realized that people in Mexico might not take them back, might think of them as different, no longer the old friends they had known.

• • •

During his year at Victory University, Isaias had earned perfect grades, a 4.0. Magaly enrolled at Rhodes College in the fall of 2014, and Isaias, no longer in school, sometimes helped with her homework. He borrowed a book Magaly had read in class, a graphic novel called *Fun Home: A Family Tragicomic* by Alison Bechdel. Isaias enjoyed it. "It's pretty cool."

He said he liked reading and discussing books like these—actually learning—but he didn't like the structured education system. "I guess if there's ever something that's like college but not the way it is today, I'd consider going there."

It hurt his parents to see him lose interest in school. "It's a year thrown in the garbage," Mario said. As Cristina saw it, the problem wasn't in the outside world, but within Isaias. She said Isaias had plenty of ways to find scholarship money if he wanted to. Their longtime painting clients loved him and would help. He could ask at churches. "If you ask me to look for scholarships, I can't, because I don't speak English, for a lot of reasons," Cristina said. "But he can. And he doesn't do it." And Mario and Cristina were willing to pay some money toward his education, too.

I asked Isaias more than a year after the shutdown of Victory University if he saw continuing college as impossible. He responded quickly. "No. No. It's not that. It's just that I don't want to." While Isaias' decision mystified and disappointed many people, including his own parents, it made more sense if you considered his relationship with another key person in his life: Dennis.

When Isaias was studying at Victory University, he spent less time on painting work, and the family seriously considered hiring someone to replace him in the business. If Isaias kept going to college *and* his parents moved to Mexico, Dennis would have to handle the painting business largely by himself, along with one or more new employees who might not share the same commitment to quality that had won the family more clients than they could handle. And any college solution would also be likely to cost money, possibly increasing the burden on Dennis.

It took me a long time to develop the theory I just described, and in 2015, I ran it by Isaias. He said it was basically correct. "Yeah, if I had just continued school, problems would have arisen," Isaias said. "I think we all saw it, everybody in the family saw it. How's Dennis going to take care of everything by himself? How am I going to go to school every day and then come home and, like, got to do schoolwork and still got to do something around the house to help? It would just be difficult."

I also asked Dennis about the scenario of him largely running the business by himself. "Yes, actually, we did think about that," he said. He said he would have had to hire other people, but it would have been possible. He also said family members had considered helping Isaias pursue school. "If he really wanted to, we would have let him continue studying," he said.

. . .

Isaias' former classmate Adam Truong said he didn't really want to go to college, either. But he did anyway. He was studying mechanical engineering at Christian Brothers University.

People told him he'd learn 90 percent of a job on the job. He'd contemplated dropping out of college, but he said his professors told him they all thought the same when they were young, and their friends who dropped out had no job security because they didn't have the degree.

Adam had imagined that college would give him a chance to explore new topics, but that wasn't the case, at least not in his major. "As a science major going into college, I feel like everything's one pathway, and they make you really good in that pathway, and that's it." He had thought about switching to chemical or biomedical engineering but concluded that he'd have to take out big loans. So he kept going on the mechanical engineering path.

Looking back at the time at Kingsbury, Adam thought he'd benefited from going to a less-privileged school. It made him understand the world better. Sometimes college students from more privileged backgrounds seemed clueless, especially those he met when he visited his sister, a student at Rhodes. "They have, like, no idea what happens to the other side of Memphis," Adam said. "No idea at all."

He and Mariana Hernandez weren't dating anymore, but they'd talk when they saw each other on the Christian Brothers campus. She'd landed there through a stroke of fortune.

After graduating from Kingsbury in 2013, Mariana had abandoned plans to go to her first-choice school, Christian Brothers, and had enrolled at the most affordable institution she could find, Mid-South Community College. She worked for the social services agency Latino Memphis helping younger students and maintained a close relationship with Jennifer Alejo, the college counselor who had come to Isaias' house on the night of the intervention.

In the summer of 2014, Ms. Alejo told Mariana of a new opportunity that would allow her to enroll at Christian Brothers after all. "Jennifer just told me to wait it out and that something would happen," Mariana said. "And she made it happen." Latino Memphis had helped create a new Christian Brothers scholarship program specifically designed for students with immigration problems. Backed by an anonymous donor's gift of $150,000, the Latino Student Success Scholarships assisted 14 freshmen and 11 transfer students, including Mariana.[1]

The transfer students took on $5,000 in loans each year and paid $50 a month toward loan repayment while enrolled in school. They also paid about $3,650 per year toward tuition. That was a lot of money, but much less than the university's tuition sticker price, about $29,000 per year. And the program also offered $1,000 per year for books.

Ms. Alejo had wanted Isaias to apply, too—this was the opportunity that she'd tried so hard to tell him about. It would have been easy. "This was simply, 'Hey, fill out a little application and tell me, and that's all I needed,'" she said.

In the summer of 2015, Christian Brothers announced that it had received another anonymous donation of $3.6 million for the scholarship program. That money plus contributions from the university would support the education of 80 additional students over the next four years, bringing the total in the scholarship program to 105.

The university celebrated the scholarship announcement at a luncheon. One of the special guests was Alejandra Ceja, leader of the White House Initiative on Educational Excellence for Hispanics. After the luncheon, backers of the scholarship met with corporate leaders at the downtown offices of the Greater Memphis Chamber, the city's top business organization. Mariana joined them, looking mature and elegant in a formfitting green dress with a leaf pattern, and she took a seat in a conference room next to another Christian Brothers student named Bryan Nunez.

The 20 or so people around the table introduced themselves. They represented some of the city's most powerful institutions and companies: the city mayor's office, the school system, FedEx. Mariana introduced herself as a CBU student and employee of Latino Memphis. Silently, she asked herself, "What am I doing here?"

But the business leaders showed an interest in her. "The Latino population is one that's actually growing in Memphis," said Phil Trenary, a former airline executive who now led the chamber. "Our population has not grown that much in the past 20 years. And this is an area that we see as a tremendous opportunity."

The chamber was trying to recruit businesses to invest in Memphis, and the companies needed educated workers. Mr. Trenary turned to Mariana and Bryan. "You two, you've got to stay here. That's part of the deal. You're not allowed to leave the chamber until you sign a pledge of long-term residence." The people around the table laughed. Mariana was sitting close to Bryan, her bare right shoulder touching his shirtsleeve. Later she said they were dating.

State lawmaker Mark White told the group that a few months earlier,

the Tennessee legislature almost passed a law that would have allowed
students like Mariana to get in-state tuition at public universities, but it
fell short by one vote. He would try to push the bill again in January, with
the backing of the business group. Mauricio Calvo from Latino Memphis
noted the progress. "Not even 20 years ago, *two* years ago, we could not
have dreamed of having an in-state tuition bill getting out of a subcom-
mittee."

The meeting broke up, and the head of the chamber, one of the most
powerful men in the city, walked over to Mariana and handed her a business card. "Okay, if you need me at all, I'm Phil." And then Mariana was
talking to Alejandra Ceja from the White House Initiative, who described
how her staff took interns to the president's mansion to go bowling in its
private recreational space.

If bowling at the White House sounds impossible for someone like
Mariana, consider this: A few months after the meeting at the Greater
Memphis Chamber, the Christian Brothers University president John
Smarrelli, Jr. traveled to Washington for a twenty-fifth anniversary cele-
bration of the White House Initiative. He brought with him a CBU student:
Franklin Paz Arita, the kid from Honduras who'd spent the first week of
school in 2012 sitting in the Kingsbury gymnasium, the one who had wit-
nessed a man threaten to kill his mother with a sledgehammer years earlier.

Franklin went to the White House reception and was one of a small number of people allowed into a VIP area. He shook hands with Vice President Joe Biden. Then Franklin met President Obama and spoke with him.

"He just said that it was an honor to have us as guests there," Franklin
recalled. "And I told him that because of him and Deferred Action and
because of CBU, my dreams have been revived. And he just said that it
meant a lot to him." They shook hands and posed for pictures.

Franklin recognized that being an honored guest at the White House
was a special privilege. "And it also motivates me to keep trying," Franklin
said. "To be the best possible version of myself that I can be, you know."

This really happened. Perhaps something like it could happen for
Mariana, too. Maybe the day after the meeting with the business leaders she

would go back to being a struggling college student. But for this moment she stood close, so close, to great things.

...

August 2015:

About two years and three months after graduation

For now, Isaias stayed on a different course.

One day Isaias and Dennis went to work in the country at a big new farmhouse-style home owned by an old client and friend, Michelle Betts. They prepped a room for painting and then used rollers and brushes to turn the wall from green to white. Isaias set his phone to play music: the French rock band Phoenix, a classical version of Ave Maria, British hip hop by Gorrillaz. The brothers' own band, Los Psychosis, still played together. Tommy the drummer had left the band and now Stephanie, the wife of Javi Arcega, had played drums in several of their shows.

Isaias felt optimistic about the future. "I guess I think of getting married. Kind of cool. I like that. Being with Magaly all day. That's pretty fun, right? I'm excited for that." They had talked about it but wouldn't rush in—perhaps they'd take that step in three or four years, after she had finished college. They'd skip straight to living in a house, not renting an apartment. Isaias thought about moving out to a Memphis suburb, perhaps Bartlett in the east. They'd figure it out later.

"I guess I like to make plans like that, but a lot of times skip the details," Isaias said. "'Cause details always go wrong."

Magaly was about to start her second year at Rhodes College, and it seemed to be working out well for her. The private school was both selective and expensive: each year, commuting students would pay $43,000, and those who lived on campus paid $54,000. Magaly was a U.S. citizen, and between the college's scholarships and federal financial aid, she didn't have to pay anything. In the second year, she anticipated she'd have to pay only $500 out of pocket.

She still lived at home with her mother and now she was driving an old white SUV onto a campus where some other students were driving Audis or BMWs.

The classes were hard. She felt she didn't have enough time in the day to do everything that was required, and she struggled, finishing her first year with a grade point average of 2.83. But despite the difficult work and the differences between Magaly and many other Rhodes students, she'd made some friends on campus and she'd taken one-on-one lessons on her favorite instrument, the flute, and learned to play far better than she ever had before. She frequently visited Kingsbury High and planned to become some sort of advisor for the senior class. "I guess I'm closer in age to them, so they might believe me more."

Though she still thought of becoming a veterinary pathologist, she'd become interested in education and imagined she'd work as a high school teacher before completing a doctorate later.

And Magaly liked the idea of marrying Isaias. "I mean, I guess like the words that come to my mind are cute, adorable," she said, smiling. "Sweet. I don't know. I look forward to it."

As Isaias and Dennis painted the house in the country and listened to the music they loved, their father and mother worked in the next room. The fact that Mario and Cristina were still working with their sons on this day in August 2015 was remarkable, since they had long talked about going back to Mexico—had in fact been on the verge of doing it. But in the end, they didn't go, at least not yet.

I had visited the Ramos home in December 2014, shortly before Christmas, fully expecting to hear details of the parents' final preparations to go. Instead, I found the house decorated for the holiday: a little tree on a table in the living room, fruits laid out for *ensalada de Nochebuena*, the holiday drink they'd make, white icicle lights hanging outside near the little American flags.

Mario told me that about four days earlier, they'd changed their minds about leaving. "Really, it was everyone's idea. We sat down here eating breakfast, and the idea came up to stay a while longer. I don't know how long. Three to six months at most."

Cristina had been excited about going. But she had worried about Dustin since he was still so young. And she thought about the people she knew, people like Michelle Betts, who lived close to their children and grandchildren. She imagined Isaias becoming a father to a grandchild that she could never see. "That's the feeling that kills me," she said, and Cristina, usually so cheerful, began to cry.

That December night, Dennis seemed puzzled by his parents' decision. He'd been trying to convince them to stay a while longer, to earn money to buy one more house to renovate and rent out. "I kept telling them, and they said, 'No, we're gonna leave.' They even got mad at me for asking. And in the end they changed their minds."

Mario and Cristina still talked about going back. They continued to prepare Dennis and Isaias for their absence by letting them handle important chores, like registering Dustin for seventh grade.

That August, Dennis and Isaias took Dustin shopping for school supplies. He followed his older brothers through the store, a young boy who walked with shoulders hunched forward. The shopping reminded Dennis of his own school days not so long before, when he and Isaias were young. It had been harder then. The family had little money and because Mario and Cristina worked such long hours, they usually shopped at Walmart at the last minute, when the shelves had already been emptied. Now, they shopped three days before school started, and when the cart full of supplies totaled $104.67, Dennis simply paid with a debit card.

What did Dustin think about going back to school? "It is unexpected," he said. What Dustin meant by "unexpected" was that he'd spent much of the summer playing video games like *Call of Duty: Advanced Warfare*. When his parents told him he had to go back to class, he wasn't prepared. "And then I have the shock in my heart that I'm going to school." His parents and brothers said Dustin actually liked school, and that he'd been doing better since advancing from elementary to middle school the year before.

What was he thinking of doing as an adult? "Uh, that's a hard question," he said as he walked with his brothers. His voice was still a boy's, high-pitched, but he spoke in the slightly accented cadences of his older brothers. "There's a lawyer and a judge that I want to be," the boy continued. "But then again, I'm in love with video games, so I could do that. Then there's a biologist."

Dennis and Isaias still talked in general terms about going back to school one day. And the older brothers would work to give Dustin a chance to study something he liked, even cooking, or art. For Dennis and Isaias, that was what education should be: something you liked. Dennis said if Dustin didn't want to go to college, that would be fine, too.

. . .

On the morning of August 10, 2015, the same day his parents and brothers would work at Michelle Betts' house, little Dustin Ramos woke up early, put on his school uniform of tan pants and white shirt and ate breakfast by himself. He was feeling a bit nervous on this first day of school, but prepared, his hair freshly cut short by his mother. He put on the backpack

(Photo by Karen Pulfer Focht)

loaded with the supplies his brothers had bought him and sat on the edge of a couch in the living room, waiting. Outside, rain began to fall.

Three years had passed since the chaotic start of Isaias' senior year in 2012. If all went well, Dustin would graduate from high school in 2021.

Maybe Dustin would prove an average student. Maybe he would drop out. Maybe he'd climb to the very top of his class, as Magaly had done.

Maybe one day Dustin's parents really would go back to Mexico, and he'd spend the next few years shuttling between them and his brothers in Memphis, a young boy walking through international airports. Maybe his parents would stay in America, and the government would grant them papers in a year, or in two years, or in ten years. Or maybe the papers would never come.

But now Dustin was only 11 years old, and all his possible lives branched out in front of him in an endless tree of potential paths. And rain or not, he had to go to school.

"Vámonos, Pato," his father said. Let's go, Duck.

The boy rose and moved to the door, and his mother hugged him and spoke to him softly. *"Recuerda todo que tienes en tu cabeza y en tu corazón."* Remember everything you have in your head and your heart.

His father stopped the green truck a short distance from the middle school, and Dustin ventured into the rainy semidarkness. He joined the children clustered under the sheltering awnings outside the locked school doors, each waiting with their own fears and desires and hopes. Then the hour arrived, the school doors opened and the children walked inside, and into the future.

EPILOGUE

...

I HADN'T ALWAYS BELIEVED that Mario and Cristina really would go back to Mexico, especially after 2014, when they'd called off their plan. But Isaias understood that when his parents spoke of returning, they meant it.

Late in 2015, a few days after Christmas, Mario and Cristina drove with their three sons to the city's Greyhound bus terminal, a modern, spacious new building near the airport. They hugged Dennis, Isaias and Dustin goodbye, then walked through a portal to a waiting bus.

And then it was over in an instant, the sons on one side, the parents on the other, only a few feet away but somehow already irretrievably gone.

That day, Mario and Cristina rode the bus to Dallas, stayed overnight in a hotel, then awoke and boarded a plane to Mexico City, using a special discount fare that Isaias had found online: only $196 for the two of them.

Within hours, an image arrived on Isaias' cell phone: an aerial view of Mexico City, the capital of the country that Mario and Cristina hadn't seen since March 2003, a full 12 years, nine months earlier.

From the moment Mario and Cristina walked through that portal at the bus station, Dennis and Isaias bore the full weight of responsibility for caring for themselves and Dustin, who had now turned 12. They worked

(Photo by Karen Pulfer Focht)

long hours on painting and remodeling projects because they would soon have to pay local property taxes on the house where they lived and the two other houses the family had bought in Memphis. And they'd need to send money to support their parents during the rough early months of preparing their old house in Mexico for sale.

A couple of weeks after Mario and Cristina left, Isaias said his younger brother appeared to be doing well. "I guess at one point I thought he was like, depressed or sad but no, it turns out he was tired that day." When the older sons talked with their parents by phone or video conferencing, Dustin was there too. "And he's okay with it," Isaias said. "We're actually having a lot of fun, the three of us."

The sons ate dinner together. Isaias took Dustin to school every morning and told him to take out the garbage, and though the boy sometimes seemed grumpy, he did it. "He's upbeat," Isaias said. "He's excited about things."

Nearby, Rigo Navarro was living a similar life—his mother and father had returned to Mexico, too, and he and two of his brothers were likewise running a household on their own. "I see myself as the man, the wife and the maid of the house," Rigo said. He said he always did the cooking, and that his mother was talking about staying in Mexico, though his father planned to come back and visit soon.

Mario and Cristina likewise spoke about trying to come back for an extended visit legally, with a visa, though an immigration attorney told me it might be very hard. The family members were considering sending Dustin to Mexico for a few weeks in the summer. Dennis and Isaias might one day be able to visit Mexico, too, if immigration authorities granted them special permission to leave and return.

The older brothers were making big changes in the house, turning their parents' bedroom, as planned, into a music practice space. Their parents hadn't liked pets, but Isaias and Dennis wanted them, and now they bought two young cats from the animal shelter. They named the gray one Cocoa and the tan one Sandy. Dustin called the cats "awesome."

The band Los Psychosis stopped playing together. The Ramos brothers said Javi and his wife Stephanie wanted to pursue their musical careers with more professional ambition than the brothers did, and they parted ways on good terms. Some constants remained. Magaly and Isaias were still together. And for now, at least, the plaque of Jesus that Cristina had carried across the desert remained on the kitchen wall, just as she had left it.

The brothers were paying close attention to the 2016 presidential election campaign, in which Donald Trump and other candidates were making extreme anti-immigrant statements. Dennis and Isaias backed the Democratic socialist candidate Bernie Sanders, even donating to his campaign, though they couldn't vote. For both the Ramos family and the country as a whole, the future was uncertain.

In the meantime, what are we to make of the story of Isaias and his decision not to continue in college?

Many people who read my December 2013 newspaper article on Isaias concluded that his story was about his immigration status and the problems it caused. Obviously, immigration problems did affect Isaias as well as his family. Yet other Kingsbury students with immigration problems, like

Mariana Hernandez and Franklin Paz Arita, found ways to continue their college careers. After spending time with the Ramos family over a span of more than three years, I'm convinced that Isaias' story isn't only about his immigration status, but that it also reflects elements of family life and thinking that are common to many children of immigrants, even those who are citizens.

I don't want to imply that immigration status doesn't matter. It does, and immigration problems crushed many dreams at Kingsbury High. America allows these young people to live in the country indefinitely and educates them at great expense to taxpayers. Then after they finish high school, the country creates artificial barriers that make it more difficult for them to fulfill their potential. All of this is pointless and wasteful.

Still, passage of the Dream Act or something like it would not magically solve all the problems of America's young Hispanics. Nationwide, the proportion of unauthorized immigrants among Hispanic kids in 2013 was only 3 percent. An additional 3 percent were legal immigrants. By far the biggest group was U.S. citizens born in this country: 94 percent.

Many students in Isaias' graduating class had unauthorized immigration status, probably because the Mexican population in Tennessee was so new. But all the data suggest that the proportion of citizens among young Hispanics will continue to rise both in Memphis and across the country.[1] The face of young Hispanics in America won't be Isaias the unauthorized immigrant, but his little brother, Dustin the citizen.

In many cases, the lives of young Hispanics with citizenship will closely resemble the life of Isaias. Many will have immigrant parents who want their children to succeed in school but don't know how to help and don't speak English. Many teenagers will juggle academic demands along with work and family obligations. And many will wrestle with doubts about the value of education.

That's why society should give children of immigrants extra supports like the ones that I've mentioned throughout the course of this book: expanded early childhood education, additional guidance counselors, scholarship funds and psychological interventions to improve students' motivation to study. Indeed, *all* children from disadvantaged backgrounds need extra support.

Of course, these extra supports often cost money, and spending public money is a political question. The politics around immigration are so often so irrational that as of this writing, at least, an overhaul of immigration law appears far away. Many more years may pass before Congress sets new rules on how many immigrants to let into the country, or how to treat unauthorized immigrant adults. In November 2014, President Obama's administration announced two more executive actions: an expansion of Deferred Action for Childhood Arrivals, and a program that would offer similar protection to unauthorized immigrant adults who were parents of U.S. citizens or legal permanent residents.[2] Both programs faced legal challenges, and neither had been implemented as of this writing.

In the meantime, our society should view the millions of immigrants' children as a powerful pool of human potential. We should handle matters related to immigrants' children *separately* from the more controversial questions of immigration policy. Because so many decisions on education take place at the state and local levels, communities can and should make good choices for their kids independently, far from the heat and grandstanding of Washington politics.

And regardless of what governments do, adults who come into contact with children of immigrants can offer advice and encouragement. Throughout the course of my time at Kingsbury, I was struck by how much the students needed guidance, and I saw that interested adults could make a big difference.

If you're an adult and you worry that you're unqualified to help, or perhaps the wrong race or ethnicity, remember that in many cases, the student might have no one else to turn to. Kingsbury graduate Jose Perez said he didn't really care who was offering help. "We'd rather get help from *anybody* than from nobody," he said. "If our next-door neighbor can help us, we'll be at our next-door neighbor's house every day."

Despite all the obstacles, many children of immigrants *are* succeeding in school and life. Students like Estevon, Magaly, Adam, Franklin and

Mariana made it to college and stayed in. And even situations that look bleak can take surprising turns for the better. I recently walked into a bank near Kingsbury High and saw a nameplate for one of the tellers: Lorena Gomez, the teen mother whose life had been marked by enormous conflict and stress. She wasn't in the bank that day, but I took her business card and later spoke with her by phone. Lorena said her daughter was well and that her relationship with her own mother had improved. She loved banking, hoped to advance in the field, and said her Spanish skills helped her work with Hispanic customers. "I feel useful for something," she said. For Lorena, the future looked far brighter than it had a few short years before.

As the proportion of Hispanic youth in America slowly rises above one in four, we have reason to hope—and reason to remember what Rigo Navarro said one day in class:

Don't give up on us.

ACKNOWLEDGMENTS

...

I WORKED ON THIS BOOK for more than five years, and many people helped along the way. But I'd like to start with just two names. When I approached former Kingsbury principal Carlos Fuller with my crazy idea of hanging out in his school for a year, he could have said no, but he said yes. I'll write here what I told him in person: while I didn't necessarily agree with every decision he made, I saw him as someone who loved the kids. Thank you, Mr. Fuller. And Margot Aleman from Streets Ministries was the first person to introduce me to individual students, including Isaias. Those introductions led to everything else. Thank you, Margot.

I interacted with well over 160 people connected to the Kingsbury universe, including staffers at the high school, elementary school, middle school and vocational center. There are too many names to list here, but I thank every teacher, counselor, administrator, student, parent, sibling as well as the people with TRIO, Young Life, Leadership Memphis, the Memphis Police and Streets Ministries.

I also want to thank the leaders of the former Memphis City Schools for their support, including former regional superintendent Kevin P. McCarthy, attorney Sybille Noble and former superintendent Kriner Cash.

At Latino Memphis, I thank Mauricio Calvo for giving me the idea for this book and former staffer Jennifer Alejo for helpful insight.

The International Center for Journalists brought me to Washington in 2012 for an excellent multi-day training session on immigration policy. I thank Patrick Butler, Johanna Carrillo and the rest of the ICFJ staff, as well as the Scripps Howard Foundation for sponsoring the program.

I also thank the organization Investigative Reporters and Editors for its excellent conference sessions on writing techniques and the book industry, the Dart Center for a useful session on youth violence that showed me for the first time that reporters sometimes hang out in schools, the Pulitzer Center on Crisis Reporting for sponsoring a series of my talks, the Education Writers Association for exposing me to ideas that influenced this book, the Mayborn literary nonfiction conference and the Power of Narrative conference for high-level training on storytelling, and Neil White for his informative seminars on book publishing.

Photographer Karen Pulfer Focht stuck with me for years and captured many of the images that appear in this book. Photographer Dominic Bracco II worked long hours with me during my critical trip to Mexico in 2013 and let me stay in his apartment before my flight home. Thank you both for your energy, enthusiasm and great pictures.

I also want to thank my friends Dr. Victor Saul Vital Reyes and Dr. Mardya Lopez for opening their home to me in Mexico City.

At *The Commercial Appeal*, I'm grateful to the people who approved my two leaves of absence: former editor Chris Peck and current editor Louis Graham. I also thank my supervisors Peggy Burch and Jacinthia Jones for backing this project and dealing with my absences, reporter Samantha Bryson for covering for me during my first leave of absence, as well as editors Zack McMillin, John Sale and Ian Lemmonds for producing the December 2013 newspaper project on Isaias. Reporter Jennifer Backer generously shared documents she'd uncovered while reviewing the shutdown of Victory University.

I thank G. Wayne Dowdy and other staffers of the Memphis Room at the Benjamin L. Hooks Central Library for helping me with archival research.

I funded my early work on this book with money I inherited from my mother's side of the family. My grandparents and my mother are gone now, but I want to acknowledge their role. I must thank divine providence, too, for the many other lucky breaks I received.

When I started this process, I didn't know how to write a book. I thank the people who helped me learn, including freelance editor Laura Helper-Ferris, as well as these writing group leaders: Sonja Livingston at the University of Memphis, Leslie Rubinkowski of *Creative Nonfiction* magazine and Paul A. Kramer at Vanderbilt University. And I thank all the members of their writing groups, too.

Each Thursday for several years, I sent "book updates" to a small group. They included some of the people I've already mentioned, plus these family members: my brothers, Matt Connolly and Michael Thomas Connolly; my sister-in-law, Jolanda Pandin; my father, Leo Connolly; my aunt Joanne Salviani; my uncle John Salviani; my stepmother, Barbara Huber, and her children, David Huber, Deborah Huber and Donna Huber; David's wife, Michelle, as well as several friends and colleagues: Jeff Reed, Rosa Ramirez, Wendi C. Thomas, Maria Cerny, Louise Julig, Kyle Veazey, Nana Sintim-Damoa and Carol Guensburg. Knowing you were out there made the long days of work less lonely.

Many of the list members helped with reporting problems and spent hours reading early drafts of the book. These people helped, too: Ian Johnson, Marc Perrusquia, Lise Olsen, Eileen Gorey and Deborah Santiago.

Many authors and journalists offered me help and advice. They include Emily Yellin, Sam Quinones, Sonia Nazario, Bruce Shapiro, Sarah Carr, Jeff Gammage, Richard Middlemas, Tom French, Lucy Hood, James Neff, Dennis McDougal, David Cay Johnston, Brooke Hauser, Lisa Hickman, Roland Klose, Roy Peter Clark, Pat Potter, George Getschow, Doug Swanson, Phil Kuntz, Buzz Bissinger, Lowell Bergman, Michèle Stephenson, Molly Caldwell Crosby, Trevor Aaronson, Charles Lewis, Bob Ortega, Linda K. Wertheimer, Virginia Morell, Josh Meyer, Rebecca Skloot, Aram Goudsouzian, Mark Greaney, Miriam Pawel, David Margolick, Kim Severson and Courtney Miller Santo.

I was extraordinarily lucky that literary agent Michelle Tessler took an interest in my project after many others passed. She improved my book proposal and quickly found me a great publishing home at St. Martin's Press. Advice to would-be authors: talk to Michelle first. Then try all other agents.

At St. Martin's Press I thank my editor, Elisabeth Dyssegaard, who immediately understood the importance of the story and my vision for the book, and reviewed draft after draft to help me say what I was trying to say. I also thank the other hardworking members of the St. Martin's team, especially Laura Apperson, Michael K. Cantwell, Donna Cherry, Georgia Maas, Christine Catarino, Katie Bassel, Claire Leaden, Kristopher Kam, Laura Clark and Kathryn Parise.

I thank these helpful professionals: my attorney, Brian Faughnan; clerical assistant Bridgett Byrum; my shorthand coach, Carolyn Bowlin and my friend Ralph Dickinson for translations when my Spanish knowledge hit its limits.

Finally, I thank the family at the center of this book: Isaias, Dennis, Dustin, Mario and Cristina, their family and friends in Hidalgo and the members of the band Los Psychosis. My interactions with the family lasted well over three years, far longer than I originally thought. Frankly, if a reporter wanted to follow *me* around for three years I'm not sure I'd say yes. At any time Isaias or his family could have said, "You know what, Daniel? That's enough." But the family members in Memphis and Hidalgo welcomed me into their homes again and again with warm hospitality and delicious meals. I was humbled by their generosity and hope I can learn to treat others the same way. Thank you.

NOTES

...

Portions of this book originally appeared in *The Commercial Appeal* under the headlines "Investing in Isaias" and "Kingsbury Student Leader Took Harrowing Path to Memphis," both published online December 19, 2013. A condensed version of the Isaias story appeared in print December 22, 2013.

Several works influenced the structure and style of this book. Among them were *A Hope in the Unseen: An American Odyssey from the Inner City to the Ivy League* by Ron Suskind (New York: Broadway Books, 1998) and *Friday Night Lights: A Town, a Team, and a Dream* by H. G. Bissinger (Cambridge, MA: Da Capo Press, 1990), both of which tell true stories about high school and the transition to adulthood. I read and re-read the book *Children of Immigration* by Carola Suárez-Orozco and Marcelo M. Suárez-Orozco (Cambridge, MA: Harvard University Press, 2001), the best academic work I've found on this subject. And obviously, I borrowed the title of my book from the Bible. At an Education Writers Association conference, I heard a talk by University of Pennsylvania professor Shaun R. Harper, who called on us in the news media to stop portraying failures among black and Hispanic boys and instead to highlight those who succeed. This led to my decision to focus my research on high-achieving students.

I know that some people find the terms "illegal immigrant" and "illegal alien" offensive, and I've tried to limit their use in this book. Those and similar terms were at one time in mainstream use in newspapers and they appear in some of the headlines that I cite below.

Prologue: Gold in a Green Town

1. The statistics on Mexican immigration compared to previous immigration waves come from Jeffrey Passel, D'Vera Cohn and Ana Gonzalez-Barrera, *Net Migration from Mexico Falls to Zero—and Perhaps Less* (Washington, DC: Pew Hispanic Center, April 23, 2012), p. 7. http://www.pewhispanic.org/2012/04/23/net-migration-from-mexico-falls-to-zero-and-perhaps-less/

2. Hasia R. Diner, *The Jews of the United States, 1654 to 2000* (Berkeley: University of California Press, 2004), pp. 79 and 88. Diner notes that the nineteenth-century immigrants dubbed "German Jews" came either from countries that incorporated into unified Germany in 1871 or that, like Austria and Hungary, had an urban elite deeply influenced by German culture.

3. Mark Hugo Lopez, Jeffrey Passel and Molly Rohal, *Modern Immigration Wave Brings 59 Million to U.S., Driving Population Growth and Change through 2065* (Washington, DC: Pew Hispanic Center, September 28, 2015), p. 11. http://www.pewhispanic.org/2015/09/28/modern-immigration-wave-brings-59-million-to-u-s-driving-population-growth-and-change-through-2065/

4. The statistic on Hispanic births in the Memphis area comes from the Tennessee Department of Health, via the Shelby County Health Department. A total of 1,761 Hispanic babies were born in 2007 in Shelby County, which includes Memphis. Per the National Center for Education Statistics, the average U.S. elementary school has 481 students; thus this number of children would fill more than three elementary schools.

5. The proportion of Hispanic youth in America comes from Jeffery S. Passel, D'Vera Cohn and Mark Hugo Lopez, *Census 2010: 50 Million Latinos: Hispanics Account for More than Half of Nation's Growth in Past Decade* (Washington, DC: Pew Hispanic Center, March 24, 2011), table 7, http://www.pewhispanic.org/2011/03/24/hispanics-account-for-more-than-half-of-nations-growth-in-past-decade/. The proportion of children of immigrants comes from my correspondence with the Pew Hispanic Center and is based on the U.S. Census Bureau's 2014 Current Population Survey.

6. Anna Brown and Eileen Patten, *Statistical Portrait of Hispanics in the United*

States, 2012 (Washington, DC: Pew Hispanic Center, April 29, 2014), table 22. http://www.pewhispanic.org/2014/04/29/statistical-portrait-of-hispanics-in-the -united-states-2012/

7. Passel, Cohn and Gonzalez-Barrera, *Net Migration from Mexico Falls to Zero— and Perhaps Less*, p. 7.

8. The description of periodic torture at the tree in Santa Maria Asunción comes from my interviews in June and July 2013 with several residents of the village, including Maria Ines Castro Vargas, 36; Margarita Tellez Vargas, 68, nicknamed Señora Mago; her sister Herminia Herlinda Tellez Vargas, 67; Demetrio Vargas, 48; Blanquita Martinez Garcia, 57; and her daughter, Blanca Vargas Martinez, 22, nick-named Blankita Chica. The August 2013 incident was documented in the local news. See, for example, Felipe Vega and Juan Manuel Aguirre, "Evitan linchamiento con-tra supuestos extorsionadores," *El Sol de Hidalgo*, August 10, 2013. http://www.oem .com.mx/elsoldehidalgo/notas/n3083671.htm (accessed August 2013).

9. This quote comes from Ponchito's mother, Esther Silva Hernandez.

10. Isaias described listening to the radio in the sewing shop in a college essay during his senior year.

11. This account is based on Ponchito's recollection. Isaias said he doesn't re-member the conversation.

12. The account of bringing no clothes other than what they wore comes from Mario and Cristina. Dennis says he believes family members must have had a few extra clothes, but not a lot.

13. The National Centers for Environmental Information said the average daily high in March 2003 in the southern Arizona city of Tucson was 73 and the average low was 47.

14. Luke Turf, "Finding Rafa," *Tucson Citizen*, December 18–19, 2003.

15. The National Centers for Environmental Information confirmed that snow fell in Denver on several days in March 2003.

16. The discussion of the wage difference between Mexico and the United States draws on my 2015 interview with economist Jaime Ros as well as my article with Jacquelyn Martin, "Seeking a Better Life: Thousands Leave Acambay, Mexico, for Birmingham Area," *Birmingham Post-Herald*, July 26, 2004.

17. This section draws on sociologist Douglas S. Massey's work, primarily on his book co-authored by Jorge Durand and Nolan J. Malone, *Beyond Smoke and Mir-rors: Mexican Immigration in an Era of Economic Integration* (New York: Russell Sage

Foundation, 2002). See also the article "Why Border Enforcement Backfired" by Douglas Massey with Jorge Durand and Karen A. Pren. At the time of writing the article was forthcoming in the *American Journal of Sociology* 121, no. 5 (March 2016): 1–44. Massey also answered some of my questions by e-mail.

18. Señora Mago's sister, Herminia Herlinda Tellez Vargas, confirmed many of the details of Mario's childhood and said that neglect by Mario's mother may have contributed to the deaths of the other children. Mario's mother can't give her side of the story since she is deceased.

19. Facts and figures on the Mexican-born population in the United States come from the report by Passel, Cohn and Gonzalez-Barrera, *Net Migration from Mexico Falls to Zero—and Perhaps Less.*

20. The 2012 Passel, Cohn and Gonzalez-Barrera report says that, beginning in 2003, the number of unauthorized Mexican immigrants was 5.5 million and the number of legal Mexican immigrants was 5.2 million. That trend of unauthorized Mexican immigrants outnumbering legal Mexican immigrants was true as late as 2011: 6.1 million unauthorized, 5.8 million legal immigrants.

21. The section on conditions in the Memphis construction industry draws on my article "Construction Takeover; Hard Work, Unlawful Tactics Help Some Hispanic Builders Conquer Industry," *The Commercial Appeal*, January 2, 2008.

22. The section on Memphis history draws on my interviews with G. Wayne Dowdy as well as his book *A Brief History of Memphis* (Charleston, SC: History Press, 2011). The section on former Mayor Willie Herenton draws from Marc Perrusquia's series "Always a Fighter," *The Commercial Appeal*, published over multiple days beginning January 4, 2009. Perrusquia notes that, technically, Herenton was not the first black mayor of Memphis. J. O. Patterson, Jr., a former City Council chairman, had served briefly in 1982 after another mayor resigned. Herenton was the first *elected* black mayor.

23. The discussion of Memphis city resources dedicated to Hispanics draws on my articles in *The Commercial Appeal*, "The Parallel Universe," September 23, 2007, and "Hispanic Population Outpaces Help," February 9, 2015.

24. This is a variation on a popular saying: *"Cruz, cruz, que se vaya el diablo y que venga Jesús."* Cross, cross, go away devil and come here Jesus. Cristina provided the account of throwing the holy water. Isaias said he doesn't remember it.

Chapter One: Chaos and Hope

1. In August 2013 I interviewed Bill White, the school system's chief of planning and accountability, and he confirmed much of what the guidance staff had told me about the technical problems.

2. Jane Roberts, "Carver High Students Boycott Class to Protest Problems," *The Commercial Appeal*, September 10, 2012.

3. Howard Blume, "School Record System Report Critical; Consultant's Newly Released Findings Bolster Complaints about L.A. Program," *Los Angeles Times*, November 7, 2014; Howard Blume and Ruben Vives, "Judge Orders State to Fix Jefferson High Scheduling Issues," *Los Angeles Times*, October 8, 2014. See also Joy Resmovits, "Settlement Seeks to Help Get Rid of 'Sham' Classes," *Los Angeles Times*, November 6, 2015.

4. I'm referring to Margot by her first name because that's what she almost always used in the school. Mario and Cristina likewise used their first names in their painting business. Some other adults, like Carlos Fuller, always used a courtesy title in the school, as in "Mr. Fuller," so I refer to them that way in this book.

5. Peter T. Kilborn, "Where the Young Are Stranded in Poverty, a Good Samaritan Stops His Van," *The New York Times*, January 31, 1993.

6. Louis Freedberg, Susan Frey and Lisa Chavez, *Recovering from the Recession*, EdSource, August 2013, http://edsource.org/wp-content/publications/pub13-school-stress.pdf. For information on rehiring, see Michelle Maitre, *Counselors Optimistic about Resurgence in Schools*, EdSource, January 22, 2015, http://edsource.org/2015/counselors-optimistic-about-resurgence-in-schools/73160 (accessed December 3, 2015), and this story on the Los Angeles public schools: Teresa Watanabe and Sara Hayden, "School Board Passes Bigger Budget," *Los Angeles Times*, June 25, 2014.

7. For more on the role of counselors, see Michael Hurwitz and Jessica Howell, "Measuring the Impact of High School Counselors on College Enrollment," *College Board Advocacy & Policy Center Research Brief*, February 2013, http://media.collegeboard.com/digitalServices/pdf/advocacy/policycenter/research-brief-measuring-impact-high-school-counselors-college-enrollment.pdf. See also Cheona S. Woods and Thurston Domina, "The School Counselor Caseload and the High School-to-College Pipeline," *Teachers College Record* Vol. 116, No. 10 (October 2014).

8. These paragraphs draw on my article "Military Culture: JROTC Instrumental at Kingsbury High," *The Commercial Appeal*, December 26, 2011.

9. These particular titles were mentioned by Franklin Paz Arita in a June 2012 interview.

10. Ginger Thompson, "Immigration Clash Leaves Vidalia Onion Farmers Bitter," *The Chicago Tribune*, May 28, 1998.

11. For coverage of Operation Vanguard, see the article by Cindy Gonzalez, "Vanguard Remains in Limbo," *Omaha World Herald*, July 16, 2000.

12. Regarding INS enforcement priorities, see Louis Uchitelle, "I.N.S. Is Looking the Other Way as Illegal Immigrants Fill Jobs," *The New York Times*, March 9, 2000.

13. The statistic on the small number of actions brought against employers for immigration violations refers to the 2004 fiscal year. See "Immigration Enforcement: Preliminary Observations on Employment Verification and Worksite Enforcement Efforts," U.S. Government Accountability Office, June 21, 2005, p. 4. http://www.gao.gov/products/GAO-05-822T. The statistic on 845 arrests also refers to the 2004 fiscal year and comes from a May 26, 2006, U.S. Immigration and Customs Enforcement fact sheet on worksite enforcement efforts.

14. See my article "Arkansas Has Few Federal Immigration Agents," Associated Press, May 16, 2006.

15. See Douglas S. Massey, Jorge Durand and Nolan J. Malone, *Beyond Smoke and Mirrors: Mexican Immigration in an Era of Economic Integration* (New York: Russell Sage Foundation, 2002), p. 105.

16. Eric Posner, "There's No Such Thing as an Illegal Immigrant," *Slate*, February 4, 2013. http://www.slate.com/articles/news_and_politics/view_from _chicago/2013/02/immigration_reform_illegal_immigrants_are_really_guest _workers.html (accessed November 23, 2015).

Chapter Two: Outclassed

1. In 2015, I requested a copy of the employment contract Mr. Fuller described, but the school system said no records matched my request. School system spokesman Shawn Pachucki wrote in an e-mail that the system believed Mr. Fuller had signed such a contract, but the office that had handled those contracts no longer existed, so it couldn't be verified. He said under such contracts, the principal's job was not at stake. "However, if all benchmarks were met, a $4,000 cash incentive was promised," Pachucki wrote in an e-mail. Since I never saw the contract itself, I'm uncertain what the exact terms were.

2. Daniel Kiel, "Exploded Dream: Desegregation in the Memphis City Schools," *Law and Inequality* 26, no. 2 (Summer 2008). http://papers.ssrn.com/sol3 /papers.cfm?abstract_id=1317854. The section on Memphis school desegregation

also draws on numerous archived newspaper articles, school profile reports and high school yearbooks, most of which were stored in the Memphis Room of the Benjamin L. Hooks Central Library. Of particular note were future mayor Willie Herenton's 1971 doctoral thesis "A Historical Study of School Desegregation in the Memphis City Schools, 1954–1970," Southern Illinois University; Richard Lentz's "Ordinance Mars CAB Bus Burial," *The Commercial Appeal*, March 23, 1972; the unbylined story "Busing Plan in Protest Second Day," *Memphis Press-Scimitar*, April 28, 1972; and an unsigned editorial, "Sad Story of White Flight," in *The Commercial Appeal*, September 13, 1973.

3. Steve Suitts, "A New Majority Research Bulletin: Low Income Students Now a Majority in the Nation's Public Schools," Southern Education Foundation, January 2015. http://www.southerneducation.org/Our-Strategies/Research-and-Publications/New-Majority-Diverse-Majority-Report-Series/A-New-Majority-2015-Update-Low-Income-Students-Now

Chapter Three: Rain

1. For more on driver's license issues in Tennessee, see "Bill to Encourage More Immigrants to Take Driving Tests," Associated Press, April 12, 2001; Paula Wade, "Vote Ok's Driver's Licenses for Noncitizens," *The Commercial Appeal*, April 24, 2001; "Tenn. Tightens Rules on Immigrant Drivers," Associated Press, July 20, 2002; and Lucas L. Johnson II, "Tenn. Halts Immigrant Driving Certificates," Associated Press, February 25, 2006.

2. Samuel Huntington, "The Hispanic Challenge," *Foreign Policy*, October 28, 2009. The section about the use of English among young Hispanics draws from *Children of Immigration* by Carola Suárez-Orozco and Marcelo M. Suárez-Orozco (Cambridge, MA: Harvard University Press, 2001) as well as these reports: Jens Manuel Krogstad, Renee Stepler and Mark Hugo Lopez, *English Proficiency on the Rise among Latinos: U.S. Born Driving Language Changes* (Washington, DC: Pew Hispanic Center, May 12, 2015), http://www.pewhispanic.org/2015/05/12/english-proficiency-on-the-rise-among-latinos/. See also David Folkenflik, "The Next Frontier in TV: English News for Latinos," NPR, August 15, 2012, http://www.npr.org/2012/08/15/158763308/the-next-frontier-in-tv-english-news-for-latinos (accessed December 2, 2015). Ravi Somaiya and Brooks Barnes, "Fusion Aims at Millennials, but Struggles with Its Identity," *The New York Times*, May 25, 2015.

3. Maki Park and Margie McHugh, *Immigrant Parents and Early Childhood Programs: Addressing Barriers of Literacy, Culture and Systems Knowledge* (Migration Policy

Institute, June 2014). http://www.migrationpolicy.org/research/immigrant-parents
-early-childhood-programs-barriers

Chapter Four: A Deck of Cards

1. Colleges typically charge application fees. Marion Mathis said it's her recollection that Estevon received fee waivers for some college applications and that
others were paid by his mother and his grandparents.

2. Sam Howe Verhovek, "Gates, 'Spreading the Wealth,' Makes Scholarship
Gift Official," *The New York Times*, September 17, 1999.

Chapter Five: Horse to Water

1. The section on Southwest Tennessee Community College draws on Maria
Ines Zamudio, "Degree of Success," *The Commercial Appeal*, December 1, 2014, as
well as Emily Ford, "Staying in College Is the Hardest Part," *The Commercial Appeal*,
May 27, 2007. The material on state funding for Southwest comes from my 2015 in-
terview with Steven P. Gentile, Director of Fiscal Policy Research, Tennessee
Higher Education Commission.

2. The statistics on graduation rates come from College Navigator, an online
tool from the National Center for Education Statistics: https://nces.ed.gov/college
navigator/. Because of differences in when I downloaded the data from the website,
the MTSU stats are for students who started in the fall of 2008, the U of M stats
are for those who started in the fall of 2007, and the Rhodes stats are for those who
started in the fall of 2006—that said, the rates didn't change much from year to
year.

3. Caroline M. Hoxby and Christopher Avery, "The Missing One-Offs: The
Hidden Supply of High-Achieving, Low Income Students" (working paper, National Bureau of Economic Research, no. 18586, December 2012), http://www.nber
.org/papers/w18586. See also Sandra E. Black, Kalena E. Cortes and Jane Arnold
Lincove, "Apply Yourself: Racial and Ethnic Differences in College Application"
(working paper, National Bureau of Economic Research, no. 21368, July 2015).
http://www.nber.org/papers/w21368

4. Anthony P. Carnevale and Jeff Strohl, *Separate and Unequal: How Higher
Education Reinforces the Intergenerational Reproduction of White Racial Privilege*
(Georgetown University Center on Education and the Workforce, July 2013).
https://cew.georgetown.edu/wp-content/uploads/2014/11/SeparateUnequal
.FR_.pdf

5. Holly K. Hacker, "Federal Data Show What Families Really Pay for College," *The Dallas Morning News*, March 7, 2014. See also Jon Marcus and Holly K. Hacker, "Colleges Continue to Put Burden of Price Hikes on Poorest, New Figures Show," Education Writers Association, November 29, 2014. http://www.ewa.org/key -coverage/colleges-continue-put-burden-price-hikes-poorest-new-figures-show (accessed December 2, 2015).

6. See the report *Student Loan Servicing: Analysis of Public Input and Recommendations for Reform* (Consumer Financial Protection Bureau, September 2015), http:// files.consumerfinance.gov/f/201509_cfpb_student-loan-servicing-report.pdf, as well as Gretchen Morgenson, "A Debt Setup That's Failing the Students," *The New York Times*, October 11, 2015.

7. Adam Looney and Constantine Yannelis, *A Crisis in Student Loans? How Changes in the Characteristics of Borrowers and in the Institutions They Attended Contributed to Rising Loan Defaults* (Brookings Institution, September 2015). http://www.brookings .edu/about/projects/bpea/papers/2015/looney-yannelis-student-loan-defaults

8. John Maggio and Martin Smith, "College, Inc." *Frontline*, May 4, 2010. http://www.pbs.org/wgbh/pages/frontline/collegeinc/ (accessed August 2015). See also Tamar Lewin, "Report Finds Low Graduation Rates at For-profit Colleges," *The New York Times*, November 24, 2010.

9. *Trends in Debt for Bachelor's Degree Recipients a Year after Graduation: 1994, 2001 and 2009* (U.S. Department of Education Report, NCES 2013-156, December 2012). http://nces.ed.gov/pubs2013/2013156.pdf. For default rates, see *The Condition of Education 2015* (The National Center for Education Statistics), chapter 4, Student Loan Volume and Default Rates, pp. 230–233. http://nces.ed.gov/programs/coe/indicator _cug.asp

10. Nicholas N. Nagle, Randy Gustafson, and Charlynn Burd, *A Profile of the Hispanic Population in the State of Tennessee* (The University of Tennessee Center for Business and Economic Research, August 2012), pp. 17–18. http://cber.bus.utk.edu /census/hisp/bfox288.pdf

11. *Between Two Worlds: How Young Latinos Come of Age in America* (Washington, DC: Pew Hispanic Center, December 11, 2009). http://www.pewhispanic.org/2009 /12/11/between-two-worlds-how-young-latinos-come-of-age-in-america/

12. Roberto G. Gonzalez, *Young Lives on Hold: The College Dreams of Undocumented Students* (College Board Advocacy, April 2009). https://secure-media.collegeboard .org/digitalServices/pdf/professionals/young-lives-on-hold-undocumented -students.pdf

13. Michael Riley, "Immigrants Shut Out of Colleges," *The Denver Post*, August 11, 2002.

14. Letter to the editor, *The Gazette* (Colorado Springs, Colorado), September 17, 2002.

15. Helen Thorpe, *Just Like Us: The True Story of Four Mexican Girls Coming of Age in America* (New York: Scribner, 2009), pp. 50–51.

Chapter Six: Motivation

1. In 2015, this student agreed to meet me for an interview, but he didn't show up. I tried to reschedule with him, but he never agreed, and I don't know exactly why he left school or what happened to him afterward.

2. I first heard this phrase from a Memphis graffiti artist named Brandon Marshall. It was a tagline for the 2011 documentary movie *Miss Representation*, about demeaning images of women in the media. I'm not sure where the phrase comes from originally.

3. See my project "Blood Trade: Memphis and the Mexican Drug War," *The Commercial Appeal*, June 27, 2010, and July 4, 2010.

4. Jody Callahan, "Off the Street," *The Commercial Appeal*, April 3, 2013. The information about the guilty plea and sentence comes from federal court records.

5. Ben Sisario, "Lux Interior, 62, Singer in the Punk-Rock Era, Is Dead," *The New York Times*, February 5, 2009.

Chapter Seven: Intervention

1. The section about the "college bound" slogan draws on several articles in *The Commercial Appeal*: Dakarai I. Aarons, "Memphis City Schools Workers Get Psyched; Hear Sobering Warning," August 10, 2006, as well as Dakarai I. Aarons, "Johnson Pushes College Message," March 5, 2007, and Jane Roberts, "MCS Must Scramble to Delay Sign-ups; Open-enrollment Changes Never Approved by Board," March 11, 2009.

2. Susan Saulny, "After Recession, More Young Adults Are Living on Street," *The New York Times*, December 19, 2012.

3. Tamar Jacoby, "This Way Up: Mobility in America," *The Wall Street Journal*, July 22, 2014.

4. Mark Hugo Lopez and Ana Gonzalez-Barrera, *Women's College Enrollment Gains Leave Men Behind* (Washington, DC: Pew Hispanic Center, March 6, 2014). http://www.pewresearch.org/fact-tank/2014/03/06/womens-college-enrollment

-gains-leave-men-behind/. See also Deborah A. Santiago, Emily Calderón Galdeano and Morgan Taylor, *The Condition of Latinos in Education: 2015 Factbook Latino Males in Higher Education* (*Excelencia* in Education), p. 18. http://www.edexcelencia.org/research/2015-latinos-higher-education

5. For more on this type of clinic, see my article "Filling a Void: Clinics Find Need, Profit by Serving Low-income Hispanics," *The Commercial Appeal*, April 8, 2007.

6. "Revisions to the 2013 Census of Fatal Occupational Injuries (CFOI) Counts," Bureau of Labor Statistics, April 2015, as well as my article "Construction Takeover: Hard Work, Unlawful Tactics Help Some Hispanic Builders Conquer Industry," *The Commercial Appeal*, January 2, 2008, and my article "Job Deaths High For Hispanics" in the *Birmingham Post-Herald*, July 27, 2004.

7. Jaison R. Abel and Richard Deitz, "Do the Benefits of College Still Outweigh the Costs?" Federal Reserve of New York, *Current Issues in Economics and Finance* 20, no. 3 (2014). https://www.newyorkfed.org/research/current_issues/ci20-3.html

8. Elizabeth Marquardt, David Blankenhorn, Robert I. Lerman, Linda Malone-Colón and W. Bradford Wilcox, "The President's Marriage Agenda for the Forgotten Sixty Percent," *The State of Our Unions* (Charlottesville, VA: National Marriage Project and Institute for American Values, 2012). http://www.stateofourunions.org/2012/SOOU2012.pdf

9. *Health, United States, 2011: With Special Feature on Socioeconomic Status and Health* (Hyattsville, MD: National Center for Health Statistics, 2012), p. 37. http://www.cdc.gov/nchs/data/hus/hus11.pdf. See also Nanci Hellmich, "Higher Education Linked to Longer Life, CDC Report Shows," *USA Today*, May 16, 2012.

10. The section on James J. Heckman's work draws on Eduardo Porter, "Investments in Education May Be Misdirected," *The New York Times*, April 2, 2013, as well as Heckman's February 2013 presentation to the Nebraska Chamber of Commerce and Industry entitled "Schools, Skills, and Synapses."

11. David Muphey, Lina Guzman and Alicia Torres, *America's Hispanic Children: Gaining Ground, Looking Forward* (Child Trends Hispanic Institute, September 24, 2014). http://www.childtrends.org/?publications=americas-hispanic-children-gaining-ground-looking-forward

12. I was in the Ramos family home the night of the intervention along with photographer Karen Pulfer Focht. We mostly stayed quiet and observed, but our presence may have influenced the situation in some subtle way.

Chapter Eight: Bianca the Guide

1. I left the Ramos family home before Isaias had this conversation with Bianca Tudon. Bianca later shared the transcript of the Facebook exchange with me, and I interviewed both her and Isaias about the conversation.

2. Isaias was part of the last senior class to graduate from the Memphis City Schools. As the result of a complex fight over school consolidation, the Memphis City Schools system formally dissolved in 2013 and Kingsbury High came under the jurisdiction of the Shelby County Schools.

Chapter Nine: A Funeral in Mexico

1. The account of Antonia's death draws on my July 1, 2013, interview in Santa Maria Asunción with Trinidad Castro Vargas, who was nearby when it happened.

2. From my October 29, 2013, interview with Memphis immigration attorney Greg Siskind.

3. Stats on Border Patrol staffing and budgets come from the U.S. Customs and Border Protection website, www.cbp.gov. See also Matt Graham, "Border Security Assets," Bipartisan Policy Center, July 2013. Numbers cited refer to the Border Patrol Program budget, which is one part of the larger budget for U.S. Customs and Border Protection.

4. Ana Gonzalez-Barrera, *More Mexicans Leaving than Coming to the U.S.* (Washington, DC: Pew Hispanic Center, November 19, 2015).

5. See my article "Not a Citizen? No Problem; Illegal Immigrants Meet Little Resistance Getting Home Loans," *The Commercial Appeal*, November 12, 2006.

6. Brian Bennett, "Figures Skew Number Obama Deports; Immigrants beyond the Border Area Are Actually Less Likely to Be Kicked Out Now," *Los Angeles Times*, April 2, 2014.

7. Samuel Huntington, "The Hispanic Challenge," *Foreign Policy*, October 28, 2009.

8. Jeffrey S. Passel, D'Vera Cohn, Jens Manuel Krogstad and Ana Gonzalez-Barrera, *As Growth Stalls, Unauthorized Immigrant Population Becomes More Settled* (Washington, DC: Pew Hispanic Center, September 3, 2014). http://www.pewhispanic.org/2014/09/03/as-growth-stalls-unauthorized-immigrant-population-becomes-more-settled/

9. The education statistics come from Mexico's Instituto Nacional de Estadística y Geografía, or INEGI, specifically the table "Características educativas

de la población." http://www3.inegi.org.mx/sistemas/sisept/default.aspx?t=medu 09&s=est&c=26364 (accessed July 2015).

10. Data on fertility rates come from Encuesta Nacional de la Dinámica Demográfica ENADID 2014, Principales Resultados, produced by INEGI and Consejo Nacional de Población (CONAPO), July 9, 2015, p. 7. http://www.inegi.org .mx/est/contenidos/proyectos/encuestas/hogares/especiales/enadid/enadid2014 /doc/resultados_enadid14.pdf

11. María del Rosario Cárdenas Elizalde and colleagues, "Informe de pobreza en Mexico 2012," Consejo Nacional de Evaluación de la Politica de Desarrollo Social (CONEVAL). http://www.coneval.gob.mx/Medicion/Paginas/Informe -de-Pobreza-2012.aspx

Chapter Ten: Victory

1. The account of Adriana Garza announcing the scholarship to Isaias and his family is based on interviews with the people involved. I wasn't present when it happened.

2. Peter Reford, "Five of the Best Computer Science Classes in the U.S.," Bloomberg.com, June 11, 2015. http://www.bloomberg.com/news/articles/2015-06 -11/five-of-the-best-computer-science-classes-in-the-country (accessed December 2, 2015).

3. From my August 2015 interview with Wesley Thorne, who formerly worked as Carnegie Mellon's point person for corporate recruiters. Stats on salary and job placement come from the Carnegie Mellon publication "Post-Graduation Survey Results 2014—College of Engineering, Electrical & Computer Engineering." https://www .cmu.edu/career/salaries-and-destinations/2014-survey/Electrical%20and%20 Computer%20Engineering5.pdf (accessed December 2, 2015).

Chapter Eleven: A Locked Door

1. James Dowd, "Slim Profits Shutter Victory," *The Commercial Appeal*, March 7, 2014.

2. See my article "Recruiters Seek Victory Students," *The Commercial Appeal*, March 11, 2014.

3. The paragraphs about the federal inquiries into Victory University draw on the government e-mail correspondence that Jennifer Backer obtained through Freedom of Information Act requests. The state regulator that I refer to was the Tennessee Higher Education Commission. On July 29, 2015, the commission notified

Victory University that it was retroactively revoking its authorization to operate. In an interview, commission lead attorney Julie Woodruff explained that the agency takes this retroactive revocation step when a university has failed to comply with shutdown procedures.

4. Tamar Lewin, "For-Profit College Company Files For Bankruptcy," *The New York Times*, May 5, 2015.

Chapter Twelve: Dustin's Destiny

1. This section draws on my article "Anonymous Donor's Gift Allows Christian Brothers University to Fund Immigrant Students' Scholarships," *The Commercial Appeal*, March 26, 2015. The financial terms of the scholarship differ slightly between transfer and freshman students.

Epilogue

1. See the previously cited report by Jeffrey Passel, D'Vera Cohn and Ana Gonzalez-Barrera, *Net Migration from Mexico Falls to Zero—and Perhaps Less* (Washington, DC: Pew Hispanic Center, April 23, 2012). http://www.pewhispanic.org /2012/04/23/net-migration-from-mexico-falls-to-zero-and-perhaps-less/. The statistics on citizenship come from my direct correspondence with the Pew Hispanic Center.

2. Jim Kuhnhenn, "Legal Scholars: Obama's Immigration Actions Lawful," Associated Press, November 25, 2014.